# Improving College Education of Veterans

Edited by

Charles Hopkins

Douglas Herrmann

Roland B. Wilson

Bert Allen

Lynn Malley

"The willingness with which our young people are likely to serve in any war, no matter how justified, shall be directly proportional to how they perceive the veterans of earlier wars were treated and appreciated by their nation."

George Washington

## Dedication

This book is dedicated to all who have served, especially who have made the ultimate sacrifice, and those who return with medical and other problems that continue, sometimes known or not known to others, long after their discharge. We are grateful to them for their faithful service and sacrifice.

This book is also dedicated to all veterans who have wanted a college education: to those who wanted to apply to a college or a university but were afraid to do so; to those who started college but dropped out; to those who started college but progressed slowly at getting a degree because they did not get assistance they needed; and to all veterans who obtained a degree with or without assistance.

iv

Contents by Section

Contents by Chapters in Sections

x

# Acknowledgements

**Conference Organizing Committee:** Bert Allen, Sonja Ferguson, Steve Fiore, Frank Gomez, Doug Herrmann, Zachary Herrmann, Charles Hopkins, Dan Hopkins, Jared Jobe, Steve Kime, Lynn Malley, Leslie Miller, David Payne, Doug Raybeck, Keith Wilson, Roland Wilson, Kathryn Snead, Jer Yates

**Origins of the Conference**: This conference grew out of Plans developed by the Academic Veterans Association (AVA) of the Vietnam Veterans Institute (VVI) to conduct a series of national conferences that focus on improving the college education of veterans. After the conference had been conceived, the College Educators for Veterans Higher Education (CEVHE) volunteered to pick up where the AVA and the VVI left off.

**Conference Donors:**
Captain Marty Block, USNR (Ret.)
President Daniel Bradley, Indiana State University
Educational Testing Service

# Description of the Conference on
# Improving College Education of Veterans

Washington, D. C. from 22 – 24 October, 2009.

The conference was held by the College Educators for Veterans Higher Education at the headquarters for the Servicemembers Opportunity Colleges (SOC), at 1307 New York Avenue, NW, Washington, DC 20005

Twenty four speakers were invited to address different kinds of difficulties that veterans are known to encounter sometimes while seeking a college degree. The speakers, who were distinguished in higher education, higher education of veterans, or research in education, were each invited to speak to one of the kinds of difficulties. Table 1 lists the affiliations represented by the speakers. [More institutions and organizations than speakers because several speakers had more than one affiliation].

Table 1
Institutions and Organizations Represented
By the Speakers at the Conference

Colleges and Universities
University of Central Florida
Federal University of Rio Grande
    do Sul, Brazil
Hamilton College
Indiana State University
Kansas State University
Milligan College
Purdue University
Towson University
Trinity University

Education Organizations
American Association of State
      Colleges and Universities
American Council on Education
Educational Testing Service
LanneM Talent Management

Military Organizations
Judge Advocate General, U.S. Navy
U.S. Marine Intelligence
U.S. Army Reserve
U.S. Marine Corps
U.S. Navy
Indiana Committee for Employer
      Support of the Guard and
      Reserve

Veterans Service Organizations
Department of Veterans Affairs
Iraq and Afghanistan Veterans of America
Operation Vets
Vietnam Veterans Institute

Veterans Education Organizations
College Educators for Veterans Higher Education
Creative Conflict Engagement Services
Operation Diploma, Military Family Research Institute
      at Purdue University
Operation Vets
Servicemembers Opportunity Colleges
Student Veterans of America
Veterans Advisory Committee on Education

The conference was attended by approximately 50 individuals who represented a variety of different academic institutions and educational organizations and who also were distinguished in a manner similar to that of the speakers. Some of the attendees came from a few of the affiliations of the speakers but mostly they originated from other institutions. These institutions of the attendees are listed in Table 2. Many of the attendees played roles at academic institutions that were similar to the roles of the speakers at their institutions: as college professors, associate deans, different kinds of deans, provosts, veterans coordinators, and/or researchers.

Table 2
Affiliations of Attendees

American Association of State
  Colleges and Universities
Argosy University
Broome Community College
Catholic University of America
Columbia Southern University
Georgetown University
The Graduate School
Grand Canyon University
Harford Community College at
  Aberdeen
Hunter College-CUNY
Illinois State Approving Agency
Indiana State University
MPR Associates, Inc.
National Center for Education Statistics
Operation College Promise
NJASCU
Prince George's Community College
Purdue University
Rose Hulman College
Southern Polytechnic State University
University of Central Arkansas
University of the Incarnate Word
University of Phoenix

# PROLOGUE

Names and affiliations of Editors are provided
after the Prologue

This book consists of 25 chapters based on a series
of presentations made at the conference, Improving
College Education of Veterans, held in Washington, D.
C., October 22 – 24. The presenters, who are
distinguished in higher education of veterans, or research
in education, were each invited to address to one of kinds
of difficulties that veterans are known to encounter
sometimes while seeking a college degree. This book was
developed from the conference presentations in order to
inform professors, college administrators, academic
researchers and others about difficulties that veterans
face in college and to propose how these problems can be
resolved so that they have the same college experience as
non-veteran students.

The table of contents lists the topics addressed by
presenters. The presentations are reported here largely in
the order in which presentations were made at the
conference. A few of the presentations were scheduled at
the conference for the convenience of the presenter but
are reported here according to four themes of the book:
introduction to some higher education problems of
veterans; broad perspectives on veterans education
problems; specific kinds of veterans education.

Emphasis is given in all chapters to how higher
education can serve the needs of veterans as they seek

college degrees. American society in total but especially college administrators, professors, and academic researchers areexpected to confer degrees to veterans. Difficulties that veterans experience as they seek a degree constitute a problem that academia must eliminate. These difficulties may be called the Veterans Higher Education Problem. Given that this problem has existed for at least five decades, the problem appears to be an enigma for higher education.

College educators are up against many difficulties in trying to help the higher education of veterans. For example, because of the poor economy, endowments for colleges have shrunk. The boards of colleges and their college administrators could also provide an extensive list of difficulties that must be attended today. The difficulties facing higher education require solutions by the officers of an institution and its board of directors. Endowments may increase when new donors are found. The number of applicants for admission to colleges may increase with ingenious marketing plans. Higher education has yet to decide what to do with veterans who apply for and attend a college or university.

During and after the Vietnam War, many schools had agreed to treat active duty servicemembers fairly in order to qualify the school as a member of the Servicememberes Opportunity Colleges. However, the institutions that promise to treat servicemembers fairly make no such promise regarding veterans in general. More recently, many institutions have indicated that they have renounced the anti-veteran attitudes of the Vietnam era. However, these institutions take care to support servicemembers and veterans without regard for how professors and college administrators feel about the military policy that servicemembers and veterans carry out.

Understandably, partly because servicemembers and veterans constitute only about 3% of students at most schools, professors and administrators focus their attention almost totally on non-veterans. Because many veterans struggle for at least part of their time in higher education, non-veterans tend to shine amidst students in general. Thus, higher education in America does a better job of educating non-veterans than it does veterans. This is the essence of the Veterans Higher Education Problem.

Many in the academic community recently have come to recognize that it is in their best interest to try to eliminate the difficulties that make up this problem. Greater success at educating veterans could be achieved by making systemic changes in American higher education. Colleges and universities can contribute to improving the American system for educating veterans in several ways. First, colleges and universities may officially adopt as part of their mission the educating of veterans. Second, those institutions that adopt such a mission must also develop pedagogy on how veterans should be instructed and how their knowledge should be assessed. Such pedagogy will require investigations about the methods of teaching and assessing the learning of veterans, while precluding mistreatment of veterans. Third, colleges and universities with a pro-veteran mission should hire professors, college administrators, and staff who are veterans. Fourth, colleges and universities may help improve the college education of veterans by embracing the changes that will encourage veterans to seek out and obtain a college degree. Fifth, colleges and universities may encourage ways to improve educational opportunities and practices by developing ways the government may produce better conditions for veterans to obtain college degrees. Sixth, higher education may seek collaboration with the veterans community, e.g. the American Legion, the Veterans of Foreign Wars, Disabled American Veterans.

If some educational institutions are to officially adopt a mission to educate veterans, that might cause higher education to move quickly to solve the higher education problem by developing programs for veterans. Also, such institutions should ask those outside of higher education to improve the situations for veterans to obtain a college degree. A comprehensive process inside and outside of higher education will help ensure that veterans who seek a college degree are treated and educated with the best practices.

The Veterans Higher Education Problem was not widely recognized until recently. Many professors and college administrators have not known about the problems of veterans because professors and administrators are not veterans themselves, thus making it challenging for them to anticipate or recognize veterans' difficulties. Many professors and administrators are not aware that their actions treat veterans poorly. Some professors and administrators are aware of these difficulties but do not talk about them because they do not see it as their responsibility to help mistreated veterans. Many educators have assumed that the poor treatment of veterans occurred only during the

Vietnam era. Finally, some educators assume that the Veterans Higher Education Problem does not exist.

As mentioned earlier, veterans constitute less than 3% of students on most campuses. Many other student groups are much larger than the veterans groups on a campus. As a result, these other groups attract attention to their problems easily due to their highly visible special interests. Veterans, due to their nature, usually do not talk or complain about the problems they encounter. Usually they merely want to get their degree and start a career as soon as possible, and, in many cases, to support the family that they started while in the service.

Veterans' problems are much greater than the financial burden addressed by the new GI Bill. The problems that veterans encounter belong to the same categories of problems that non-veterans encounter: attending class, taking quizzes, completing exams, and writing term papers. In addition, both veterans and non-veterans must select an appropriate college; make the transition to college life; acquire the academic skills needed in college; adjust to the culture of a college; interact with professors, administrators, and other students; finance college; obtain transfer credits; participate in college educational programs; maintain health; and find employment on graduation. However, the difficulties in these categories challenge and affect veterans differently than the ways they challenge and affect non-veterans.

Many educators today are aware that veterans have unique challenges that should be addressed and recognize that the elimination of these problems will need the cooperation of other educators, leaders in society, and leaders in veterans organizations who are able to rectify the situations that lead to the problems. More attention to the difficulties of veterans in higher education, such as is provided in this book, will be needed in order that veterans and servicemembers have the same opportunity to obtain a college degree as exists for non-veterans. Once educators are properly informed about the Veterans Higher Education Problem, they will be able to set about to eliminate it. Moreover, leaders in higher education will move quickly to develop higher education programs for veterans if those outside of higher education urge higher education institutions to make the necessary changes promptly. In order to help this process, the authors of chapters in this book propose various ways to eliminate this problem.

Names and Affiliations of Editors

Charles Hopkins
Emeritus Professor of Education
Indiana State University

Douglas Herrmann
Emeritus Professor of Psychology
Indiana State University

Roland B. Wilson
USMC (Ret.), MA Linguistics
U.S.Marine Corps Intelligence

Bert Allen
Professor of Counseling,
Milligan College

Lynn Malley
JD; MA, LLM
Creative Conflict Engagement Services

# Section I. Introduction to Aspects of the Veterans Education Problem

## Chapter 1

## From Boots to Books

### Mr. John Powers
Independent Consultant, Operation Vets and Executive Director, Student Veterans of America (SVA)

### Mr. Patrick Campbell
Chief Legislative Counsel, Iraq and Afghanistan Veterans of America

This chapter examines how schools and the Veterans Administration (VA) can develop better practices for dealing with the nearly half a million veterans, spouses and children who will be going to school on the Post 9/11 GI Bill. This chapter will give an overview of the college problems of recent veterans and the need to support veterans in higher education.

The transition from military to civilian life is often a difficult transition for veterans. Many veterans seek to attain a college degree after completing their military service. As the Post-9/11 GI Bill has now been implemented, thousands of service members, veterans, and their dependents are eligible for increased GI bill educational benefits. Student veterans bring a unique perspective to a college campus. Their military experiences shape the ways they view and interact with the campus community.

Higher education institutions have an excellent opportunity to recruit these individuals and help them meet their post-secondary educational goals. Campus administrations should value student veterans as a vital component of their campus community. Their life experiences contribute to the educational environment and support higher education's commitment to diversity.

Operation Vets

A college education can be an important factor in helping veterans transition back into civilian life. Operation Vets is dedicated to ensure colleges and universities have support systems in place to welcome these veterans.

John T. Powers
Veterans Advocate
Operation Vets


Operation Vets Mission:
• To assist colleges and universities in creating programs to support service members, veterans, and dependents on campus
• To support veterans transitioning from military life to higher education
• To provide innovative service and training to colleges and universities supporting veterans pursuing their educational goals

4

# Chapter 2

Keynote Presentation

# Education and Transformation

## Dr. Douglas Raybeck

Emeritus Professor, Hamilton College
Founding President, College Educators for
Veterans Higher Education

This conference was developed to inform professors, college administrators and academic researchers about the challenges veterans encounter in college and how these difficulties can be eliminated. In so doing, veterans can be educated and transformed while completing a college degree in the same manner as are non-veterans.

Social scientists are largely agreed that reciprocity is probably the most fundamental social rule across a wide range of cultures (Becker, 1986). It is enshrined in virtually every major religion and appears in Christianity as the Golden Rule: "Do unto others as you would have them do unto you." In a more secular vein, major philosophers also argue that reciprocity is basic to most value and belief systems (Quine, 1978). Indeed, there are numerous accounts of reciprocity appearing among primates (De Waal, 2000; Watts, 2002). It has even been argued that reciprocity has been manifested among laboratory rats (Rutte & Taborsky, 2007).

Why begin an essay on education with a discussion of reciprocity? Quite simple. This book seeks to improve the circumstances of veterans who wish to further their education. Many of them have made striking gifts to their country. Some have surrendered limbs, some, their emotional well-being. Both men and women have given greatly to their country and it would seem that some fundamental reciprocity is called for.

As an educator, my natural concern is with education and, I would argue that this profession is peculiarly well-suited to repay veterans for the sacrifices they have made on our behalf. Unlike financial compensation, or material gifts, the provision of education, a true education, furnishes the wherewithal for a better life and continued growth. True education has been and can always be transformative. I mean transformative in the broadest sense. Not only can it change one's life, it can change the way one views the world and relates to it. It both widens and deepens one's perspective and leads to a more thoughtful and aware citizen.

The remainder of this brief essay will be taken up with three extended examples of just the kind of transformation to which I refer. In the first instance, education clearly improved the attitude, understanding, and even nature, of a given individual. In the second instance, education resulted in a remarkable alteration in social, cultural, and economic circumstances culminating in a greatly improved condition. Finally, we will encounter a veteran of the Gulf War who experienced many of the difficulties we seek to alleviate and yet, through perseverance, and some small assistance, overcame these to achieve considerable success.

Example 1:

Perhaps the least noteworthy case in point, our story begins with a somewhat refractory young lad who displayed neither academic talent nor motivation. In primary school, he flunked spelling twice and had to take remedial reading three times. While the opportunities were before him, he declined to grasp them. Instead, he was something of a behavior problem, disturbing other classmates with pranks and jokes.

He may have been bored or simply disenchanted, but this sorry pattern persisted through half of the seventh grade. During the first half of that year he was one of two ringleaders who sought to create an inhospitable environment for new teachers. As a consequence of their successes, the small, rural primary school went through five teachers in a bit more than 5 months. The sixth teacher would profoundly affect this youth's life. The teacher in question was a short, stocky, balding man of French Canadian extraction. As it eventuated, he too had had a somewhat checkered youth and was not about to tolerate this sort of misbehavior. He identified the two ringleaders, marched them out into the hallway, shoved them hard against the lockers and said, with a very red face, "There will be no more of this shit!" He had made his point most impressively, and both boys greatly improved their behavior.

This teacher took our recalcitrant lad quite seriously and encouraged him to try to do better academic work. The boy applied himself and discovered a range of skills he did not know he possessed. The teacher further persuaded him that academic achievement was a means to escape the confines of the small, bucolic, somewhat repressive town in which he had lived all his life. Lacking any means to afford college, the lad realized he would have to apply himself in high school in order to earn a significant scholarship.

He worked hard and successfully in high school and obtained a full tuition scholarship to a good liberal arts college. He needed to work to cover the expenses of room, board, books, and incidentals, but he also needed to keep his grades up, for the nature of the scholarship required that he maintain at least a B average. As a result of his hard work and application as an undergraduate, he was able to gain admission to a good graduate school and a fellowship sufficient to cover living costs.

Thus, education and the good work of a primary school teacher transformed our youth from an unruly bumpkin to an active academic capable of writing papers such as this one.

Example 2:

Our next example was born in Chicago in 1956. His mother raised him in a very modest two-room apartment on Chicago's South Side. The schools in that area are notoriously poor, overcrowded, and even violent. Here is an extended excerpt that describes the conditions of his early life:

`Good home training'
Patrick was born in his grandfather's bed July 31, 1956, in a two-story brick apartment on South Wabash Avenue in Chicago. He was immediately put in the oven to keep warm, he would later say, recalling that his family told him the doctor suggested it because his body temperature was low.

Patrick, his mother, Emily, and sister, Rhonda, returned to his grandfather's apartment for good after being on welfare -- not long after his father, Pat, left them for New York as the baritone sax player for cosmic-jazz legend Sun Ra. Patrick was 5 or 6. He, his mother, and his sister shared a set of bunk beds.

The family was small but tight. His mother worked- a lot at a dry cleaners, a currency exchange, and later sorting mail at the post office. His grandmother planted roses, tulips, peppers, and tomatoes behind the apartment, in the shadows of the towering Robert Taylor Homes, a rough public housing development a block away. The smell of fresh bread from Schulze Baking Co.

filled the streets. Patrick was ``Boopy" to his relatives, though no one remembers where the nickname came from.

``Their family was like a pillar of the community," Brigandi said. The neighborhood was a kind of family, too.

You couldn't sneak down an alley, Patrick said, without someone calling your mother. For several summers, Patrick helped Brigandi's father sell ``Snow Balls" - snow cones - out of a white converted Jeep.

The family had its struggles. Patrick's uncle, Sonny, was a heroin addict. Patrick recalled catching him shooting up In the living room, prompting a huge fight between his mother - who tried to kick Sonny out - and his grandmother, who ``wasn't tough enough," Patrick said.

``His presence in the apartment, especially when he was dirty, was a real source of tension between my mother and my grandmother," he said. (Hellman, 2006)

Despite the many disadvantages of being raised in such an area, his mother encouraged Patrick to apply himself in school and he managed to make a positive impression on his teachers. Largely because of his efforts to succeed, in the eighth grade he was recommended to and recruited by an educational program called A Better Chance. ABC relocates students from difficult environments to more constructive ones and can provide scholarship assistance when necessary.

While his former classmates were encountering problems with gangs and drugs, Patrick was attending Milton Academy outside of Boston. Having displayed the same kind of motivation and ability that gained him admission to this program, he was later accepted to Harvard University where he earned an A.B. degree. He was the first in his family to enter and complete a college education. After winning a Rockefeller Fellowship and spending a year working for the United Nations, this industrious young man gained admission to Harvard Law School where he again manifested a distinguished performance.

By this point Patrick was well-equipped with the educational tools to succeed in a highly competitive world. He gained a position clerking for a federal appellate judge and subsequently joined the NAACP Legal Defense and Education Fund. His own experiences as an African-American growing up in Chicago's South Side were melded into the work he did for the NAACP. It was through this organization that he encountered the range of civil rights problems still confronting this country. It was also through this organization that he encountered a young woman whom he married in 1984. They have gone on to have two fine daughters.

Patrick's efforts on behalf of the NAACP and the exceptional work he did while a partner with a Boston law firm brought him to the attention of the Clinton administration. In 1994, at the age of 38, he was appointed Assistant Attorney General for Civil Rights by

President Clinton. He served in this position with distinction for somewhat more than three years before retiring to the private sector where he held a variety of prominent and very remunerative positions with different large corporations.

With this remarkable range of accomplishments one might think our tale would be over, but such is not quite the case. You may have thought the reference to Patrick was a first name; instead it is the surname of Duval Patrick, the 71st governor of the Commonwealth of Massachusetts. The remarkable trajectory of what was once a disadvantaged and impoverished African-American youth is adequate testimony to the power of education to transform and enrich one's life.

Example 3:

Our last case study is of a young man, Derrick Johns, who at the age of 17, with a waiver from his mother, was accepted into the Marines. He was a well-built, athletically inclined youth of significant size, and possessed of attractive facial features. Partly as a result of these qualities, he spent the first two years of his tour stationed in Washington, DC as part of the Presidential Honor Guard. He then transferred to northern Kuwait with 1600 other Marines. Derrick was tasked with working at the very front, employing laser designators to paint targets for laser guided bombs. The responsibilities of these Marines exposed them to both enemy and friendly fire. As a consequence, they would frequently seek refuge in Iraqi tanks that were too damaged to provoke anyone's fire.

Unfortunately, as it eventuated, our tanks were firing depleted uranium rounds. These very effectively pierced enemy armor and incapacitated a many of the tanks in which Derrick sought shelter. Apparently, the armed services were unaware of the long-term effects of exposure to depleted uranium rounds. The problem is due less to the radiation than to the nature of uranium itself. Uranium is a toxic metal and it is now generally recognized that exposure to it can result in serious health issues (WHO, 2001).

After two years in Kuwait, Derrick's tour of duty was completed and he returned to the States. He was fond of his grandfather and decided to investigate the college from which his grandfather had graduated. At age 22, in the spring of 1990, he came to Hamilton College for a pre-freshmen meeting and a discussion about financial aid. When the college was unable (unwilling?) to meet his needs he approached the football coach who took one look at the large, well conditioned, young man and arranged for a football scholarship.

I first encountered Derrick when he elected one of my anthropology classes. While Derrick impressed me as a bright student, he seemed to suffer from what one might term 'tunnel vision'. The range of his interests was narrow and he took a very pragmatic approach to his education. Initially Derrick intended to be pre-law and majored in government. His exposure to a range of courses broadened his interests and his perspective. In 1993, Derrick became my advisee and an anthropology major. Shortly after making this change he rather rapidly went deaf in one ear and suffered significant hearing loss in the other. His vision also suffered some impairment and it was later discovered that he had narrow angle glaucoma in both eyes. Both the nerve damage and the glaucoma are consistent with uranium poisoning, though Gulf War Syndrome is also a possibility.

Not surprisingly, these problems increasingly interfered with his studies. By his senior year, Derek was sick much of the time and never really felt healthy. As a consequence of missed classes and a reduced ability to concentrate, he failed two courses. The committee on academic standing refused to consider the extenuating circumstances and separated him from the college for a semester. He was told to demonstrate that he could do college-level work and then he could return. Shortly after he left Hamilton Derrick's mother died, adding additional emotional burdens to an already troubling situation.

Throughout this period, Derrick sought medical assistance from the Veterans Administration, which steadfastly denied any responsibility for his problems. This was before Gulf War Syndrome was acknowledged as a serious problem affecting many who served in that theater. Derrick sought what medical treatment he could and worked in a variety of jobs to defray the costs of medicine and doctors. He met and married his wife in 1996 and they had two daughters.

In 1998 he obtained a job with Morgan Stanley, which led to increasingly challenging and remunerative employment in a variety of companies, the last of which was Abbott Labs. In 2008 he became President and CEO of a new company, Diffusion Technologies, Inc., which manufactures medical devices. It has introduced novel means of reducing the likelihood of infection at surgical sites, particularly those involving the spine.

Obviously, Derrick has profited from and employed the education he received while at Hamilton for 3 1/2 years. However, in this instance his success is more a reflection of his character, perseverance, and motivation, than simply his education. He has, despite his many difficulties, managed to build a very good life for himself and his family. He has done all of this without a formal degree, which he would now like to obtain. Here is an excerpt from the communication he sent in 2006 to an Associate Dean at Hamilton College:

> In the spring of my junior year I lost my hearing 100% in my left ear and 20% in my right ear virtually overnight, which made me severely depressed and not able to function very well for some time. I returned to Hamilton in the fall of my senior year only to find out my mom was diagnosed with ovarian cancer to which she finally succumbed 18 months later. At this time I was 26 and failed two classes in the fall of my senior year (I did however complete my Senior Thesis).

> The Committee on Academic Standing (CAS) treated me like a pack of hungry wolves handing down a punishment more in line with a freshman whose grades suffered from too much socializing rather

than a 26 year old senior who had health and family issues to deal with.

I am now 37 with a wife and two daughters. For the first time since I was forced to leave Hamilton I have the time and financial ability to complete the 6 credits I need to matriculate. I currently live in Austin TX and have access to UT at Austin. I know this sounds hokey but I did make a promise to mom to finish what I started and would much rather have a Hamilton degree rather than a UT degree, especially since I am still paying back loans to Hamilton for a degree I have not yet received.

Any guidance you can offer as to how I would petition the powers at Hamilton to allow me to complete my degree at UT would be most appreciated.

Unfortunately for Derrick, Hamilton College has a limitation of seven years within which one may complete courses for a degree. Derrick's petition was unsuccessful. Although he only lacks six courses to graduate, he was informed that he must take all of these at Hamilton College and that he could not transfer them in from the University of Texas. Thus, despite his personal successes, he remains without degree. However, he did get an excellent education despite the obstacles placed in his path. Indeed, he credits his education for much of his success in the business world.

That Derrick has succeeded as well as he has despite his many travails, is a testimony to his unusually strong character and powerful motivation. We cannot expect these strengths of all returning veterans. Derrick's life could have been much more pleasant if the college had recognized his special circumstances, provided appropriate supports, and allowed him adequate time to overcome the many difficulties that beset him. The authors of the following chapters are committed to promoting the provision of these kinds of assistance for veterans seeking a higher education.

Education is capable of transforming ordinary or even problematic lives into ones of promise and fulfillment. Education can also provide vital tools for success in a highly competitive society such as our own. We seek to ensure that those veterans who wish to seek further education will find a hospitable and helpful environment in which to thrive. Recalling what both male and female veterans have given their country, simple fairness and reciprocity suggests we can do no less.

## References

Becker, L. (1986). Reciprocity. Boston: Routledge & Kegan Paul.

De Waal, F. B. M. (2000). Attitudinal Reciprocity in Food Sharing among Brown Capuchin Monkeys. Animal Behavior, 60(2), 253-261.

Hellman, S. (2006). Beating odds, a uniter rose from Chicago's tough side. The Boston Globe.

Quine, W. V. (1978). The Web of Belief. New York: Random House.

Rutte, C., & Taborsky, M. (2007). Generalized
    Reciprocity in Rats. PloS Biol, (7), e196.
Watts, D. P. (2002). Reciprocity and Interchange in the
    Social Relationships of Wild Male Chimpanzees.
    Behaviour, 139(2/3), 343-370.
WHO, W. H. O. (2001). Depleted Uranium. Geneva,
    Switzerland: U World Health Organization.

# Chapter 3

# Do You Hear My Silence? Listening to the Untold Stories of Military Students

## Kathleen Marie Heath
Professor of Anthropology
Indiana State University

This presentation reviews the ongoing problems of today's veterans and those to whom veterans are related as they seek a college degree. Many examples are discussed that capture the difficult experiences entailed by these problems and indicate the need for higher education to eliminate these problems.

Researcher: "On a scale of one to seven, how satisfied are you with Veteran Services on your campus?

Respondent: "Six".

Researcher: "Is there anything else you want to add?"

Respondent: "No".

I am a scientist. I form testable hypotheses and work with quantitative data. I am also an anthropologist. I know that such data do not represent the whole story. The missing pieces are frequently the unsolicited stories - the stories told by many over a long period of time. As a tenured - faculty with an open - door policy, I have the privilege of being a participant/observer of student life on campus, the successes, the failures, the highs, the lows, the listener of the untold stories. Here are my impressions of a compilation of stories listened to over the last ten years from men and women veterans, servicemembers currently enlisted in military service, and their immediate family members who are on campus as students.

As I enter the classroom on the first day of the semester, I can usually identify the military students in my course. Some will be women others men, some very young, others older but they all are well groomed and sit tall in their chairs. They listen intensely but tend not to ask questions. As one student so elegantly phrased it, "how do you go from boots to books?" This is when I began to listen.

I just returned from Iraq and wanted to take advantage of my GI educational benefits. Most of my old friends didn't go to college and I don't relate to these students, I don't fit in with the study groups. My military friends are scattered all over the country, the nearest one is over two hours away.

Civilian life on campus is so different from the infrastructure of the military where you have clear instructions, guidance, and support. I didn't figure it out until I was a junior.

Excuse me Professor, do you know if there are other vets in the class? It would be nice to have a classmate who was a vet to study with.

I've been repeatedly deployed, four years is now approaching ten years – It's hard being a 30 year old college student with a family and my military duties, no wonder so many student-vets drop out of college.

These phrases I have heard many times from many different GI Joes & Janes, if I only had a place to go on campus, if I only had a support system. That is when I coined the term student-vet. Although I could listen and in some cases even get them together with fellow student-vets, several of their concerns I had no idea how to address.

I am getting deployed two weeks before the semester ends. What affect will that have on my grade? What should I do? All my professors are telling me different things.

Although we have a great veterans administrator on campus – he is only one

and over worked. Do you know of a place on campus where I can maintain my military records and keep current on veteran benefits?

Vets get the run around when trying to get help on campus; the staff is ill prepared to meet the needs of vets.

The military offers a lot of programs to help vets with their transition but when it comes to the educational benefits, they are in so many different places and so far away. I didn't even hear about some of them until it was too late.

Then I became aware of another group of students who were having difficulty, the relatives of vets. Many students have spouses in the military, some deployed leaving a single parent to maintain the household and raise the children. Some have brothers and sisters in the military. The student-vet-relatives have their own stories.

The military is holding a meeting for returning vet family members during finals week. What am I to do?

I need to miss class several times this semester to go to the veterans hospital, it is more than an hour drive each way and each trip will take me the entire day.

My sister is in the military in Iraq. We were very close. I worry all the time. My brother doesn't want to talk about it and my parents are so worried that I don't want to bother them with it.

I use to be a good student until my brother was killed in Afghanistan. My family was so sad, I had no one to talk to. My grades went down, I just couldn't cope. I only made it this far because a veteran faculty member helped me. I am spending this year repeating courses. If only I had a place to go, people to talk to who would understand.

Not all is a story of woe. Since 9/11 the military personnel and their family members are respected for their sacrifice and dedication to all of our security. The Vet Culture on campus has changed with the times. Unlike the 1960's and 1970's, other students do not shun student-vets in uniform. On the contrary, they volunteer to aid them in need.

Debbie, the wife of GI Joe who was deployed in Iraq, had to drive over two hours for military services several times during a semester. The appointments were during regular business hours, which meant she would miss several class periods in several different courses. Several Debbies had children and some with unreliable cars. Students helping out the Debbies of campus is more the norm than the exception – taking notes, catching them up on class-work during off hours, babysitting, and even lending them their cars. Professors too record classes and provide extended office hours to help them succeed.

GI Joes & Janes may need to miss a few weeks within a semester or be employed to duty before completing a semester. Faculty have made special arrangements for GI Joes & Janes to complete their assignments and even take exams online. Fellow classmates have volunteered to fax or e-mail notes and even present oral presentations for absentee vets.

The most difficult of all is the student who has a relative injured or killed in the line of duty. Fellow classmates and faculty alike have shown great empathy in this regard. Calling them and checking up on their well being, spending time with them so they are not alone, and offering them space when they need to be alone.

The Vet Culture has changed. The image of the student-vet and the student-vet-relative has moved to one of compassion, empathy, and respect. In addition, the Campus-Culture has changed since the economic crisis of 2008. Today, more and more students hold part-time or full-time jobs off campus, are married/divorced, have families, and represent the non-traditional student returning to school for retraining. The student-vet is no longer isolated from the general campus population but blends in and shares many life experiences with her fellow classmates. Nonetheless, The vet-Student and vet-student-relative have special needs that must be addressed as soon as possible-not put-off, not ignored.

The 'silence' tells the story. But we can listen, we can learn, and we can implement change to alleviate many of the unique problems facing the student-vet and the student-vet-relative. First, we need to assure that each campus has a Student Veterans Organization. This is a simple, low cost solution to fulfill the need for a "Troop-Group", a buddy system of student-vets and student-vet-relatives to share activities amongst themselves as well as being part of the other student organizations. All student organizations are centered on a common theme aimed at uniting a sub-culture of campus students to give a student who may feel isolated a sense of inclusion, a member of a social network.

Second, administrators need to develop protocols for the absentee Student-Vet. Withdrawal from classes or the entire semester should be the last resort for students who have attended more than half of the semester. These students are serving their country, serving us; they are not taking an extended spring break. Repeated withdrawals are discouraging, extends the time needed to complete a program, and may result in failure to complete the program. With computer access and blackboard availability, classroom videotaping, and skype, student vets should be able to complete most of their coursework online. Although many professors are willing to work with student-vets during deployment or military activation, protocols need to assure all professors provide reasonable means for students to complete coursework during such circumstances.

Third, colleges and universities need a one-stop-shopping Veterans Center on campus. The center needs to provide comprehensive services not only to the Student-vet but also the Student-Vet-Relative, who have unique needs not common to the general population of college students. As the stories above show, these services fall into three broad categories. Veterans Educational Benefits represents a tangled web of opportunities and limitations that can be virtually unique to each student-vet. The students do not want another brochure handed to them, nor do they want an automated phone number or webpage. They really want and need an informed person capable of sifting through the bureaucratic paper work to help them select the optimum educational package and file necessary forms and applications.

Fourth, colleges and universities have counseling and disability services for students but are frequently not equipped to deal with the special needs of the student-vet. This is not to say that an on-campus Veterans Center is to replace Veterans Administration or Veterans Hospitals but to provide equal services for the student population. As the population of Student-Vets and Student-Vet-Relatives grow, campuses should have counselors trained to deal with PTSD (Post-Traumatic-Stress Disorder), grief, and reentering civilian life as well as disability services capable of dealing with the myriad of physical and head trauma injuries. Finally, a Campus

Veterans Center should provide a social networking system for integrating vets into campus life. Freshmen and sophomores could be paired up with a junior or senior support partner and student-vets could be grouped together into basic general education courses to help the transition between military life and civilian campus life.

Such implementations are not only good for the Student-Vet and Student-Vet-Relative but also for colleges and universities as well as the community. A win-win scenario should not be passed by, listen to the silence.

Chapter 4

# Improving the College Education of Veterans

## Dr. Steve F. Kime
### Past President, Servicemembers Opportunity Colleges
### Former Chair of the Veterans Advisory Committee on Education

Upon returning from the war, many veterans are attending college. Unfortunately, some of these veterans are encountering problems like those encountered by previous generations. Recent examination of this situation indicates that higher education officials are largely unaware of, or are ignoring, these problems.

Many details of the circumstances that veterans face at college are addressed during this Conference. The problems that they face run from the straightforward and mundane to flaws in national policy. All of the issues are important and everyone involved in the education of veterans needs to be aware of them.

We need, however, to place veteran education issues in a broad policy framework if we are to get the attention of legislators and policymakers. During this Conference you are encouraged to remember that, if change in the way veterans are treated is to be made, it will most likely happen because policymakers at the national level have taken action that causes progress on campuses and in the federal bureaucracy.

We must remember the unhappy past lest it be repeated, but it does no good to address current issues overburdened by the baggage of the past. It is time to help a new generation of professors, administrators, fellow students and Veterans Administration (VA) staffers make college the best it can be for veterans.

We need to recognize clearly the mistakes of the past and present, but understand that a new day is dawning and a precious opportunity to affect policy has been ushered in by the new G.I. Bill. Conference deliberations will do the most good if we understand the broader context in which they fit. Here are some policy categories to bear in mind:

Cultural Reform in Veterans' Affairs is badly needed. The Department of Veterans Affairs (DVA) operates in a culture that is firmly stuck in the past. Attitudes about veterans and those who educate them are in place that must be changed. These attitudes have roots in real, but outdated, experience. Today's veterans, supported by modernized technology and management, can be treated better and far more efficiently. A cultural revolution at DVA must be launched either from the top or from outside the Department.

Congress, Department of Defense (DoD), and Office of Management and Budget (OMB) stifle imagination and initiative at the Department of Veterans Affairs (DVA). No agency is more minutely managed, or more than the DVA. The Department still behaves like a subordinate agency rather than a Cabinet level policymaking Department that is charged with fulfilling the nation's promises to veterans. This is a major national policy issue. Many of the straightforward, practical, issues that plague veteran-students would go away or be mitigated if the DVA behaved like the major player that it could be.

The new GI Bill presents an opportunity to break old molds and outdated attitudes in veteran education. Hopefully, the Secretary will perceive this opportunity. The country is in the mood to see veterans treated logically and fairly, and increased participation in the G.I. Bill process by younger, savvy, players will inevitably increase pressure for reforms. The more active role of modern academe, this is heavily invested in new technology, can have a positive effect. Leadership in Congress is crucial. Today, unlike the past, hope for reform lies more in the Senate, Defense, and Veteran Committees than just those in the House. This may help.

Academe must stand up and be counted. Past performance was awful, but there are hopeful signs. Attitudes toward warriors, if not war, are changing in academe. The whiff of lots of federal money helps.

As the new GI Bill becomes institutionalized, there will be increasing opportunities for colleges and universities to participate. They can relegate veteran outreach to an obscure, underfunded and underappreciated corner of the university as in the past, or they can recognize the educational and social value of these opportunities at the policymaking level of their institutions. There needs to be "Command Attention" to veterans at every college and university.

There is a revolution going on in academe and veteran education must join it. A conceptual revolution has taken place in higher education. Adult and Continuing Education, not the care and feeding of 18-year olds, is already becoming the guiding concept. This, of course, applies readily to veterans who are adult students and not recent escapees from Mom's apron strings.

Adult students come to higher education with experience and education under their belt. Some of this is creditworthy. Adult learners have an idea why they are in college. Their focus on their future place in the world of work imposes reality and relevance on academics that they are unaccustomed to. This is healthy, and it portends great change in academe.

Veterans are very special adult learners who come from a unique and demanding workplace. Many have growing families and must hold outside jobs. It is time for the administration and management of veteran education, in academe, in Congress, and in the Veterans Department, to adjust policies to the Adult and Continuing Revolution in higher education.

A Management Revolution has taken place in America and Veteran education has been left out. It is high time that the Department of Veteran Affairs becomes at least as efficient as Home Depot.

Why haven't the management concepts of the big retailers and credit-card companies penetrated the Veterans Department, even though such concepts have gained some acceptance at such progressive bastions as the IRS?

The concept of Management by Exception is decades old, but it has never seen the light of day at DVA. Why hasn't the notion ever occurred to the VA? Instead of assuming that every veteran and every educational provider is a potential crook, why not set up effective processes to spot and punish lawbreakers?

The Rules and Regulations for the GI Bill make the federal tax code look transparent. A sweeping change is needed. The Byzantine accumulation of micromanaging generations of public servants should be swept away and replaced by a new, brief, simpler set of rules. Again, the opportunity to do so has been ushered in by the new GI Bill. Management reform to match the boldness and imagination of the new BI Bill is needed.

The technological revolution in America has not been applied to veteran education. There needs to be prompt and significant attention to upgrading technology in educational management if DVA is ever to discharge its duties under the new GI Bill. Health Care, a vital priority, has been allowed to smother out upgrades to veteran educational technology.

But more needs to be considered. It does little good to computerize bad practices. The reasons that the DVA is always behind in handling educational claims o of veterans are only partly technological. Too much information is demanded too often. There are far too many complex rules for fairly straightforward management problems. It is no wonder that time consuming decisions must be made one at a time by an analyst. The bottom line here is that technological upgrade must be done in conjunction with an overhaul of the regulations and procedures, and the "culture."

Recognize what veterans bring to the table. There has long been an active institution in academe dedicated to the education of active duty military members. Servicemembers Opportunity Colleges (SOC) has managed a Consortium aimed at facilitating attempts by men and women on active duty to attend civilian colleges and universities and earn regionally accredited civilian degrees. Hundreds of colleges and universities agree to military-friendly SOC policies on credit transfer, acceptance of military vocational learning that is creditworthy, and support of highly integrated and articulated degree programs.

The problem for veterans is that many of them choose to matriculate at colleges and universities that either do not usually serve active duty servicemembers or will not apply SOC's practices to veterans. It is time to form a seamless web between recognition of military learning of active duty servicemembers and that of veterans.

Such an effort cannot be merely tacked on to SOC's program for active duty servicemembers. DoD has a strong interest in the education of active duty military members and discharges its responsibilities for active duty military education well. DoD's interests fade when the servicemember becomes a veteran for good reason:

> DoD's mission is warfighting. DoD has never been the primary advocate for veterans, and it should not be. This is why we have a Department of Veterans Affairs, and why it is at the Cabinet-level. The Partnership that DoD has developed over the decades with higher education needs to be emulated by DVA.

Care for veterans in college. Veterans bring notable strengths to the classroom that should be recognized. They also have vulnerabilities and weaknesses that must be addressed. Many of them will spend their immediate post-service years on campuses, so the nation's responsibility to care for veterans falls at least partly to colleges and universities. It is their duty.

Veterans are very special adult learners. Many have served in Hell, and they carry the burden with them. College counseling and health care service must proactively address the need here. It is the nature of these vulnerabilities that they may or may not readily manifest themselves.

It should not be necessary to point out that veterans with physical handicaps must be accommodated. Accommodating the physically handicapped is firmly entrenched in the law. It needs to be added that injured veterans have been handicapped in especially traumatic ways, and their care is complex and urgent. Handicapped veterans did their duty. Colleges must do their duty, too.

Finally, advocates of educating veterans need to aggressively take advantage of the fact that we are at a key juncture. There is a new, very promising GI Bill. Veterans can actually attend college on it! Colleges and universities are changing their attitudes and they have powerful incentives to do better. Congress has awakened to the nation's responsibilities. The public is on board. It remains to get the administrative, managerial and academic policy houses in order.

We should be thinking of ways to put those houses in order to face the issues that we confront.

# Chapter 5

# Hallowed Halls

## Dr. R.W. Trewyn
### Vice President for Research
### Kansas State University

In 1995, Jim Stever and I published an article entitled, "Academe: Not So Hallowed Halls for Veterans" [1] which was based upon our experiences at the University of Cincinnati and Ohio State University, respectively, and on veterans' employment data we had collected from other universities. Because of the hostile reception we had experienced from the higher education community when we returned from Vietnam many years ago, we were hoping Desert Storm veterans would be welcomed on campus in the '90s. Sadly, their reception was less than enthusiastic most often, which led to our 1995 critique.

It would be nice to believe things have improved at universities for today's military veterans returning from

Afghanistan and Iraq, but that doesn't seem to be true; at least, not universally. Fortunately, the book Educating Veterans in the 21st Century [2] confronts the issues veterans are facing on campus and the authors are to be commended for recommending solutions and for undertaking this conference. To help delineate the foundation for some of the problems that still linger, here are a few highlights – or, perhaps more accurately, lowlights – from our 1995 article:

❖ THE CAMPUS WARS; THE 1960S AND BEYOND: The campus riots of the 1960s and '70s are emblematic of a period in American history that should not elicit kudos at most universities. Moreover, even though the antiwar rhetoric subsided after Vietnam, an anti-military culture remained on campus.

❖ AFFIRMATIVE INACTION: Few Vietnam-era veterans seeking employment on campuses after 1974 realized they were granted affirmative action rights equivalent to women and minorities if the university held federal contracts [3]. Veterans didn't know because universities didn't tell them.

❖ VETERAN CLEANSING: When universities discovered they were employing Vietnam veterans or others who had served during that era, many responded by terminating the vets. Affirmative action in reverse occurred ... campuses acted affirmatively to purge the system of all things military related.

❖ TRUTH; A CASUALTY OF WAR: The way some universities responded when confronted about their low employment levels for military veterans was to file a new federal report with inflated numbers. The fact that they hadn't hired enough veterans to account for the bigger total didn't matter.

❖ RIGHTS VERSUS WRONGS: Hopefully, veterans' rights have reached a place in the new millennium where military service can be listed proudly on employment applications. The expectation Desert Storm vets faced was that only "unrepentant veterans" would note their service. That's just wrong!

❖ PAYING THE PRICE FOR PATRIOTISM: For Vietnam veterans, the financial cost of military service was determined to be substantial in lifelong earnings. However, the price for receiving lower grades from anti-military professors has not been established. Those costs may not be trivial either.

There could be many reasons for the problems we described in 1995. One likely relates to graduate enrollments that underwent a massive and unprecedented surge in the 1960s until graduate school deferments ended in 1968. A significant number of those individuals are employed on college campuses yet today, many at high levels. Although very few of them were probably among the anti-war zealots who were spitting on the troops returning from Vietnam, many avoiding the draft by this means seem uncomfortable around those in uniform or with military experience, even decades later. They may not have felt the pride of military service, but they can see in those who have. Keep that in mind.

Finally, thank you for serving America! Your patriotism matters, even to those in the Hallowed Halls.

References

1 Trewyn, R.W. & Stever, J. A. (1995). Academia: Not so hallowed halls for veterans. Journal of the Vietnam Veterans Institute, 4, 63-75.

2 Herrmann, Douglas, Hopkins, Charles, Wilson, Roland B. & Allen, Bert (2009) Educating Veterans in the 21st Century. Charleston, S.C.: BookSurge," www.booksurge.com..

3 Vietnam Era Veterans Readjustment Assistance  Act of 1974; Title 38 United States Code Section   4212.

# Section II. Broad Perspectives on the Veterans Higher Education Problem

## Chapter 6

# Veterans and Higher Education: Barriers, Solutions and Successes

## Mr. James Selbe
### Master Sergeant, U.S. Marine Corps (Ret.)
### Assistant Vice President of American Council on Education (ACE)

> Several initiatives have recently been developed by ACE to serve those who serve. The goal is to promote access to and success in higher education for more than two million service members and their families who seek college degrees.

Campuses across the country, representing every sector in higher education, find themselves confronting a potential cohort of more than 2 million military provides these veterans with an education benefits package that makes a college education truly affordable. But it is going to require more than enhanced benefits to ensure that our nation's returning veterans can attain a college education.

Today's student-veterans demonstrate many of the characteristics of the nontraditional student. Veterans include older students with work and family responsibilities, students whose college entry has been delayed, first-generation students, and students from the lower and middle quartiles of socioeconomic status. Equally important when considering programmatic initiatives is that more than 1.6 million veterans have served in a combat environment since September 11, 2001. These experiences lend themselves to a whole new set of barriers to the attainment of postsecondary aspirations.

Further defining the current cohort is made more difficult by the absence of data to indicate enrollment trends, persistence rates, and other information specific to veteran engagement in higher education. "It all starts with the way we count", according to Cliff Adelman, senior associate at the Institute for Higher Education Policy. "Currently, the U.S. Department of Education does not collect annual data on the veteran student population and what data are collected are not representative. We don't see veterans in the data. They're not counted and we have to find out what happens when they participate in postsecondary education."

Despite the lack of data, findings from the ACE focus group research have delineated some factors that positively affect veteran participation in higher education—namely, greater access to accurate and timely information; streamlined processes for accessing education benefits; academic credit for military training and experience; and transitional support programs on college campuses. At the same time, ACE found that an alarming number of veterans are not considering higher education despite the increased benefit.

Focus group research revealed a number of reasons, most predominantly the needing to find a job right and not seeing the need for more education. Others assumed that the administrative process would be too much of a hurdle, or that college was not a reasonable option. Said one veteran, "Some of my friends are intimidated. . . . They have been in the military for a long time. They didn't have the mindset to look forward to go to school. They were of the assumption that school isn't for everyone. They would rather go out and get a job."

Many veterans indicated that lack of awareness is a major obstacle. Student veteran testimonials and the focus group findings confirmed that veterans are often unaware of the specifics of their education benefits and even less aware of the national, state, and campus programs intended to serve their needs. Specifically, focus group participants stated that they did not have as many information sources after transitioning from the military as they did when in the service.

A second major administrative hurdle that many veterans face is a lack of recognition of their military training and experience during the admissions process. Comparing the high school grade point average of a 26-year-old veteran to that of a high school senior doesn't do justice to the range of experiences and leadership skills the veteran will bring to campus. Veterans also want academic credit recommendations for their military training and experience to count toward their degrees. Unfortunately, veterans may spend hours traipsing from one campus office to another, trying to figure out why their documented training won't count toward a degree program in a related field. "Transfer credit is one nightmare we have to overcome," says California State University Chancellor Charles Reed. "While vets are going through transition, the paperwork and bureaucracy are unbelievable."

"What veteran-friendly colleges don't do is coddle veterans. Instead, they create environments in which vets have the tools to engage in debate and make use of resources."—Luke Stalcup, Army combat veteran and Georgetown University student. On top of administrative snafus with education benefits and transfer credits, veterans sometimes experience a less than welcoming campus climate. Stalcup recalls being told by a staff member at another institution, "Go stand over there. You are not special. We'll deal with you when we can deal with you." Stalcup added, "It's not that we'll get our feelings hurt. We're a tough bunch. But words carry the weight of the institution, determine the resources we get, and reflect respect that others on Campus show."

Veterans also report examples of isolation. "I didn't know other veterans on campus. And I wasn't able to relate to younger students not in the military," said Derek Blumke, cofounder and president of Student Veterans of America and a senior at the University of Michigan. "A student in one class asked me: "Were you in the military? Did you kill anyone?" After that, I became hesitant to tell people I had been in the military." With these kinds of encounters, veterans may want to lower their visibility—all the more reason why institutions must make greater efforts to foster an environment where veterans are apt to sense a feeling that they belong within the academic community.

Providing opportunities for contact with peers is a good place to start, especially during the first semester, when colleges and universities often lose veterans. To counter feelings of isolation and to increase retention, institutions and veterans groups are looking at a number of approaches, including one-stop services, veterans' centers, and peer organizations. Through the national organization Student Veterans of America, for example, veterans are becoming more visible and more vocal on their campuses, highly motivated as they are to make the college experience a positive one for future student veterans. As one veteran noted, "Once you find a peer, you become visible."

As colleges and universities give thought to creating a veteran-friendly campus, the key is to give veterans a voice as early as possible. Bring together senior level campus administrators and student veterans. Veterans are as diverse as any other students that colleges serve and it's important to understand the range of their needs and hopes, from housing options and opportunities for career networking, to peer mentors who foster their academic advancement.

As the number of returning veterans continues to dramatically increase, institutions of higher education can once again position their programs and services to ease the transition from soldier to student. In turn, this generation of veterans will be poised to contribute to their communities as civilians—filling the nation's workforce shortages in teaching and health care, leading successful nonprofit organizations, or starting up small businesses to reinvigorate a depressed economy. As we welcome an influx of returning soldiers who are eager to take advantage of expanded education benefits for themselves and their families, we must remember that just getting veterans to campus isn't enough.

We must also organize our programs, services, and policies to reflect veteran-friendly approaches that help these students set and meet educational goals. Simply put, we owe our veterans — and ourselves — the best higher education has to offer.

Chapter 7

# The History of Efforts to Educate America's Veterans

## Mr. Roland B. Wilson

MA Linguistics. U.S. Marine Intelligence. Gunnery Sergeant, U.S. Marine Corps (Ret.)

During World War II and subsequently, many discussions took place about whether it was a good idea to provide the veterans of that war with support to go to college during and after the end of the War. Since that time, the government and society have supported and at times have interfered with the efforts of veterans to obtain a college degree. This chapter will discuss historical events important to properly understand and support the education for today's veterans.

The purpose of this chapter is to provide a foundation background and history of veterans and their fight for a "fair" education, to provide insight into just some of the problems veterans in the past and present have; to have a common starting point in which we can all begin to help veterans more and to educate (educate the educated) those who want and some who may not want to know and help push for veterans change.

## Military Contributions of Veteran

The contributions of veterans are many. America's veterans have risked and at times sacrificed their lives for more than 230 years to protect the freedoms established by the founders of our great nation. Our service men and women have participated in one or more of approximately 40 conflicts at a cost of over 1,294,039 who never returned home.

## History of Veterans' Education

Education was not a necessity for veterans in the late 1700s, the 1800s, and in the 1900s prior to the end of World War II (Herrmann, Hopkins, Wilson, & Allen, 2009). In those years, veterans returned to their farms or to the jobs they held before joining the military. The practice of giving veterans help in order to attend college began in earnest with World War II.

An assessment of how educational opportunity for veterans has grown can be better appreciated by considering how educational opportunity has grown for another class of students, that class being women. Both veterans and women have had similar problems becoming accepted at higher education facilities and getting a "fair and equal education." Veterans have struggled for education since the 1700's and that prior to WWII benefits did not exists. Similarly, Barbara Miller Solomon described In the Company of Educated Women that the educational opportunity of women was non-existent in our society in the colonial era to the 20th century it increased across the Civil War, World War I, and World War II. The development of educational opportunity of women may be compared to that of veterans as follows.

I. From 1600~early 1700's

Centuries ago it was assumed that women had smaller brains and weaker minds than men. Women's roles were set from birth. Labor consumed most of the waking hours of females.

Comparatively, in the past and even today some people say such things as "veterans can't learn", "they are dumb" or "college is not a place for them." Some argued that veterans would not be sufficiently intelligent to succeed in college. Some were concerned about whether the typical college students would have difficulty getting along with those veterans who originate from a "lower socio economic strata." Luckily for women, shifts in science such as to the advent Newtonian in religion to evangelism, and in philosophy to Locke's associationism slowly undermined the assumption of female inferiority, bringing about a change in attitudes about them.

## II. During the 1700-1800's

Events such as the American Revolution gave women ways to enter the public arena, helped women redefine their identities, led to growth in schooling and made it possible for women to be more independent. During this time, veterans began to be more aware of what they could and could not do without an education.

## III. From the mid 1800's to the early 1900's

Due to the Civil War and WWI, women who gained invaluable experiences as substitutes for the young men turned soldiers furthered their professional goals, and developed a new expectation for advanced and equal education. Returning veterans not only wanted their jobs back, but wanted to become better educated to help further themselves as well.

## IV. From the early 1900's to the 1940's, the phase of Independence

Finally, higher education did become more accessible to highly motivated youth from various racial, ethnic, and religious backgrounds including women, especially the wealthy. In addition to this, women were finally regarded as equals in the political sphere. Veterans voices were finally beginning to be heard as well with the passage of the first GI Bill (Mettler, 2005). However, their education has never caught up to that of other groups or classes.

Women's education is said to nurture their identity and conversely, women's identities develop their education. Similarly we believe veterans education nurtures their identity and that their identities as veterans "can" help develop their education.

Needs of American Society

Manufacturing, business, and commerce, are increasingly more technical and need well-trained and educated veterans. American society and government could benefit from the contributions of veterans due to their unique education, as well as their military, world and leadership experiences. As of 25 May 2009, out of 435 Representatives and 100 Senators who serve in the Congress, veterans consist of only ninety-six members of the House and twenty-five members of the Senate. In the early 1970s and before, as many as three out of four members of Congress were veterans. "Since the beginning of the 20th century, the percentage of veterans in Congress was 10 percent to 15 percent higher than among the same age group of men.

However, wars such as the Vietnam War, and bad publicity given to that war, tarnished the idea that serving in the military was a civic duty (Burkett, 1998; Roth-Douquet & Schaeffer, 2006). Many college students found ways to avoid it along with others who would become the current educators of our children—and leaders of our country. Every post-World War II president until 1993 wore a uniform. But when Bill

Clinton was elected after he actively avoided military service during the Vietnam War, the precedent was broken. Society, both in civil education and our local and federal governments need the respectability of military service to change back to veterans.

## Lack of Support for Veterans Education

Foreign students are required by the Department of State (DOS) to have all the education and living funds they need prior to receiving their U.S. Visas and education on the United States. Nevertheless, many colleges and universities provide scholarships, internships, assistantships, and tuition assistance to foreign students. The vast majority of these institutions do not offer these same benefits to veterans. Why? Foreign students are already coming to study for their education and have the funds to do so. Many veterans do not or cannot afford to start a college education.

Many institutions give athletes substantial support. The amount of support depends on the sport and an athlete's contribution to the success of an institution's team. The financial support of some athletes in college is just an example of how certain students are educated at the expense of other students including veterans.

The GI Bill provides substantial support for veterans' opportunity to acquire a college education. Nevertheless, foreign students, athletes, and other special interest groups of students are supported better than veterans. Why can't veterans be supported as well as other groups on campus?

What Do Today's Veterans Need?

What veterans need is a question that has been posed for many years, but how many listened or searched for the answers? Veterans need a future that a good education can bring. Many veterans do not want to or can't return to the jobs that they had before service/war. Many veterans want new employment because they find that the job they had before serving no longer exists or cannot serve a family.

Also many veterans do not want to return to the jobs they had before leaving to serve because the military has trained them to use new technologies. They either want to use their new skills or at least employment that is more challenging than the job they had when they left. Additionally, many veterans want jobs involving leadership or management. All veterans receive an abundance of leadership training and most have held leadership positions in the military. Consequently they want leadership positions in American society—if possible.

Variety of Efforts to Help Veterans

A variety of efforts have been made to help veterans with their education needs. At least five kinds of efforts have been made These five kinds are listed in Table 7.1 and discussed in the following paragraphs.

## Table 7.1
## Kinds of Efforts to Help Veterans Get a College Degree

Organizations of vets to help vets
Businesses dedicated to help veterans
Government programs to support the
efforts of veterans to get an education
Government efforts to help veterans
find a place in society
Societal efforts to help veterans get
educated and find a place in society

Organizations That Help Veterans.

Veterans Service Organizations (VSOs) do a lot to help veterans with all aspects of life and continue to provide a large voice for veterans. Veterans groups hold meetings so that veterans can talk with others of the same background in a social non-threatening atmosphere. Veteran Student Organizations are appearing across the United States and on campuses. However, sometimes these organizations receive very little support from the schools, if any compared to other groups on campus. Universal Student Organizations such as the Student Veterans of America were established to give support and provide information to veterans who are in college.

Business dedicated to help veterans

There are commercial sites, books, and organizations that claim to help veterans with their higher educational needs. However, many of these are not for veterans as much as to make money at a veteran's expense.

GI Bill programs to support the efforts of veterans to get an education

On June 22, 1944, President Franklin D. Roosevelt signed into law the "Serviceman's Readjustment Act," better known as the "G.I. Bill of Rights." Under this legislation, the federal government provided World War II veterans with education, vocational training, loan guarantees for homes, farms, or businesses, unemployment pay, and assistance in job searches. This benefit was subsequently cut for the Korean and Vietnam era veterans.

A new Montgomery GI Bill was established in 1985. It was supposed to encourage veterans to go to college by having "them" invest in their education. Servicemembers were required to deposit a fixed sum into an account that could be used later to attend college. This was a very unpopular program and was considered a failure by many.

Service members were also able to withdraw this money a year after a year it had been put into an education account. When they did so, they lost their eligibility for the GI Bill. Unfortunately, many young service members withdrew the money from their account and spent it on other things. When these service members became veterans, there were no funds in savings to use to pay for their education. The Montgomery GI Bill was a failure in it denied GI Bill funds.

In 2008 Congress passed yet another GI Bill, the Post 9/11 GI Bill. Unlike the Montgomery GI Bill, the post 9/11 GI Bill does not require service members to contribute to a college account. As a result it will provide college support for nearly all veterans, those who served in the regular service branches and the National Guard and reservists. The Post 9/11 GI Bill is the most comprehensive veterans education bill ever established. However, there are vast delays in not only the implementation of this bill, but now congress is eating away at other veterans benefits such as "Tricare for Life."

As many of you know or may remember, "free and lifetime" health and dental care was a promise given to all who agreed to serve 20 or more years. This promise was taken back in the 1980's. In the current bill, there are things that hurt the veterans such as giving the service branches the choice of when to start to allow veterans to pass this education benefit to their children. The Department of Defense (DoD) has picked up on this and said that this is a retention incentive and would not be given to those who already retired.

Societal efforts to help veterans find a place in society.

Servicemembers Opportunity Colleges (SOC). Other programs to help veterans include the Servicemembers Opportunity Colleges (SOC), which consists of over 1800 colleges and universities in the United States who have promised to provide service members and veterans with the same services offered non-veterans such as the flexibility and transfer of military credits in conjunction with the American Council on Education (ACE). SOC was established in 1972 and is funded by the DoD (Servicemembers Opportunity Colleges, 2004). SOC is cosponsored by the American Association of State Colleges and Universities (AASCU) and the American Association of Community Colleges (AACC), in cooperation with educational associations, including the Military Services, the National Guard, and the Coast Guard.

Although 1800 members of SOC may seem like a lot, it is estimated that there are about 4146 colleges and universities in the United States. Therefore, more schools do not belong to SOC than do belong to SOC. Table 7.2 lists the general categories of services promised by SOC.

Table 7.2
Services Promised by SOC

The institutions of this organization promise to offer the same services to active duty military and veterans as are offered to non-veteran students

These institutions also promise to provide services needed by servicemembers and veterans: flexible residency requirements; transfer of military credits; transfer credits from nationally standardized tests.

Unfortunately, some of the schools on the SOC list have not provided all of the services promised. Some SOC schools do not provide proper credits and flexibility, let alone advice on how to transfer credits or convert their military earned credits/experience.

National Association of Veterans Research Foundation (NAVREFs). This is a membership organization of the VA affiliated nonprofit research foundations, also known as the nonprofit research and education corporations, and its mission is to promote high quality management and communication among the VA-affiliated nonprofit research and education corporations and to pursue issues at the government level that are of interest to its members.

National Association of Program Administrators (NAVPA). This is a professional organization for people working in both campus and community-based veterans' programs.

Veterans Advisory Committee on Education (VACOE). This committee was created by statute, Title 38, United States Code, §3692. The provisions of this statute provide for an Education Service within the Veterans Benefits Administration and is responsible for providing support to the Committee. The objectives and scope of this committee is to provide advice to the Secretary of Veterans Affairs on the administration of education and training programs for veterans and servicepersons, reservists and guard personnel, and for dependents of veterans. (under Presentations 30, 32, 35 and 36 of Title 38, and Presentation 1606 of Title 10, United States Code).

American Council on Education (ACE). This organization has done a very good job at providing an easy to use site for veterans to evaluate how many credits they may have based on their military occupational specialty (MOS) and training. However, the amount of credit given to military training and experience are often only approximate. The ACE evaluations of credits sometimes do not take proper account of Military Occupational Specialty and the amount of experience (grade level) that a veteran had while in the service. This is not as much of an ACE problem as it is a service problem, since the services must request ACE come and evaluate their courses. Also the amount of credits awarded differs between one service's MOS and the identical MOS in another service, sometimes even if the MOS is studied at the same school/place. This too, must be worked out by the services to ensure their service personnel are getting equal credit for equal work.

Corporate Veterans-Education Programs. There has been an increased interest in veterans' education through the corporate effort of America and key companies such as Walmart, and the Lilly foundation leading the way. Walmart has helped higher educational institutions in a number of states. Lilly has helped such institutions in Indiana (described by Hitt in this book). Certain universities have developed programs specifically for veterans. George Washington University (GWU) Efforts has created three new programs to assist veterans with tuition and adjustment to college life.

Creating Next Generation Leaders. This GWU program helps female students connect with leading women across a variety of fields and develop their roles as future women in leadership, which includes sitting down with female leaders in government including ambassadors. This program is exactly the type of detailed assistance that veterans also need. One of the primary reasons I believe it is not also a veterans program is that Veterans are NOT considered a minority or protected class (something addressed by Admiral Gordon, in this book).

Department of Veterans Affairs' Yellow Ribbon program. Slots are generous, but unfortunately limited and to qualify for the Department of Veterans Affairs' Yellow Ribbon program a veteran must have at least 36 months of active duty service post 9/11. Student veterans also have support from Student Veteran Services Coordinator at universities that serve as a liaison to student veterans, assists veterans in logistical needs, and helps raise awareness in administrative departments about student veteran issues.

Development of Attitudes About the Education of Service Members and Veterans. After World War II the American citizenry quickly accepted the idea that veterans deserved a college education in return for their military service. On college campuses some faculty and students were unsure about whether veterans would succeed academically and socially. After just a few years it was recognized that veterans would be successful.

Educational Benefits. As is well known, during and after the Vietnam War some professors and administrators adopted negative attitudes about service members and veterans (Trewyn & Stever, 1995). Subsequently, many politicians, celebrities, other public figures and citizens concluded that America had learned that, regardless of their political affiliation or stance on war, people should not attack those service men and women who are sent to defend the nation. Society decided that it was unfair to blame our military and veterans for participating in a war that the public disapproved.

Nevertheless, some veterans feel that some people in higher education still possess these negative attitudes, partly because some professors and administrators have adopted the practice of some politicians, celebrities, and public figures who have recently concluded that they could voice anti-war attitudes if they claim that they supported the troops while being opposed to a particular war. However, claims to support the troops, while opposing a war, give the military no more cover than it had before and statements of opposition to a war are held by many veterans as disheartening. Also, veterans feel strongly that these anti-war attitudes are a slap in the face to their faithful service.

Also some veterans fear that some people in higher education still possess negative attitudes because some politicians feel comfortable making outright anti-veteran comments. For example, a ranking member of the House recently stated that some homecoming veterans are "potential right-wing extremists." Such statements damage the status of veterans and, as believed by many service members and veterans, embolden the enemy and encourage them to attack American forces more often and more aggressively.

Besides anti-veteran statements, the absence of pro-veteran statements and actions by prominent politicians is conspicuous and suggests they may hold anti-veteran attitudes. For example, in the summer of 2009 at 8 am in the morning, Congress held a moment of silence for the pop star Michael Jackson. It makes those men and women who defend this great country wonder why doesn't Congress and higher education do this for the servicemen and women? When was the last time congress held a moment of silence for those men and women killed and wounded in action? They give their blood and lives, but have no voices in the halls of Congress. Why cannot Congress take a few minutes each week to hold a moment of silence and read out the names of those from their states who have been killed or wounded during that week while protecting our freedom?

What Have We learned?

Since the advent of the GI Bill, the notion of giving veterans a fair and equal higher education has begun to blossom. However, we still have a long way to go to ensure that veterans get a good college education, one that is comparable to that given to non-veterans

## References

Burkett, B. G. (1998). Stolen valor: How the Vietnam generations were robbed of its heroes and its history. Sunnyvale, CA: Verity Press.

Herrmann, D., Hopkins, C., Wilson, R.B., & Allen, B., (2009). Educating veterans in the 21st Century. North Charleston, South Carolina: Booksurge Llc.

Mettler, S. (2005). Soldiers to citizens: The GI Bill and the Making of the Greatest Generation. Cambridge: Oxford Univ. Press.

Roth-Douquet, K. & Schaeffer, F. (2006a). AWOL: The Unexcused Absence of America's Upper Classes from Military Service—and How It Hurts Our Country. New York: Collins.

Servicemembers Opportunity Colleges. (2004). What is SOC? Retrieved on February 5, 2005, from http://www.soc.aascu.org/socgen/WhatIs.html.

Trewyn, R. A. & Stever, J. A. (1995). Academia: Not so hallowed halls for veterans. Journal of the Vietnam Veterans Institute, 4, 63-75.

# Chapter 8

# The Best Practices in Educating Veterans and Servicemembers

## Command Sergeant Major
## W. Douglas Gibbens

US Army Reserve (Ret), Executive Director, Indiana Committee for Employer Support of the Guard and Reserve

At the request of Indiana's Governor and the Adjutant General of the Indiana National Guard, leaders of Indiana's higher educational institutions developed a list of "best" practices that professors and college administrators should follow in their interactions with Servicemembers and Veterans. These best practices will be proposed as a guide for academics everywhere.

After a series of events that can be left unspoken, in 1967 I found myself as a member of the United States Army Reserve and attending college at the University of Illinois attempting to obtain my Bachelor's Degree in Agricultural Economics. During this time, I was the victim of several events that illustrate the concerns of today's Servicemembers and Veterans as they attempt to complete their higher education and serve their country at the same time.

Specifically, I found myself called to attend Annual Training for 17 days during the middle of a semester, which meant that I would be unavailable to attend class during this time and that I would also miss at least one "hourly" examination. In addition, there were times that I was scheduled for additional training or military schools that conflicted with my class attendance or examinations. There was no specific policy by the University of Illinois to address these challenges, so each professor treated them in his or her own manner. On more than one occasion, I received a failing grade on an examination because I had to attend training at the time of the exam. I also had challenges on attendance as class attendance was tightly monitored and played significantly into a student's grades. Sometimes my grades suffered because my training kept me from attending class. I mention my own experience only to illustrate that I have empathy for the challenges raised by today's members of the Guard and Reserve as they face geometrically increased pressures for training and mobilization from what I faced at that time.

Currently I work for the Indiana Employer Support of the Guard and Reserve (ESGR, 2007; U.S. Department of Labor, 2006). This organization is an agency of the Department of Defense that seeks to ensure that servicemembers do not lose their civilian jobs when they are deployed. ESGR attempts to encourage employers to retain the jobs of servicemembers during deployment (Bauman, 2009; Johnson, 2009; McGrevey & Keher, 2009). The organization tries to promote a culture in which all American employers support and value the military service of their employees. ESGR recognizes outstanding support, increases awareness of the law, and resolves conflicts through mediation. ESGR is primarily a volunteer organization with only a very limited staff. I am the Executive Director for ESGR in Indiana, which means that I am the senior full time staff member in Indiana.

Nationally the ESGR has nearly 5,000 volunteers and in Indiana we have about 120 volunteers. We work to ensure that Guard and Reserve members will return to the same or better employment they had prior to deployment. ESGR really believes and practices the idea that positive recognition of employers is far more effective in dealing with employers than pointing out to them that not saving the jobs of servicemembers is against the law.

I am the Executive Director of the Indiana ESGR in part because I have extensive experience counseling and assisting servicemembers. I am a retired Command Sergeant Major (CSM) from the US Army Reserve and served a total of 35 years in the Army. A Command Sergeant Major is the highest enlisted rank that can be attained in the Army and typically serves as the Senior Enlisted Advisor to a commander at the Battalion and higher level. Because I had the privilege of serving my last nine years as Command Sergeant Major for Major Generals (2 stars), I have had exposure to thousands of soldiers and their varied challenges and concerns.

Since the spring of 2002, the Indiana ESGR has assisted in the mobilization and demobilization of servicemembers at Camp Atterbury, Indiana. Camp Atterbury has become a major mobilization center for members of all branches of service, not just the Army. Through this source, as well as concerns raised directly to the Indiana ESGR, we have become aware of the problems that members of our Guard and Reserve have had with our colleges and universities.

Although the ESGR is commissioned to investigate any employment problems of Guard members or Reservists before or after deployment, the Indiana ESGR decided to investigate the reports of problems concerning higher education to determine what, if any action was merited to solve the higher educational problems of their Guard and Reserve members. This decision was made because Guard and Reserve members engage in higher education to improve their chances for employment, improve the status of their current employment, and better position themselves for advancement within the military. As a result, in 2007 and 2008 the Indiana ESGR conducted a program to investigate whether Guard and Reserve members actually do encounter problems at their higher educational institutions.

First, the web was searched in 2007 to determine whether Indiana colleges and universities posted their policy for students who were Guard and Reserve members and were deployed. For example, policies might address whether deployed students would be given back the funds they used to pay for their tuition. Another issue might be whether deployed students were given the right to take an incomplete and complete a course after returning from deployment. Posting a school's deployment policy helps Servicemembers take account of their college or university's practices when a student is deployed.

Second, CEOs of Indiana higher educational institutions, or their representatives, were surveyed about their school's practices concerning the deployment of Guard and Reserve members. The survey also asked about the educational practices of Guard and Reserve members in general (Herrmann, 2007; see also Sternberg, MacDermid, Wadsworth, Vaughan, & Carlson, 2009). Slightly more than 60% of institutions surveyed completed and returned the survey. 30% of those surveyed reported that their Guard and Reserve members encountered some kind of problem at their school. Educational problems pertaining to deployment were noted at about 10% of these schools. Other problems were as high as 25% of the schools surveyed reported that Guard and Reserve members encountered problems getting transfer credit for military training and experience. 23% of the schools reported that some Guard and Reserve members felt that one or more educational programs at their school did not take account of their military background when it should have. About 19% of the schools heard that the campus climate did not welcome servicemembers. Similarly, 17% of the schools felt that servicemembers and veterans did not get sufficient help with college adjustment issues, such as getting along with non-veteran students. The least common concerns (reported by about 15% of schools) had to do with difficulties of Guard and Reserve members in obtaining financial aid and in obtaining health care on campus.

The survey results indicated that a substantial proportion of Guard and Reserve members were being treated poorly on campus according to the CEOs or representatives that returned the survey. It was concluded that such poor treatment was serious and the results of the research were reported by the Indiana ESGR to Major General R. Martin Umbarger, the Adjutant General of the Indiana National Guard. The Adjutant General then conveyed these results to the Governor, Mitchell E. Daniels Jr. The Governor and the Adjutant General decided that Guard and Reserve members would be better served in college if the leaders in higher education formed a taskforce that developed guidelines for professors and administrators to use when interacting with servicemembers and veterans.

Accordingly the Governor and the Adjutant General sent a letter outlining the problem and encouraging the CEO or a representative of each school to participate in the taskforce. The ESGR was delegated responsibility for arranging the meetings and communication of the taskforce. ESGR then contacted the CEOs of all Indiana schools and universities both by letter and by e-mail and invited them or their representative to serve on an Advisory Committee that would be responsible for approval of guidelines developed by a Steering Committee. A Steering Committee was also formed being made up of representatives of ten colleges and universities, of which eight institutions were supported by the state and two were private institutions.

The Steering Committee met in person once and several times over the web in the autumn of 2008. The goal of this committee was to develop some Best Practices that Professors and Administrators could use when interacting with servicemembers and Veterans. In October, a preliminary draft of Best Practices was presented to the Advisory Committee that then offered suggestions about the initial draft of the Best Practices. In November members of the Steering Committee met with some members of the Advisory Committee and developed a revision of the Best Practices available at that time.

In late November, the latest draft of the Practices was sent once again to entire Advisory Committee for revisions or comments. Twenty two of the 79 institutions gave their approval of the Best Practices; the remaining institutions gave tacit approval in that they did not give any negative feedback. In December, minor revisions were made in the wording and grammar of the Best Practices and then this final draft was unanimously adopted by the Steering committee. (It should be noted that around the same time, the American Council on Education, 2008, also developed a list of Best Practices similar in content to Indiana's Best Practices).

The final draft of the Best Practices was then submitted to Governor Daniels and Major General Umbarger in January 2009. The Governor approved and "highly recommended" the adoption of these Best Practices to all institutions. In June, the Governor and Adjutant General mailed the final draft of the Best

Practices to the CEOs of Indiana's 79 colleges and universities, inviting them to implement those Best Practices that were appropriate to their institution. The Best Practices recommended by the Governor and Adjutant General consisted of four categories of guidelines.

Best Practices #1

Designate a highly visible office with appropriate staff to serve as an institutional single point of contact for students with any type of military affiliation to coordinate services, provide advice, create programming, and advocate for students with issues related to their military experiences and student status. Within this Best Practice #1, the Steering and Advisory Committees included three sub-points.

1. Ensure that the person who is the Point of Contact is knowledgeable about and sensitive to the needs and experiences of servicemembers and student veterans

2. Appoint staff at an appropriate level to deliver direct student support and services as well as to advise decision-makers on campus policies and procedures related to military servicemembers and veterans

3. Facilitate peer-to-peer interaction for servicemembers and veterans through options such as designation of space for gathering and networking, sponsorship of a student club or organization for military students, or organization of other student activities

Best Practices #2

Develop transition programming and ongoing assistance specifically designed to meet the needs of military servicemembers and veterans. Within this Best Practice #2, the Steering and Advisory Committees included three sub-points.

1. Develop orientation programs specifically for students with a military background that is appropriately flexible in both content and timing.
2. Ensure that staff is knowledgeable about the counseling, advising, and potential health care needs of students with a military background and that they can support, refer, or inform them appropriately.
3. Create an efficient process for students departing for or returning from deployment or other military duty.

Best Practices #3

Develop and communicate to students, staff, and faculty administrative policies and procedures to cover the unique situations and experiences of students who are servicemembers or veterans. Within this Best Practice #3, the Steering and Advisory Committees included a list of activities to support and communicate.
1. Academic credit articulation for military training and military experience.
2. Fee deferments for students when educational benefits such as the GI Bill or tuition assistance are

delayed beyond normal payment dates.

3. Withdrawal and/or course completion procedures for students called for deployment or other military duty during the academic year, including withdrawals.

4. Absence policies related to military duty.

5. Fee refund policies for military withdrawals.

6. Mechanisms for communication with students while deployed.

7. Procedures for returning students following deployment or other military duty.

8. Sensitive consideration for surviving family members of students who died while in military service to include resolution of grades from the student's final semester and potential posthumous award of degrees

Best Practices #4

Institutions are encouraged to communicate with each other to develop and implement additional best practices to serve Servicemembers and Veterans. Finally, the Steering and Advisory Committees encouraged institutions with small numbers of servicemembers and veterans to maximize their services by collaborating with other similar institutions. Additionally, institutions were advised that they should take advantage of opportunities for their designated staff members to meet with peers from other schools – or in other words, develop a networking system to share best practices and policies.

Follow Up

In the November, 2008 meeting of the members of the Steering Committee and Advisory Committee a suggestion was made that follow-up should be conducted to determine the usefulness of the different Best Practices. The ESGR also plans to hold a celebratory meeting to congratulate institutions for their support of our servicemembers and veterans. In addition the ESGR plans to provide Indiana academics who so desire the opportunity to go to Camp Atterbury in May of 2010 so that they can observe training and mobilization efforts of our Men and Women in uniform. All academics who attend will be given a military briefing that will explain how certain weapon systems operate, about the kinds of duties conducted by our soldiers in Iraq and Afghanistan, and the capabilities of Camp Atterbury for training.

A copy of Best Practices sent to the CEOS of Indiana's Colleges and Universities in June, 2009 follows this chapter.

References

American Council on Education. (2008a). Serving those who serve: Higher education and America's veterans. Retrieved March 5, 2009, from http://www.acenet.edu/Content/NavigationMenu/ProgramsServices/MilitaryPrograms/serving/Veterans_Issue_Brief_1108.pdf

Bauman, M. (2009) The mobilization and return of undergraduate students serving in the National Guard and Reserves. In Ackerman, R. & DiRamio, D. (Eds.), Creating a Veteran-Friendly Campus: Strategies for Transition and Success, New Directions for Student Services, No. 126, Jossey Bass: San Francisco.

Employer Support for the Guard and Reserve (2007). Retrieved on December 5, 2007 from http: www.esgr.gov

Herrmann, D. J. (2007) Investigations s into the treatment of servicemembers by Indiana Higher Educational Institutions. Terre Haute, IN: Veterans Higher Educational Group.

Johnson, T. (2009). Ensuring the success of deploying students: A campus view. In Ackerman, R. & DiRamio, D. (Eds.), Creating a Veteran-Friendly Campus: Strategies for Transition and Success. New Directions for Student Services, No. 126, Jossey Bass: San Francisco.

McGrevey, M. & Keher, D. (2009) Stewards of the public trust: Federal laws that serve service members and student veterans. In Ackerman, R. & DiRamio, D. (Eds.), Creating a Veteran-Friendly Campus: Strategies for Transition and Success. New Directions for Student Services, No. 126, Jossey Bass: San Francisco.

Sternberg, M., MacDermid Wadsworth, S., Vaughan, J., & Carlson, R. (2009). The higher education landscape for student Servicemembers and Veterans in Indiana. West Lafayette: Military Family Research Institute at Purdue.

U.S. Department of Labor (2006). Elaws - employment laws assistance for workers and small businesses - USERRA Advisor. Retrieved in 2006 from http://www.dol.gov/elaws/userra.htmport.

## Best Practices for Support of Military and Veteran Students in Higher Education

❖ Designate a highly visible office with appropriate staff to serve as an institutional single point of contact for students with any type of military affiliation to coordinate services, provide advice, create programming, and advocate for students with issues related to their military experiences and student status

▪ Ensure point of contact is knowledgeable about and sensitive to the needs and experiences of service members and student veterans

▪ Appoint staff at an appropriate level to deliver direct student support and services as well as advise decision-makers on campus-level policies and procedures related to military service members and veterans

▪ Facilitate peer-to-peer interaction for service members and veterans through options such as designation of space for gathering and networking, sponsorship of a student club or organization, or organization of student activities

❖ Develop transition programming and ongoing assistance specifically designed to meet the needs of military service members and veterans

▪ Develop orientation programs specifically for students with a military background that is appropriately flexible in both content and timing

▪ Ensure that staff are knowledgeable about the counseling, advising, and potential health care needs of students with a military background and can support, refer, or inform them appropriately

▪ Create an efficient process for students departing for or returning from deployment or other military duty

❖ Develop and communicate to students, staff, and faculty administrative policies and procedures to cover the unique situations and experiences of students who are service members or veterans

▪ Credit articulation for military training and military experience

▪ Fee deferments for students when education benefits such as GI Bill or tuition assistance are delayed beyond normal payment due dates

- Withdrawal and/or course completion procedures for students called for deployment or other military duty during the academic year including withdrawals, incomplete grades or award of partial credit as appropriate

- Absence policies related to military duty

- Fee refund procedures for military withdrawals

- Mechanisms for communication with students while deployed

- Returning student procedures following deployment or other military duty

- Sensitive consideration for surviving family members of students who died while in military service to include resolution of grades from the student's final semester and potential posthumous award of degree

❖ Institutions are encouraged to communicate with each other to develop and implement additional best practices to serve military members and veterans

- Institutions with small numbers of military members and veterans may be able to maximize services by collaborating with other similar institutions

- Institutions should take advantage of opportunities for their designated staff members to meet with peers from other schools

Chapter 9

# Update from the Veteran Affairs Advisory Committee on Education (VACOE)

## Dr. Kathy M. Snead
VACOE Chair, 2009-2010
President, Servicemembers Opportunity Colleges

The Secretary of the Department of Veterans Affairs is advised on education matters by the Veterans Affairs Committee on Education (VACOE). This chapter addresses the college problems of veterans that might be considered by the VACOE and possibly called to the attention of the Secretary.

It is my pleasure to update you on the mission and proposed actions of the Veterans' Advisory Committee on Education. The purpose of the Veterans' Advisory Committee on Education is to advise the Secretary on the administration of education and training programs for veterans, servicepersons, and dependents of veterans. I recently completed my second year as a Secretarial appointee to the Committee. In September when the 2009-2010 Committee appointments were announced, I was appointed Chair for the coming year. Our Advisory Committee will not formally meet until January 2010, so I have little to share in terms of directions and priorities our committee will focus upon in support of veteran education.

Instead, today I will present a Department of Veterans Affairs (VA) update that Mr. Bill Spruce, Yellow Ribbon Program Manager, provided at Servicemembers Opportunity Colleges' (SOC) annual Advisory Board meeting on October 5th. The majority of the VA update to the SOC Advisory Board was to provide details of the Post 9/11 GI Bill workload that has consumed VA personnel at all levels. According to Bill Spruce, the VA has received 277,403 claims for Post 9/11 GI Bill. The Education benefits unit has received 249,668 requests for eligibility determinations, and 27,735 enrollment certifications. Just a reminder, eligibility determinations may contain an enrollment certification that is processed simultaneously. To date, VA has completed action on 205,074 of those claims.

VA currently has 72,329 claims pending: 60,071 of those claims relate to eligibility determinations and 12,258 of those are enrollment certifications. Veterans Affairs personnel estimate that 25% of eligibility determinations also include a school enrollment certificate. Bill also shared information about how long it takes to process a Post 9/11 GI Bill claim. On average, it takes approximately 35 days of waiting to process a claim due to the work backlog. The time to process claims increases each year during September and October as the fall enrollments is the most common time for veterans enrolling in college. VA has asked schools to continue submitting their enrollment certificates timely.

Other VA Education Division statistics that might interest you are that since August 1, 2009 the VA has authorized payment of $997 million in non-presentation 33 education benefits. And they have authorized payment of $1.05 billion for all education benefit programs (including the Post 9/11 Bill). So while the Post 9/11 GI Bill has been the educational benefit program in the news, it is important to remember that the VA is authorizing education payments for two major benefit programs at the same time with different payment schedules, eligibility requirements, and monitoring procedures in addition to several others (1606 and 1607).

The higher education community has responded positively to Yellow Ribbon Program. As a reminder, the Yellow Ribbon GI Education Enhancement Program is a provision of the Post 9/11 Veterans Educational Assistance Act of 2008. This program allows degree-granting institutions in the United States to enter into an agreement with VA to fund tuition expenses that exceed the highest public in-state undergraduate tuition rate. Participating institutions can contribute up to 50% of those expenses and VA will match the same amount as the institution. VA has signed 3,539 agreements for the 2009-2010 school year. The highest contribution from a school is $66,150 for 25 students. More than eleven hundred of the Yellow Ribbon agreements are for an unlimited number of students at that institution.

Approximately 25 new education bills amending the Post 9/11 are currently on the floor of Congress. One amendment that has already passed into law is the Marine Gunnery Sergeant John David Frye Scholarship which amends Chapter 33 to include the children of servicemembers who die in the line of duty after September 10, 2001.

This concludes the Veterans Affairs update portion of my chapter. The proposed legislation is a great segue into my own observations on some of the legislative concerns that the higher education community have been engaged in regarding the Post 9/11 GI Bill during the past few months.

SOC participates in the Partnership for Veterans Education, a unique consortium of military, veterans service organizations, and higher education associations that collaboratively has identified a number of technical and legislative policy recommendations to enhance and improve the Post 9/11 GI Bill for our veterans. We are certainly interested in discussing these legislative change recommendations at the appropriate venue later in the conference. For now, I'll merely summarize the key issues:

• Modifying the regulatory language related to "established charges" as the combination of tuition and fees charged the individual for the term, quarter, or semester thereby providing a single metric so that the state tuition and fees chart reflects the typical enrollment pattern of most college students at the highest priced public institution in the state where the veteran resides. [Creating a state tuition and fees chart based on two separate caps artificially inflates the stated cost of an in-state undergraduate program of education and generates wild discrepancies in the maximum benefit available from state to state (TX, UT.CA, DC)];

• Establishing Presentation 33 program eligibility for Title 32 Active Guard Reserve service;

• Allowing all veterans enrolled in programs of education on a greater than half-time basis to be eligible for living allowances regardless of the educational mode of delivery (enabling living allowance to be paid to veterans engaged in online learning);

• Expanding the definition of approved programs of education to include those non-degree certificate and vocational programs funded under the Montgomery GI Bill (Chapter 30);

• Including Apprenticeship and On-the-Job training programs funded under the Montgomery GI Bill (Chapter 30) as approved educational programs under Chapter 33:

• Changing the irrevocable decision condition nature on veteran benefit election between types of benefits (transferring from MGIB to Post 9/11) There likely will be additional legislative concerns raised as the first enrollment cycle under the new bill comes to a close in December.

It seems to me that the legislative concerns voiced by the Department of Veteran Affairs early on have taken a back seat to the claims processing "crises" that the department is experiencing. Clearly, the Department was not and is not sufficiently prepared to process the large number of eligibility determinations and claims that the Post 9/11 GI Bill generated. In their defense, Veterans Affairs had fourteen months from the time the bill was signed into law to conceive, plan, and execute implementation procedures that were not fully automated.

There simply wasn't sufficient time to implement the complexities of the legislation. Congress did authorize the Department to develop an automated eligibility processing system but that system won't be operational until close of 2010. In the meantime, VA will use their outdated system to process nearly 300,000 veteran education claims. Until that automated system is fully developed, human intervention and data manipulation are required to handle the eligibility decisions and to initiate the financial processing cycle. I would remind you also that this educational benefits legislation requires that the VA process two or more financial transactions for each eligible veteran: the tuition expenses which are paid directly to the institution, the book stipend paid directly to the veteran, monthly housing paid directly to veterans enrollment greater than half-time, and one-time payments to certain veterans relocating from rural areas.

The workload generated by the Post 9/11 GI Bill did not keep pace with the resources of the Department of Veterans Affairs and as a result, veteran benefit claims have gone unfilled. Veterans who registered for the fall semester found that their tuition expenses were not paid in a timely manner to the institution with whom they are registered. Institutions were asked to defer tuition costs, waive late fees, and/or extend loans to students until the VA could process the veteran payments rather than drop them for delinquent accounts. Overall, the higher education community has accommodated the processing delays and backlog with great empathy. Many institutions have filled the financial gap for veterans in terms of tuition payments and fees. Veterans have experienced personal financial challenges when monthly housing allowances that should pay for food, housing, and transportation were delayed or not yet processed.

According to Veterans Affairs, there are 26,000 veterans whose educational benefits, including tuition, fees, housing allowance, and book stipend have yet to be paid. For other veterans, some but not all payments have been processed. Because the administrative burdens of processing veteran education benefits have exceeded the department's resources, veterans with earned entitlements are forced to rely on stop gap measures and bear financial hardships and accrue personal debt until the VA works through its backlog of claims. One intervention strategy employed by the Secretary of Veterans Affairs to help offset the financial challenges to our veterans using their educational benefits this fall was authorization of emergency payments of $3,000 directly to Veterans. Clearly these challenging transitions to postsecondary education was not the scenarios that Congress envisioned when they passed the Post 9/11 GI Bill in July 2008.

Chapter 10

# Improving the College Education of Veterans: A Valuable Resource in a World of Challenges

## Mr. Frank Gómez

MS Public Administration, Strategic Alliances Executive, Educational Testing Service

The United States must ensure better education for all its citizens if it is to emerge productive and competitive from the current economic crisis. Educational declines in literacy and numerical skills, and changes in the workforce put our nation in peril. Professors and college administrators can join the fight for America's future by ensuring that veterans are provided a hassle-free college education that takes advantage of their military training, knowledge and experience.

I hope that this chapter presents you with new insights that can help make veterans education advocates more effective. Although Educational Testing Service is best known by such tests as the College Board's SAT® (that ETS administers), the GRE® and the TOEFL®, it is also a leading educational research institution. Its research includes the area of public policy as it relates to education. For example, its Policy Evaluation and Research Center (PERC) has carried out 12 symposia on the achievement gap, the most recent, on out-of-school learning, earlier this month here in Washington, DC. Most of the symposia have been subsequently turned into policy reports.

"America's Perfect Storm" is one such report. It was issued in 2007, and has since received significant notice in the media and attracted the attention of policy makers, educators, administrators and others across the nation. Copies of the report are available at www.ets.org/stormreport or CD video of relevant information, called the Perfect Storm, can be obtained by contacting me). The video illustrates vividly the causes, dimensions and impact of the convergence of three forces in our society:

1. Inadequate literacy and numeracy skills among large segments of our student and adult populations.

2. An ongoing shift in the demographic profile of our population, powered by the highest immigration rates in nearly a century.

3. The continuing evolution of the economy and the nation's job structure, requiring higher levels of skills from an increasing proportion of workers.

This convergence of forces imperils our society unless it is addressed. As described in the report and shown in the video, the United States is not among the world's leaders in any area of educational achievement. Among 29 industrialized nations, we have allowed ourselves to slip to 24th in math, 15th in reading and 20th in science. Part of the cause of this decline may be that high school graduation rates peaked at 77 percent in 1969 and have remained in the 70 percent range ever since.

Also as the report and the video indicate, immigration patterns have changed dramatically in the last 100 years, with the vast majority of new immigrants coming from Latin America and the Caribbean and Asia. They are changing the nature of our society – and of our workforce. Most come with inadequate numeracy and literacy skills to qualify for the jobs that require high levels of education and skills that will account for almost half of the job growth over the next decade.

Wage and salary earnings in the United States used to reflect a shared prosperity until about 1975. Since then and through 2007 – and likely still today – we have witnessed growing inequality. The much wider wage/salary gap has created economic, social and educational disparities that are likely to persist.

To summarize, the consequence of the Perfect Storm are that education, skills and economic opportunity are more closely related, and an uneven growth of education and economic outcomes threatens economic potential and our democratic ideals. A looming question, therefore, is whether we will continue to grow apart or, as a nation, we will invest in policies that will help us to grow together.

Veterans and Adult Education

This is the societal, economic and global competition context in which we gather to assess learning opportunities for veterans. Clearly, adult learning is critically important for individual, community, national aspirations and well-being. Despite recent progress in this area, adult learning remains an overlooked topic – not just for veterans but for many other Americans, too. Most public and policymaker attention tends to focus on K–12 and postsecondary education; but adult learning is a huge, growing problem that threatens our long-term productivity and competitiveness.

Now, for a speech I gave early this year, I extrapolated data in an ETS report on Hispanic education. I cite them here because they can help you make a stronger argument. If Hispanics were educated at the same rate as non-Hispanic whites:

- A half million more would be in college, and 175,000 more would be graduating.

- Benefits would accrue as Hispanics enter the workforce, contributing to diversity of thought and action.

- They would add more than $225 billion per year to the economy.

- That new wealth would add $100 billion to public revenues, helping all Americans.

- The number of Hispanic families with less than adequate incomes would decline from 40% to under 20%.

Experts who know the numbers can do the math. Clearly, if veterans had the range of educational opportunities to which they are entitled, the benefits to society would be significant. Improved access to educational opportunity for veterans would boost our productivity and global competitiveness and at the same time counter the disparities in our society that we have seen in the "Perfect Storm."

A Congressional Report stated that each dollar invested under the 1944 G.I. Bill has yielded $5 to $12 in economic activity and increased tax revenue. For me, the key word here is "invested." Because we should not think that aid to veterans is charity or "pay back." It is a national necessity. Surely, our veterans can help us navigate through the "Perfect Storm."

The Perfect Storm is very real and very perilous; but like a real storm, it is seemingly an unstoppable force of nature. We can moderate its impact, however, if we:

- Recognize the peril.

- Muster the political and economic will to shape public policy accordingly.

- View veterans as resources to be shaped and tapped and made fully productive members of society.

Veterans are a proven cadre of disciplined, experienced skilled human resources that, although having varying levels of educational attainment, have much to contribute. Our economy and global competiveness can be significantly advanced by harnessing their talent through increased educational opportunity. Every dollar "invested" will reap exponential-benefits.

In conclusion, I quote the "father of American education," Horace Mann: "Let us not be content to wait and see what will happen, but give us the determination to make the right things happen."

Chapter 11

# Protected Class Status and Veterans

## Rear Admiral John E. Gordon
JAGC, USN (Ret.), former
Judge Advocate General U.S. Navy

It is either unlawful or against higher educational policy to discriminate against college students on the basis of sex, race, religion or sexual orientation. There is some apparent evidence that US military veterans students are subject to various discrimination by our higher education institutions. This chapter makes the case that veterans should receive protected class status and discusses how this can be achieved.

My topic today relates to the various forms of discrimination that a veteran of a U.S. Military Service may be exposed to as a student or a potential student at an institution of higher learning. Some forms of discrimination are protected by law. I am not going to discuss those here. There is a substantial body of law regarding discrimination in job hiring practices and in processes and standards for admission to colleges and universities, but very little if any applies to overt, subtle or perceived discrimination based on an individual's status as a veteran.

A great deal of this discrimination resulted from the severe emotion that this country experienced during the Vietnam War. Prior to that event, military service was honored by our schools and was often considered an advantage. No one can dispute that the World War II GI Bill was the vehicle that had a huge and historical effect on expanding the university system in our country. Sixteen million people qualified for significant assistance in attending post high school educational institutions. Schools everywhere were beneficiaries of the vast amount of money appropriated and the result was a population that became more educated across the board from liberal arts to highly technical areas. In a substantial way, this helped make the United States the world's greatest industrial leader in both manufacturing and research and development. Veterans of that war were clearly mainstream and universally revered and respected.

But all that changed during the Vietnam War. The lack of popular support for the war itself spilled over to the people who served even though in most cases those who served were not volunteers but were conscripted. Being spit upon and being called "baby killers" became commonplace for people in uniform. This in turn put pressure on many universities to shut down their ROTC units and deny military recruiters access to students. It was only a natural evolution that the college culture took on some of those feelings, resulting in various forms of discrimination to those students who have served their country.

Today's student veterans are faced with issues of discrimination that may tend to separate them from other students. There are two categories of veterans who are students, those who have served their enlistments and are now civilians and those who currently serve in reserve or National Guard units. The challenges facing each are similar but the latter category has additional issues especially when ordered to active duty during a semester.

It is not my intent to outline and discuss all the various forms of discrimination veterans experience in higher education, but I would like to discuss a few, mostly in general terms. A most comprehensive list of these kinds of problems are listed in Chapter 3 of "Educating Veterans in the 21st Century" by Douglas Herrmann, Charles Hopkins, Roland B. Wilson and Bert Allen. They categorized the problems into these nine distinct categories.

I. Selection of a College or University to
II. Attend
II. Transition
III. Acquiring Academic Skills
IV. Campus Culture
V. Educational Program Problems
VI. Financial Problems
VII. Academic Credit Problems
VIII. Health Problems
IX Employment Problems at Graduation

My own experience is that those issues surrounding getting successful grades and finances are the most relevant.

Those veterans with stressful combat experience have the most difficulty. Their powers of concentration can be a challenge. Add that to the experience for new college students of being truly alone and isolated for the first time and one can see how much more complex it is for veterans. Oddly enough an individual while in the military rarely finds oneself alone. The military fosters team work and soldiers are taught to seek support from other soldiers and peer units. In the military a young enlistee's daily life and routine is pretty much arranged for him or her. So even an experienced veteran can find college a lonely and frightening experience.

Most higher learning institutions have some sort of program to assist veterans, but I am sure their programs are quite diverse and range from poor to excellent.

Those issues related to study skills are very important. Some veteran's expectations may at times be unrealistic. A student veteran should not expect the spoon feeding experienced in the military. All enlistee's go through a basic course, and afterwards are assigned to a school where specific skill training is taught. Each individual may have some modicum of choice, but in the military all such decisions are made on the basis of the "needs of the service." For example a pilot coming out of basic flight training may want to fly jet fighters, but if there is not a current requirement for fighter pilots, he may be involuntarily assigned to fly helicopters (even though that pilot was the best in his flight class). But a student veteran because of status should receive equal assistance of academic counseling that members of currently legally protected classes.

Financial assistance. Virtually every student veteran receives some financial assistance from the Federal Government and the amount can sometimes be substantial. So how do schools discriminate against veterans when they are all already getting some aid. Such assistance is rarely sufficient to cover all expenses. It is often the case that a veteran needs financial aid from the college or university to continue towards a degree. Some schools reportedly use the last years veterans compensation as a base for financial aid and a student veteran may fail to qualify even though that income is no longer available.

One problem recently widely reported by the press is that the Government pays out assistance at its schedule, not the requirements of the university. During September of this year there were numerous stories of schools requiring upfront payments even knowing that the veteran's assistance was a month away. This can prevent a student veteran from enrolling for the current semester, and may result in the Government denying payment because the veteran is not properly registered, a vicious cycle for sure.

There are schools that understand and help student veterans with these types of problems, but help is sporadic. Most schools are very careful not to discriminate against those in a legally protected status, and since student veterans do not qualify on the sole basis of being a veteran, mistreatment can occur.

I believe that a few words regarding campus culture are important. Since all of today's veterans are volunteers, there may be some common personality traits among them. For one thing illegal drugs are strictly forbidden in the military and anyone caught using them may be court martialed and is certain to be discharged from military service with a minimum or an "other than honorable discharge." While I am sure there are some drug abusers in the military, there is nonetheless a no tolerance policy that has serious consequences. I am not inferring that all college students are drug users, but the presence of illegal drugs on many, if not most, college campuses is there. A student veteran's exposure to this can be very tempting. It would seem that a school should have a strong veteran's counseling program.

But a student veteran has the undeniable right to be treated equally with other protected students. There have been reported incidents of some professors making anti-military or anti-veteran statements. Can you imagine the furor if that same professor were to make anti- gay or racial or sexist statements? In other instances professors can be so anti-military that they discriminate against veterans by refusing them assistance at the same level as regular students, or worse, to not offer help at all. Neither of those actions should be acceptable. I submit veterans deserve legal protection because of their status, equal to that given protected classes. What higher sacrifice and service can a person offer than a commitment to defend one's country and subject oneself to harms way and all that it brings?

Let's turn to the students who are members of active reserves or the National Guard, who not only experience the same discrimination as veterans, but have some additional issues to face. Our country has a rich tradition of using citizen soldiers for national defense. They are often called to sacrifice their time which can affect their careers and to prevent normal life by subjecting themselves to being involuntarily called to active duty. This may not only be called to war, but for duty involving natural emergencies such as storm disasters. These calls are rarely programmed and can be quite interruptive of an orderly life.

Ask yourself, if you were a full time student in the middle of a semester when Uncle Sam or your Governor called on you to report for duty. How would that impact you? What are the schools obligations? Should a grade of "incomplete" be assigned ? Should the transcript state that the student veteran "withdrew"? Should a failing grade be assigned? Upon return should the individual called to duty be placed in the same student status they were in when called? Or should each professor have total discretion on how to handle the situation? Do colleges and universities have a duty to foster national defense by encouraging its students to serve? I am not saying there is a current foundation in law to solve these specific problems, but wouldn't a school that was interested in student veterans at least have a written policy on these issues?

Well we have spent some time on the problem. It is now time to discuss the solution. It seems clear that all U.S. veterans have made some sacrifice for their country. One is the amount of time spent doing their job when on active duty. Some are wounded, often seriously and others pay the ultimate sacrifice. Those people who have never deployed with a combat unit may find it difficult to comprehend what it is like. One often hears a military person describe his life as hours and hours of boredom followed by a brief period of sheer terror. During all of those hours of boredom, a servicemember's life is controlled by superiors. Every daily aspect such as when you eat, what you eat, when you sleep and where you sleep are all specified for you.

Being in the military is not like being employed. In my past role as Judge Advocate General of the Navy I was often queried about military justice. For example some wondered why a separate criminal justice system was needed when there plenty of jurisdictions that can try acts of crime committed by service personnel. The answer is easy. The Code of Military Justice is not a criminal system, but is rather a "good order and discipline" system. What might be a behavioral problem on the outside might be a crime in the military. Failure to show up at work can cause a civilian to lose a job, but failure to show up for work in the military is a crime and depending on the circumstances can land a service member in jail for years.

The reason I make these statements is to demonstrate what the veteran has done to assure his fellow citizens are kept safe. An individual who experiences low pay and long hours and serious risk of harm in defense of his or her country deserves the same safeguards in an academic setting that many others who are members of a statutorily protected class receive. Many student veterans experience actual or perceived discrimination in our schools from school administrators, faculty and other students who simply disagree with that veteran's lifestyle. It is time to make it right and give student veterans equal protection under the law similar to that given to other classes who have received legally protected status.

The best solution would be to make students who are veterans members of a legally protected class. To digress just a moment, I sometimes wonder how we ever got to any protected classes under our constitution. The Declaration of Independence is fairly much based on forming a classless society. That all ended when the Civil Rights Act of 1964 passed. It created legally protected classes. Over the years the courts have sustained this law.

Not all discrimination is illegal. Legally protected status as a member of a certain class results from specific legislation guaranteeing specified rights to certain people. Members not in the class may or may not have the same rights but lack a specified law making them members of a specific class makes those rights general in nature.

Given that there is certain discrimination against veterans, should those individuals who are student veterans be made the beneficiary of a protected class? Is the discrimination experienced by our student veterans in colleges and universities severe enough to impose a legal sanction? While I have attempted to discuss some of the problems veterans experience there is insufficient time here to prove the case conclusively. I leave such proof to others. But accepting that there is serious discrimination against veterans, I am proposing some alternative solutions for your consideration.

One idea to resolve these issues might be an academic standard imposed by some administrative authority. A strong veterans advocacy program might be part of an accreditation program. We could discuss a myriad of similar ways to accomplish the intended goal of equal treatment for veterans. However, in the end you would likely experience uneven, widely divergent programs, some better that others. Enforcement would be a major problem.

It is no secret that most institutions of higher learning receive federal funds. given by the Federal Government is for research and development. A recent Washington Post article by Daniel de Vise sites a 2008 National Science Foundation report which ranks all schools by how much money has been received for research and development from the Federal Government. The number one ranked school was Johns Hopkins University and it received $1.7 Billion. Then numbers go down from there but the article cited, for example, George Washington University as being ranked 111th and it received $143 Million.

Everyone knows that whenever the Federal Government gives away money, there are strings attached. One of those strings is that veterans who work for a higher educational institution are protected from discrimination by that institution. Veterans who are students at the same educational institution are not protected from discrimination by that institution outside of employment. However, veterans could be protected from discrimination while students by conferring guaranteed protected class status for student veterans regardless of employment by an institution. There are two ways to do this. One way is to have the President issue an Executive Order and the other is legislation made into a law.

One may assume that an Executive Order would be the simplest way to accomplish this. No one can argue the validity of the power of the President to write rules and regulations on how federal grants may be spent. What could be easier than simply preparing and issuing a presidential document that requires implementation of a program at each institution that gives student veterans protected status.

Sounds simple but Executive Orders can be extremely difficult to execute. It would be simple if the President felt strongly enough about the issue to order a draft prepared and presented to him for signature. But unless the President has strong desire to do that, any preparation of an Executive Order would be subject to the whims of a vast bureaucracy. A proposed Executive Order is usually sent to all parts of the government by the office of Budget and Management. All interested parties have the ability to comment and make changes. There may be hundreds of interested parties. Once all the inputs are in changes are made and the new order is sent out to the same offices. The process is iterated as many times as necessary until a proposal is agreed to by all. This process can take years. Moreover, an Executive Order need not last beyond the President who created it. After an Executive Order is signed it can be reviewed, changed, or rescinded by any subsequent administration.

A much better solution is the passing of a statute. This is particularly preferred because Congress has a distinct responsibility to protect veterans. Not every person in Congress has large industry or other special interest groups located in his district that requires his attention, but every congressman has veterans in his district. And veterans do vote and votes are what all members of Congress pay attention to. So the incentive for them to act on an issue involving veterans is 100 per cent.

It would not be difficult to come up with short legislative language that would make student veterans a protected class. The rules of how a proposed bill becomes law can, however, be cumbersome. Most bills follow the prescribed path. Essentially a congressman writes a bill and submits it for action. After the bill is referred to the appropriate committees, hearings are held, mark ups are made and the bill finds it way to the floor for a vote. It can be amended at any point during that process. Once a bill passes either the House or Senate is referred to the other body where the process may be repeated all over again. Once a Conference Committee agrees the final bill goes back to the Senate and House for final passage and eventual signature by the President. This process can be long and tedious.

There is however, a commonly used short cut as any lobbyist can tell you. Just as the bill we talked about previously can be amended at any point, so can any other bill. It only takes one member to offer an amendment to any appropriate bill at the right time and place. The most common way to a quick fix is to offer an amendment to the target bill in final mark up before it goes to the floor. This usually goes unnoticed. But the most lethal place for such an amendment is during a conference committee mark up. Conference Committees usually meet in executive session and involve only selected members or conferees. Amendments there are a technical violation of the rules, a violation which is more often than not waived. If such an amendment is successfully placed on a bill that is in conference, it cannot be amended on the floor of the House or Senate. Each body only gets to vote yes or no on the entire bill.

An amendment that makes student veterans members of a legally protected class may be received quite favorably in Congress. Taking care of veterans in Congress is very popular in Congress and most members would love to take credit for voting a benefit for such a large number of people. This is especially true when such an amendment can be passed into law and not cost the Federal Government anything.

Some people may have reservations about creating Protected Class Status whether by Executive Order or by Statute. It might be argued that such status would make veterans a group that non-veterans would envy. Envy could lead non-veterans to not accept and help veterans. This outcome is not necessarily bad. Envy might lead some non-veterans to enlist. But for those who would not choose to enlist, it is unlikely to lead to real envy. Few students and academics want to risk their life and limb as do veterans. Actually, protected class status might call attention to the sacrifices of veterans and lead members of the academic community to not only stop any discrimination against veterans but may also lead some members to help veterans to catch up academically with non-veteran students.

So academia has four choices regarding what to do for veterans in higher education. One choice is to continue to allow for members of the academic community to sometimes treat veterans poorly. That choice seems intolerable and requires some action. Protected class status for veterans seems possible to establish in one of three ways.

First, academia itself may create procedures by which accreditation is denied to institutions that permit discriminatory behavior toward veterans. Second, the President may be persuaded that there is a need for an Executive Order that would establish protected class status for veterans. Third, such status may be established by Congress passing a statute making discrimination toward veterans illegal, thereby establishing protected-class status.

You can probably discern which option strikes me as the best. But despite my position on these three options, you have your own viewpoint on what should be done. Regardless of which option you choose, I am confident that you do not want our veterans to be the object of abusive and unfair treatment in higher education, treatment that makes it harder for them to get a degree than it is for non-veteran students to do so.

# Section III. Specific Kinds of Problems of Veterans in Higher Education

## Chapter 12

## Selecting a College or University to Attend

### Dr. Leslie A. Miller
#### Ph.D., PHR
#### LanneM Talent Management, LLC

Some colleges and universities make false promises to service members and veterans to get them to enroll. On attending these schools, students with a military background experience problems, such as not being provided promised transfer credits. The most common false promises, and what can be done to avoid potential problems, will be reviewed.

In a 2009 text titled Educating Veteran's in the 21st Century, Herrmann, Hopkins, Wilson, and Allen (2009) discussed how the new GI Bill provides incredible opportunities for today's veterans. However, they also stated:

Many citizens feel that the new GI Bill will essentially eliminate any problems of veterans and put them on a fast track to get a college degree....money alone will not ensure that veterans avoid problems in college. Veterans need help with problems other students will not encounter. The additional problems that they encounter discourage them and lead them to perform less well in their pursuit of a college degree. In some cases, the discouragement leads some veterans to drop out of college. (p. 3)

Unfortunately, it appears a lack of information exists on non-monetary problems or challenges veterans face when using the GI Bill. One such non-monetary problem has to do with what we are calling false promises made to veterans as they search for a college or university to attend. Specifically, some colleges and universities, in their zest to get service members to enroll, and perhaps unknowingly, make promises to college or university, veterans experience problems, such as not being provided promised transfer credits.

The purpose of this chapter is to discuss some of the potential false promises made to veterans during the college search process and to discuss what might be done to eliminate the problems and enhance the veteran college experience. To achieve this purpose, two issues will be discussed. Discussed first will be some of the problems or false promises veterans might encounter when searching for a college or university. Discussed second are some things that can be done to avoid the problems that might occur from the false promises. The information in this paper may provide individuals with the information they need to help veterans (a) make more informed decisions about school choice, (b) ask the right questions during the college search process, and (c) avoid problems after enrollment.

## My Qualifications

As I was preparing to write the current chapter, I asked myself what qualified me to speak on such a topic as a performance improvement business consultant, when there are other experts who are much more informed about the new GI Bill and veterans. It did not take me long to convince myself, and hopefully you as well, that I bring an interdisciplinary and unique, perspective to the topic. Yes, I am a business consultant. What I do is work with organizations to uncover the problems they are experiencing with their talent (e.g., lack of performance, turnover), identify the root cause of the problem, and then work to implement solutions to the problem. Well, we have a problem here that veterans are facing and I want to help get to the root cause and eliminate the problem. But, besides that, I was an Army brat and have a special place in my heart for our military personnel – I care about their success. I have experience as an Assistant Dean of Admission and know the promises we make to students. I am an Academic Cabinet member for the University of Phoenix, where I work with college administrators to enhance the learning experience for many non traditional learners. I am a college professor (at the University of Phoenix School of Advanced Studies and Rollins College) and know about what students experience on campus and in the classroom. Last, I recently mentored a doctoral student on his dissertation where he conducted a qualitative phenomenological study to explore the transition assistance program, specifically the challenges veterans face when transitioning out of the military into the civilian life. So, I have touched many different aspects of a veteran's experience transitioning out of the military, searching for a college or university to attend, and participating in the college experience.

The College Search Process

A great deal of information exists on the typical college search process. Typically, individuals (such as parents, friends, counselors, and college administrators) advise students to search for a college that is a good fit, academically and financially. Academically, we typically advise students to (a) ensure the school is reputable, (b) gain clarity on what they want to study, (c) determine how they want to study (i.e., in the traditional or online environment), (d) ensure the school has the program or major they need and offers the environment they are seeking, (e) talk with others (parents, faculty, administrators) to gain perspectives, (f) search college catalogues and online to learn more about the college or university, (g) take a campus (or virtual) tour, and (h) take the time to visit the school and participate in an interview with admission officers. Financially, students are typically advised to search for a school that is affordable, but to avoid ruling out a specific school because it is too expensive.

Indeed, veterans should participate in the above college search activities, because the activities are important to all individuals searching for the best school to attend. However, in addition to these strategies, veterans must consider many other factors when selecting a college or university to help avoid the additional problems unique to the veteran experience. If veterans do not consider the other issues, there will likely be many different consequences. With the ultimate goal of receiving a college education, veterans might experience increased time solving problems after enrollment, years of extra study, spending more money than necessary and extreme frustration.

## Potential Problems and False Promises

Some of the most significant problems veterans may experience are outlined as follows.

1. Diploma mills – Many colleges and universities want veterans to attend their school because of the funds available through the new GI Bill. Administrators promise veterans they will receive a quality education and promise they will get credit for their life skills. The reality is, some schools do not provide a quality education, and regardless of whether they provide experience for a veteran's life skills, they are diploma mills.
2. Time to deliver the GI Bill funds – Veterans sometimes find that it can take quite a while, up to

three months, for the college or university to receive their GI Bill funds from the Veterans Administration (VA). Some college administrators and counselors promise veterans delayed payment will not be an issue since their tuition is being paid by the VA. However, the reality is, veterans are often pestered to pay their tuition and face unpleasant consequences, such as having their classes dropped.

3. Denial of academic credit – Some administrators and counselors inform veterans they will have no problem transferring their military credit. The reality is, when the actual evaluation and transfer occurs, they sometimes find they were denied academic credit for training and experience in the military that is similar to the content of college courses.

4. Failure to acknowledge/meet personal and academic needs – As with most students, veterans are often told that the school has a number of services and programs for students-that they will have no problem getting all of their personal and academic needs met. The reality is, veterans have unique personal and academic needs – needs many college programs do not acknowledge and even if they do acknowledge them, fail to meet them. For example, many new student orientation programs are designed to address traditional student concerns. Many orientation programs do not deal with the concerns of older and often married, veterans. Also, many veterans would like to build upon specialties they acquired in the military (e.g., law enforcement) through additional course work in a specific subject or through other experiential

activities. Many experiential activities, such as work study and internship opportunities, are designed for the traditional student and not based on the varied experiences of veterans.

5. Unprepared to help with military acquired disabilities, illnesses, and disorders – As other students are told, veterans are informed there is a health facility on campus to meet their health needs. The reality is, college health services do not always have the staff or expertise necessary to effectively handle the disabilities, illnesses, and disorders veterans sometimes acquire in the military. For example, some of today's veterans experience post-traumatic stress disorder, a specific type of anxiety disorder that often develops after exposure to a traumatic event; many college health services are not prepared to diagnose, treat, or refer veterans for appropriate treatment.

6. Uncomfortable campus and classroom climate – As other students are informed, veterans are often told the school is diverse and how college staff, faculty, and students respect and value diversity on campus. The reality is, some veterans experience something totally different. They experience war demonstrations on campus or perceive professors making derogatory statements (although often unknowingly) about the military during lectures. Such experiences may make veterans feel uncomfortable interacting with others on campus and participating in class.

Potential Solutions

As I thought about how to position potential solutions, I recalled all of my training in sales and leadership development – which constantly reinforced how important it is to put yourself in other's shoes – that is, use a technique we call the Ben Duffy approach. We have a diverse group in the audience; for example, we have professors, administrators, and academic researchers. What each can do to help solve the problems veterans face may differ. Therefore, what I have done is put myself in veteran's shoes and focus is on those things veterans can do when searching for a college or university. While I will also share some ideas for what others can do, I would encourage all of us to think about what we might be able to do to help veterans implement the ideas shared – or what we might be able to do to proactively address each issue.

1. Diploma mills. Perhaps we should encourage veterans to ensure the schools they are considering are listed with the Department of Education (DOE). The DOE has a database of currently or previously accredited colleges and universities. Colleges and universities in the DOE database are "recognized by the U.S. Secretary of Education as a reliable authority as to the quality of postsecondary education" (U.S. Department of Education, 2009, paragraph. 1). However, the DOE database does not include those schools that do not seek accreditation, yet may offer a quality education. Perhaps those institutions that want to provide education to veterans should consider seeking accreditation.

2. Delayed delivery of GI Bill funds. We should encourage veterans to raise the issue of delayed payment of GI funds when speaking to admission counselors and obtain written verification they can delay payment of their tuition and fees. They should request financial support while awaiting the GI funds. Similarly, colleges and universities might consider delaying required payment of tuition and bills until arrival of the GI Bill funds. They might consider modifying their systems so that veterans do not receive hounding letters about failure to pay their tuition. Colleges and universities might consider creating financial support programs (such as grants and loans) to support the living expenses of veterans and their families as they await their GI Bill funds.

3. Denial of academic credit. Before submitting their transcripts, we should encourage veterans to ask questions to be sure they understand exactly how their credits will be evaluated and who will do the evaluating. The American Council on Education (ACE), after World War II, established a system for how to transfer military credits. Veterans should ensure the ACE system will be used and that a staff member trained on evaluating military credits will be responsible for reviewing his or her transcripts.

4. Failure to meet personal/academic needs. We should encourage veterans to ask what specific programs exist to meet their needs as a nontraditional learner. Schools should consider the unique needs of veterans and implement and communicate programs specifically designed to meet these needs. For example, colleges might consider having a separate orientation program for

veterans. Schools might also consider offering online or evening courses, and identify internships and work-study programs that build on veterans' experience and knowledge which could save veterans time, money, and potentially years of extra study.

5. Unprepared to help with military acquired disabilities, illnesses, and disorders. Because college health services are often unprepared to help veterans with emergency care for disabilities, Illnesses, and disorders acquired in the military, we should encourage veterans to inquire about the specific health services offered for veterans. For example, veterans might ask if the school health center partners with the VA. Campus health services should consider, in conjunction with VA medical centers, providing veterans with the care they need.

6. Uncomfortable campus and classroom climate –We should encourage veterans to ask what the school does to promote meaningful integration of veterans with other students. That is, what does the school to so ensure veterans do not experience discomfort in the classroom and on the campus? Some things schools might want to consider include:

    1) Apprising the faculty how they might make veterans feel during their lectures and of the need to be mindful of the effects of their actions on veterans.

    2) Implementing special social gatherings for veterans. Developing programs for veterans to speak to campus organizations about their military experience and learning – such as

student organizations.

3) Implementing consequences for students who vilify or harass veterans.

## A Rating System

If veterans are made so many promises, and experience so many unique problems, it might be a good idea to have a standardized system for rating schools on the extent to which they really understand the needs veterans and are veteran friendly. A few rating systems exist; however, a rating system reflecting all of the best practices (for example, the best practices shared in Educating veterans in the 21st Century) does not appear to exist. As a psychometrician, designing assessment and measurement tools to help select and develop leaders, this really excites me. It would be extremely valuable if we created an assessment checklist containing observable and measureable best practices. We could then grade colleges, as we grade primary and secondary schools, using an A – F system, to reflect their veteran friendliness. We could even rate over time to see sustained programs or progress.

## Summary

The new GI Bill definitely helps veterans pursue a college education. Obtaining a college education benefits veterans in many ways. First, a college education can provide veterans a competitive edge. Second, a college education can provide veterans a greater earning potential. Third, a college education can improve career enhancement opportunities. Fourth, a college education can help veterans develop a sense of culture. Last, a college education can provide a sense of self-satisfaction. Knowing how valuable obtaining a college education can be, our task is to help veterans eliminate the specific problems they face and do what we can to help them experience a fulfilling and successful college experience.

What can we do? We can (a) acknowledge the challenges veterans face, (b) help veterans ask the right question, (c) proactively find solutions to problems, and (d) implement best practices for making our schools veteran friendly.

## References

Herrmann, D., Hopkins, C., Wilson, R.B., & Allen, B., (2009). Educating veterans in the 21st Century. North Charleston, South Carolina: Booksurge Llc

U.S. Department of Education. (2009). U.S. Department of Education Database of Accredited Postsecondary Institutions and Programs. Retrieved November 10, 2009, from http://ope.ed.gov/accreditation/

Chapter 13

# From Soup to Nuts: A Look at Veterans' Education and Transfer of Credits Problems When They Enter College

## Roland B. Wilson
MA Linguistics. U.S. Marine Intelligence.
Gunnery Sergeant, U.S. Marine Corps (Ret.)

Discharge from the military provides veterans with different kinds of credits that can be transferred to higher education institutions. Some credits are for military training and military experience. Other credits are typically college level exams taken by veterans before discharge. Unfortunately, some schools sometimes transfer fewer or none of these credits. Educators who want their student veterans to get a degree as quickly as possible should know the injustices involving transfer credits.

For someone in the military, there are two things in life that are very difficult and take a lot of effort to adjust to: joining the service and discharging from the service. When someone enters the Armed Forces, they have at least 2-3 months to learn the "basics" of their service, and then years to get used to it. However, when they discharge, they may have a few weeks of class to prepare them for the rest of their lives. What chaos and culture shock this can be.

When service members are discharged from the military they become veterans with a variety of potential college credits that can be transferred to higher education institutions (American Council on Education, 2008; Association of Veterans Education, 2006). Some credits are for military training and experience (Wenger, Rufflo & Bertalan, 2006). Other credits may be from prior school or college level exams taken by veterans before discharge. Unfortunately, many schools sometimes transfer fewer or none of these credits (Herrmann, Hopkins, Wilson & Allen, 2009). These same schools or others may not even counsel the veterans on these potential credits. Educators who want their student veterans to get a degree as quickly as possible and succeed in life should know the injustices involving transfer credits and other problems veterans face when they discharge.

This chapter presents real examples of problems that average veterans have with discharge and when attempting to transfer credits. Then short term and long term answers to these problems are considered. These problems and answers given will provide a common starting point in which we can all begin to help veterans.

A case study

To illustrate a variety of discharge and transfer problems of veterans, I will refer to a fictional character John Stryker Wayne. Table 13.1 summarizes some salient details of John's career record, details pertinent to discharge and obtaining transfer credits.

Table 13.1
An Example of a veteran's service

| Veterans name: | John Stryker Wayne |
|---|---|
| Years of Service: | 14 years |
| Type of Discharge: | Honorable |
| Why Discharged: | Leg Injury while serving in Combat |
| Primary MOS: | Radio Communications and Computers |
| | Received training at primary And advanced leadership schools |

After his injury in combat, which he had last year, John received word from his command that he would be discharged from service and that he no longer was eligible to reenlist. Even though he wanted to make it to twenty years and loved the service, he was no longer found "medically qualified." As he waited his day for discharge, he was told that he needed to go to separations training. Separation training typically lasts two weeks and is required of service members who are to be discharged from the service. This training and information given is supposed to be complete, and informs the service member about civilian job opportunities and how to prepare a resume, how to apply for jobs, educational opportunities and other aspects of transition to civilian life. Instruction is also given on how to file a VA claim, and information on money management in the civilian world.

Due to work demands and an extreme shortage of personnel due to so many being deployed to the war zone, John's unit would not let him go to separations training until a month before his discharge. They said they needed him to keep the equipment at the unit up and running and train the new personnel. Finally when he made it to the separation classes, it seemed like many of the speakers were thrown into the schedule at the last minute. Many did not seem as knowledgeable as the service members had hoped. And in fact, some speakers did not even show up. However, there were some good briefers.

As you can see from the separation training given to John, not all separation training classes are put together as well as we would like for our veterans. Veterans need training by subject matter experts who can answer all the questions of those who are about to be discharged. If they do not have an answer, they should be able to get back with the veterans in a timely manner before discharge.

During one of the breaks in the separation training, John heard some other servicemembers talking about taking CLEPT Tests and that they are "free" while they were on active-duty. Also, these tests and others could count for credits in college. John knew he wanted to go back to school and even had written to the school he wanted to attend. Although he only had a little over two weeks left after these classes, he went back to his unit and requested time off from work to go to the base education and testing center to find out more and hopefully test.

The College-Level Examination Program® (CLEP) gives you the opportunity to receive college credit for what you already know by earning qualifying scores on any of 34 examinations. It is also possible for a service member to take tests provided by Defense Activity for Non-traditional Education Support Agency (DANTES, 2004), such as the Dantes Subject Standardized Tests (DSSTs). These tests consist of an extensive series of 37 examinations in college subject areas that are comparable to the final or end-of-course examinations in undergraduate courses. ACE recommends 3 semester hours of credit per test. DANTES funds paper-based DSST testing for eligible Service members and civilian examinees at DANTES Test Centers and at national test centers (colleges and universities) offering the Internet-based (bit) DSSTs.

John went to the base education and testing center the next morning and started to take tests. He found out about the DANTES tests just mentioned. Over the next two weeks, he took 12 tests (all the CLEP tests and three DANTES Subject Standardized Tests). He asked to have the results sent to the school he has been looking at: Iwo Jima State College.

What are the Differences Between a CLEP Exam and a DSST Exam? As of October 1, 2006, DSST

(DSST - Dantes Subject Standardized Tests) exams are computer based at all testing locations with a two-hour time limit. CLEP tests are administered by a computer and start with a tutorial. Once the student begins the timed portion of the exam, he or she has 90 minutes to complete it. Students should answer ALL questions on both DSST and CLEP exams, as there is no penalty for incorrect answers. The time allowed for CLEP exams may be extended if the student has a documented learning or physical disability. A student must contact the Testing Center in advance of registering.

Active-duty military service members have had the opportunity to take funded CLEP exams since 1974. This benefit has now been extended to military veterans. If you are an eligible veteran, you can receive reimbursement from the U.S. Department of Veterans Affairs for CLEP exams and fees, saving you time and money while you pursue a college degree.

Veterans can claim reimbursement for CLEP exams and exam administration fees under provisions of the Veterans' Benefits Improvement Act of 2004 (Public Law 108-454), which enhances the education benefits of the Montgomery GI Bill. For more information about who is eligible for the CLEP benefit and how to submit a claim, visit the U.S. Department of Veterans Affairs.

John arrived home in late July and went to Iwo Jima University the following day to register. Since he had a disability and had been in contact with the VA since before discharge, John was required to see a VA counselor who would advise him about his choice of a college program.

When he arrived at the school he went to the registration office and asked to speak to a school VA Rep about attending this school and transferring credits. The staff member in the registration office said that the VA Rep was down the hall and asked what schools he attended for college credits. John replied he had been in the service for 14 years and had credit from his branch of the military. The registration staff member said "I am sorry, but we only transfer from accredited institutions." John said "Well, this does not make sense to me, let me see the VA Rep."

One of the biggest problems that veterans face the first few days when arriving at campus is to find someone to turn to for correct information, guidance and help. Many of the staff on these colleges and universities has very little experience helping veterans. Many universities also use students in their offices when new students arrive. Thus, they give the veteran no advice or wrong advice that sends the veterans down the wrong path, which can cost the veterans time, money and at the least, raise the frustration level even before they start their first day of class.

John went to see the VA Rep at his school. He told her who he was and that he would like her help him getting started in school. Her reply was: "I only take care of reporting to VA that you are attending school/enrolled here (full or part-time) and then ensure the school gets the funds from the VA. I can't help you with your registration or credit issues. I suggest you talk with the VA Regional Office or the local VA Office at the- city's unemployment center."

John contacted the VA Rep at the regional office. He said "I do not work with credits or registration at the school. We are here only to ensure that you are qualified for the program—meet our guidelines, and then that you are receiving your money. You probably need to go back to the school or see the local VA Rep."

John contacted the VA Rep at the local unemployment office. She said "I can't help you. Our job is to try and keep track of how many local veterans are unemployed and need help with unemployment benefits. Maybe you need to go back and ask someone at your school."

As you can see, veterans like John waste a lot of time as no one seems to even be able to give them correct advice to lead them in the right direction to begin with. John went back the next day to school, but since he knew a lot about computers, he spent the night researching what to do on the Internet. He found some good information on the Web that said "Colleges that belong to the Servicemembers Opportunity Colleges (SOC) must accept not only the tests he took, but his military training and education too (all depending on his degree and found out that he could take other tests at his school that would allow him to possibly skip some classes and take courses of interest to him at a higher level.

Even if the staff at a school knows a lot, veterans must do their own research as well to ensure they have a full understanding and are in agreement with what transfer credit that they are going to get. Of course, this is not easy to do when you are tyring to get ready for discharge, a move and a new way of life. If you have a family or disabilities, this is even more difficult.

John went back to registration and told them what he had found out at the different VA offices. He had a few "brief" discussions with different staff members at the registration office and continued to tell them he wanted to speak with someone that could help him, the veteran. After a difficult and long time searching for the right person, he was introduced to Tom who was permanent staff and a registrar. Tom listened to John's story of what had happened at the school thus far and what he was trying to do to enter the school.

Tom told John "I will see what I can do to help you with your credits." However, Tom confessed that he did not know a lot about the military so it would take a few days to determine what credits he would receive. Tom asked John for all his paperwork.

John gave Tom a copy of his DD214 that showed most of the military schools he had attended. [The DD214 presents a summary of a service member's military training and experience]. John told Tom that ACE approved these schools for credit and even gave Tom a copy of the pages that described his military occupational specialty that he had printed out from the ACE website. John also said that he had sent many CLEPT and DANTES test scores to the school for transfer credits and asked Tom to check on these. Tom told John he would work on John's eligibility for transfer credits and to come back in two days while he tried to work his details out.

Tom immediately began to look at all of John's potential credits from the military on the basis of other colleges attended, college level exams (such as CLEPT and DANTES), military training, and military experience. Tom called Iwo Jima's admission's office and asked for John's tests that he arranged to be sent to the school. The Admissions Office staff member said: "We could only find three of them." When Tom asked why? The staff member replied that they normally do not keep letters and things unless the student has already registered at their school." In other words, these scores were most likely thrown away. Yet, how can a new student such as John know to register before he sends scores to be transferred?

John's experience indicates that a veteran unfortunately needs to tell the Admission office at a school the kinds of test scores that are going to be sent to them. Also a veteran apparently needs to find someone in the Admission office who will keep a folder labeled with the veteran's name and containing the reports and tests sent to the school. A veterans' rep at the school would certainly be helpful for this kind of things.

John and Tom met to review John's transfer situation. Tom told John that the Admissions office did not have all of his test scores. However, Tom told John that he had found about 40 hours of credit including some upper level ones in foreign language and others due to his communication and computer schooling.

Subsequently, Tom and John went to see the Department Chair for Computer Science, the degree John wanted to major in to determine whether the Chair would approve John's transfer credits concerning computer science and discuss any more credits for military training and military experience (American Council on Education, 2008; Wenger, Rufflo & Bertalan, 2006). The conversation was constructive, but the Chair said he would accept only 9 credit hours toward a Computer Science major. Tom, on behalf of John, told the Chair that did not seem correct and that they needed to discuss this again, but wanted the Chair to take some more time to think about it. John asked the Chair about course-specific tests—the Chair said that he did not have any ready, but might consider this after John has taken some classes.

Two days later John and Tom went to see the Dean that heads general education. Unfortunately, the conversation did not go well. The Dean told John and Tom: "General Education is a requirement and I will not waive any of my courses including P.E., even if he has had a lot in the service!" John and Tom went back to Tom's office and finished the enrollment. Tom promised John that he would contact The University President about the problems with the Dean and Chair, and see what he could do about more credits.

When veterans have problems or when decisions are made, a veteran should ask for information in writing, take notes and follow-up. If you believe in what you should get, continue on it, even if it means going to the Provost or President and ask for written justification why professors, Chairs or Deans will not do something.

Tom told John before he left his office to keep in touch and also to go see financial aid. John went to Financial Aid and asked for information on grants and scholarships for veterans. The financial aid staff person replied: "We do not have anything for veterans specifically, do you have another qualification such as being a Native American or other factors?" John said he did not know about any other qualifications or "factors" for aid. The staff person had him fill out a form for a PELL Grant. However, the school wanted him to put his last two years of income on the application. Doing so entailed that John would not get a Pell Grant for two years. John said that this practice is not fair, as he does not have that income any longer. Financial aid office staff said it was the policy of the school to subtract income of the past two years regardless of fairness.

All schools have the power to mitigate any problem that is not fair. If veterans find policies that are unfair or unequal, they must see someone about it and fight it, as needed and possible. If colleges and universities can provide grants, scholarships and work programs to other groups, including international students, and special classes of students. Why can't they do it for veterans?

John did all he could to obtain transfer credits, and started school. He continued to push the issues for his credit and to seek out more types of financial support. However, he was already—with the first day of school, disappointed at what had taken place with his new start in life, and most of all, very tired of a system that was supposed to be there to educate everyone fairly and equally.

John's difficulties with financial aid show that his credit problems were not just limited to the transfer process. These were just some of the many problems that real veterans have experienced while trying to get an education. Social problems are another example, and were thoroughly discussed at this conference. There are many more examples that can be given for veterans and they can get quite complex. Regardless of the problems and examples given, they need to listen and help veterans is paramount.

In conclusion, how do we help veterans get what they deserve and need in school? Common sense, fair rules and regulations are needed to take into account the needs of this special group of individuals while looking at their experiences as well.

Finally, a good dose of understanding and openness for these veterans will help them become not only great students, but tomorrow's leaders.

## References

American Council on Education (2008). A Transfer Guide: Understanding Your Military Transcript and ACE Credit Recommendations. Military Programs: Washington D.C.

Association of Veterans Education (2006). Association of Veterans Education Certifying Officials, A Non-Chartered Organization. National Headquarters

Address, 9813 104<sup>th</sup> Avenue Ottumwa, IA
52501.Retrieved from
http://www1.va.gov/vso/inde.cfm?template=viewr
eport&Org_ID=338-13k-

Herrmann, D., Hopkins, C., Wilson, R.B., & Allen, B.,
(2009). Educating veterans in the 21st Century.
North Charleston, South Carolina: Booksurge Llc.

Wenger, D., Rufflo, M., & Bertalan, F. J. (2006). ACME
project, internet based systems that advocate credit
for military experience and analyze options for
veterans in career transition. Proceedings of the
IEEE International Conference on Advanced
Learning Techniques, IEEE The Computer
Society.

Chapter 14

# Cognition, Curriculum and Culture: A Preliminary Look at the Experiences of Veterans in Higher Education

Stephen M. Fiore
University of Central Florida

Amanda da Costa da Silveira
Federal University of Rio Grande do Sul, Brazil

This chapter describes a preliminary look at a set of research issues facing veterans upon their return to college. This tremendous influx in student veterans, coupled with the vast change in context when moving from the military to academia, creates an important need to ensure that the experience of student veterans is positive and productive. To enable conceptualization of the multifaceted factors impacting upon the veteran experience, three broad categories consisting of Cognition, Curriculum, and Culture were created. In this chapter these are first described and are followed with a discussion of initial data collected from student veterans who provided some insights on these issues.

Currently thousands of veterans are enrolling in college and the numbers will continue to climb. This can be seen emerging from policy level changes at the Department of Veterans' Affairs (VA) where support includes $78 billion in educational benefits. This will be implemented over the next decade under the Post 9/11 Veterans Educational Assistance Act of 2008 (the "new GI Bill") program, which took effect in late 2009. Thus, according to the VA, it is expected that the number of student veterans receiving benefits will increase by as much as 25%, a figure representing up to 460,000 people. This chapter describes a preliminary look at a set of research issues facing veterans upon their return to college. This tremendous influx in student veterans, coupled with the vast change in context when moving from the military to academia, creates an important need to ensure that the experience of student veterans is positive and productive. To enable conceptualization of the multifaceted factors impacting upon the veteran experience, three broad categories consisting of Cognition, Curriculum, and Culture were created. In this chapter these issues are first briefly described. Then some initial data, collected from student veterans and providing some insights on these issues, is then described.


Cognition, Curriculum, and Culture

First, from the standpoint of cognition, an important issue for understanding is the degree to which educational experiences differ in the military when compared to educational experiences in college. For example, how different are the methods of training commonly used in the military from methods of classroom teaching? Second, from the standpoint of curriculum, research must explore the experiences of veterans when they deal with both academic and government bureaucracies such as university curriculum committees and financial aid offices as well as the Veteran's Administration. To what degree do these experiences help or hinder the progress of veterans? For example, this encompasses issues of earning credit for prior training and/or coursework as well as problems that could emerge if active duty military personnel are deployed in mid-semester. Finally, a critical component of the veteran experience has to do with the culture of the college campus. This encompasses differences in the maturity level of college student peers when compared to veterans as well as the attitudes of non-veteran students/faculty towards veterans.

With this guiding framework, two important epistemological distinctions appear to be important for a research approach. First, an important distinction of this approach is that veterans be surveyed directly. The goal was to gain an understanding of the subjective experiences of veterans enrolled in higher education. This difference is important in that many statistics currently reported on veterans and higher education are based upon data collected from administrators to understand veterans' services on campuses (e.g., Sternberg, Wadsworth, Vaughan, & Carlson, 2009). While such surveys are important and provide useful information, data specifically collected from a first person perspective, so as to get a more direct sense of the veteran experience was preferred. Prior research that has attempted to gain some first person understanding from veterans has found, for example, that veterans perceive their experiences as something that makes them different from other students (DiRamio, Ackerman & Mitchell, 2008). Related to this, others have found that veterans may have a sense of isolation and feel a need for some form of social integration with the campus community (Chickering & Reisser, 1993). Although such data collection is limited, these findings highlight the importance of understanding the direct experience of veterans. Specifically, these findings are important because they show that veterans may not be experiencing the type of social connectedness which has been linked to student success (Elkins, Braxton, and James, 2000). Second, this survey collected data that were quantifiable in some form. The issue is that it is not uncommon to hear anecdotal evidence of veteran experiences being provided during discussions of the needs of veterans in higher education. While anecdotes provide important insights into experiences, they are no substitute for data. Thus, preliminary data were collected to help us get a more quantifiable sense of the experiences of veterans enrolled in higher education.

This survey focused mainly on the issues of "cognition and learning" as that represents an area little examined in prior studies of veterans enrolled in college. Although there are numerous programs in place to help veterans acclimate psychologically (e.g., university counseling programs or veteran's administration programs), as well as help them financially (e.g., veteran aid offices), little is being done with regard to the learning and cognitive experience of veterans. In particular, as noted, some speculate that veterans are trained using methods of instruction typically different from those experienced in college classes (e.g., Herrmann, Hopkins, Wilson, & Allen, 2009). Whether or not there is a vast degree of difference between methods of training/learning, little is known about how veterans respond to a more academic context after having been taught in a military context. For example, military training may be very hands on and used to teach very concrete tasks. If this is a predominant method, it is in stark contrast to college courses that typically require reading and related homework assignments on sometimes very abstract material. Further, military training sometimes uses a variety of multimedia that includes high-fidelity simulations for teaching. Such methods are either completely absent or used very little in colleges today.

With this as a stepping off point, the goal of this chapter is to describe the findings from a preliminary survey developed to examine the subjective impressions veterans enrolled in higher education experience after enrolling in college. This survey represents the first step in a program of research to more fully study the experiences of veterans in the United States. Specifically, many of the questions are open-ended and designed to be used as the foundation for a broader survey that can more fully cover the cognitive, curriculum, and culture issues that may impact veterans. The long-term goal is to use this information to make recommendations for how to improve the educational experience of veterans enrolled in college.

## Method

### Participants

In order to explore the experience of veterans in higher education, participants were recruited through various organizations such as veterans' affairs offices at universities and student veterans organizations. To be eligible for the study, a participant was required to be a veteran (i.e., a former member of the armed services), and enrolled in a higher education institution. Seventy participants (mean age of 32.13 years, standard deviation of 6.22, and a minimum age of 23 and maximum age of 68), answered an anonymous online survey. Of the participants, 75% were men, and nearly 50% of the sample (47%) was from the United States Army. Although the sample can be considered small and not representative, the balance of gender seems to be in accordance to demographic characteristics of the military, since women represented 27% of all military undergraduates in 2007-08, according to the American Council on Education (2009). More detailed information about the characteristics of the sample can be found on Table 14.1.

Table 14.1. *Branch of service and sex information of the study sample.*

| Branch of service/ Sex | Army | Navy | Marines | Air Force | Total |
|---|---|---|---|---|---|
| Female | 41.18% (7) | 17.65% (3) | 11.76% (2) | 29.41% (5) | (17) |
| Male | 49.02% (25) | 21.57% (11) | 13.73% (7) | 15.69% (8) | (51) |
| **Total** | **47.14% (33)** | **20.00% (14)** | **12.86% (9)** | **20.00% (14)** | **(70)** |

*Numbers between parentheses represent the number of participants for each case.

## Procedure

The online survey presented a set of multiple-choice and open-ended questions concerning participant experience as a veteran enrolled in college. Participation was voluntary and neither money nor course credit was earned for completing the survey. Participants first completed an informed consent form and then provided demographic information (age, gender, branch of service, highest rank/grade earned and any prior college credits earned). After this, six multiple-choice questions about the participant's training experiences in the military were presented. Participants were asked to choose their answers based on a drop-down menu showing percentage alternatives. The six multiple-choice questions are presented in Table 14.2. Participants were then invited to write down their answers to ten questions concerning their experience as a student enrolled in college (see second half of Table 14.2)

Table 14.2. *Protocol of questions included in the survey.*

**Multiple-Choice Questions**

1. Approximately how much of your training in the military involved face-to-face instruction in a classroom that was primarily lecture based?
2. How much of your training involved face-to-face instruction in a classroom that involved lecture based training but also included "hands-on" training with a computer or with object(s) relevant to the training need?
3. How much of your training involved computer-based distributed learning such as reading lectures or course material online or viewing online lectures or videos?
4. How much of your training involved computer-based distributed learning such as reading lectures or course material online or viewing online lectures or videos, BUT also involved the inclusion of simulations (animated models/graphics) where you observed relevant components of the training need (e.g., how a particular machine worked)?
5. How much of your training involved low-fidelity computer-based simulations where you interacted with a simulated task to learn about, or practice, particular skills or procedures for that task?
6. How much of your training involved high-fidelity computer-based simulations where you interacted with a simulated task to learn about, or practice, particular skills or procedures for that task?

**Open Ended Questions**

1. 1. When you started college, if you did not have any college prepatory experience, experience, did you feel

challenged when starting your education? Why or why not? (If you had college preparatory experience, please skip to the next question).

2. Did you seek out assistance for veterans in preparatory instruction in academic skills for college (e.g., note taking techniques, learning/studying approaches, how to participate in laboratories for courses that require them, using study groups outside of class). Why or why not?

3. What did you think was the most surprising difference about how you were trained in the military versus how you were being taught in the classroom?

4. What did you find most challenging about your classroom education when you started college after the military?

5. Do you think it's important that a university take into account a veteran's military occupational specialty when providing veterans with advice about what courses to take? Why or why not?

6. Do you think veterans would benefit from having support in designing a plan of study and curriculum based upon their experience?

7. Did you try to transfer credit for military training and experience? If so, did you have any problems?

8. Have you experienced any negative reactions by peers or faculty because of your veteran status?

9. Have you had non-veteran students ask inappropriate questions about hazardous duty or combat experiences?

10. Do you feel that, as a veteran, you are a part of a minority campus group, but one without appropriately recognized help and status?

# Results

The quantitative data from the multiple choice items were submitted to descriptive statistics analysis. The qualitative written data were analyzed using content analysis in order to systematically identify and specify characteristics of the sentences the veterans typed as their answers.

## Quantitative Analysis

Descriptive analysis of the sample showed that 45% of the participants had earned some college credit prior to enlisting. More than half of the participants (52%) had a sergeant/E-5 rank as their highest grade earned. When asked about how much of their military training involved face-to-face instruction in a classroom that was primarily lecture-based, the sample of consulted veterans was well distributed, since 6.06% of the veterans said they had all their training based on face-to-face lectures, whereas 12% had half of the training that way. Only 2.67% of the sample claimed to never have had face-to-face instruction. Lecturing, a traditional pedagogical method in university classroom settings (Saville, Zinn, Neef, Norman & Ferreri, 2006), was reported to be the instructional form used in more than half of the trainings in the military education for 50.67% of the participants. The distribution of the face-to-face training based on lectures can be seen on Figure 14.1 and Table 14.3 presents the results according to each branch of military service.

Table 14.3. *Percentage of participants and lecture-based training.**

| Percentage of lecture-based training/ Branch of service | None (0%) | 10% -40% | 50% | 60% -90% | 100 % |
|---|---|---|---|---|---|
| Army | 3.03% (1) | 57.57% (19) | 12.12% (4) | 21.21% (7) | 6.06 % (2) |
| Navy | 7.14% (1) | 35.72% (5) | 0% (0) | 35.72% (5) | 21.4 3% (3) |
| Marines | 0% (0) | 33.33% (3) | 11.11% (1) | 55.55% (5) | 0% (0) |
| Air Force | 0% (0) | 21.42% (3) | 28.57% (4) | 50.00% (7) | 0% (0) |
| **Total** | **2.86%** **(2)** | **42,86%** **(30)** | **12.86%** **(9)** | **34.29%** **(24)** | **7.14** **%** **(5)** |

*Numbers between parentheses represent the amount of participants for each case.

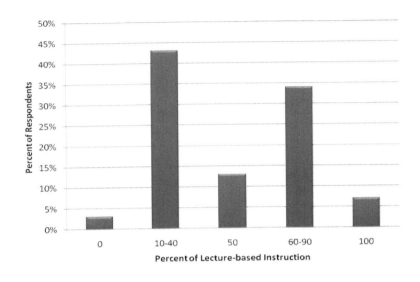

*Figure 14.1* Percentage of participants and the amount of
lecture based-training they had in the military.

Concerning the military training that involved
face-to-face instruction in a lecture-based classroom that
also included hands-on training with a computer or with
objects relevant to their training need, almost all veterans
said that at least some of their training involved a hands-
on component. Nearly 30% said that the majority of their
training involved hands on tasks, whereas only one
participant mentioned not having experienced a hands-on
component in their training at the Air Force. The
complete distribution of the answers on training
involving hands-on components can be viewed in Figu
14.2. Table 14.4 presents the results according to each
branch of military service.

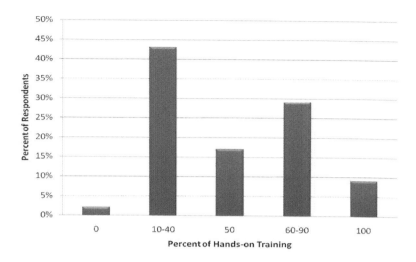

*Figure 14. 2.* Percentage of participants and the amount of hands-on training they had in the military.

Table 14.4. *Percentage of participants, lecture-based and hands on training.*

| Percentage of lecture-based training/ Branch of service | 0% | 10%-40% | 50% | 60%-90% | 100% |
|---|---|---|---|---|---|
| Army | 0% (0) | 39.39% (13) | 24.24% (8) | 24.24% (8) | 12.12% (4) |
| Navy | 0% (0) | 50.00% (7) | 7.14% (1) | 35.72% (5) | 7.14% (1) |
| Marines | 0% (0) | 22.22% (2) | 33.33% (3) | 44.44% (4) | 0% (0) |
| Air Force | 7.14% (1) | 64.28% (9) | 0% (0) | 28.57% (4) | 0% (0) |
| **Total** | **1.43% (1)** | **44.28% (31)** | **17.14% (12)** | **30.00% (21)** | **7.14% (5)** |

150

*Numbers between parentheses represent the amount of participants for each case.

For the questions involving distributed learning most participants claimed less experience with such learning methods. The majority of the participants (88.57%) claimed that their training involved less than 50% of distributed learning elements such as reading online materials and viewing online lectures. Approximately 39% of those had no experience involving distributed learning. Yet, about 9% of the inquired veterans claimed to have had more than 60% of their training involving distributed learning. The complete distribution of the answers on training involving distributed learning with online components can be viewed in Figure 14.3. Table 14.5 presents the results according to each branch of military service.

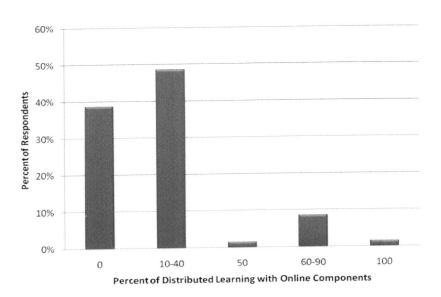

*Figure 14 3.* Percentage of participants and distributed learning (reading/viewing lectures/material online).

Table 14.5. *Percentage of participants and distributed learning (reading/viewing lectures/material online)*

| Percentage of online training/ Branch of service | None (0%) | 10%-40% | 50% | 60%-90% | 100% |
|---|---|---|---|---|---|
| Army | 39.39% (13) | 51.51% (17) | 0% (0) | 6.06% (2) | 3.03% (1) |
| Navy | 57.14% (8) | 28.57% (4) | 0% (0) | 14.29% (2) | 0% (0) |
| Marines | 50.00% (4) | 50.00% (4) | 0% (0) | 0% (0) | 0% (0) |
| Air Force | 14.29% (2) | 64.29% (9) | 7.14% (1) | 14.28% (2) | 0% (0) |
| **Total** | **38.57% (27)** | **48.57% (34)** | **1.43% (1)** | **8.58% (6)** | **1.43% (1)** |

*Numbers between parentheses represent the amount of participants for each case.

When asked about experiences with distributed learning where they observed simulations, 95.71% claimed to have had less than 50% of their training involving such methods. From those, half of the sample had not observed simulations at all, whereas 4.29% had had more than 60% of their training involving such methods. The complete distribution of the answers on training involving distributed learning with observations of simulations can be viewed in Figure 14.4. Table 14.6 presents the results according to each branch of military service.

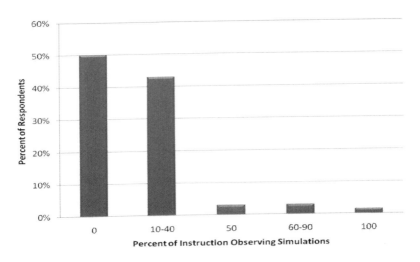

*Figure 14.4.* Percentage of participants and distributed learning (observing simulations).

Table 14.6. *Percentage of participants and distributed learning (observing simulations).*

| Percentage of observed simulations Branch of service | None (0%) | 10%-40% | 50% | 60%-90% | 100 % |
|---|---|---|---|---|---|
| Army | 51.52% (17) | 42.42% (14) | 0% (0) | 3.03% (1) | 3.03 % (1) |
| Navy | 78.57% (11) | 21.43% (3) | 0% (0) | 0% (0) | 0% (0) |
| Marines | 44.44% (4) | 44.44% (4) | 11.11% (1) | 0% (0) | 0% (0) |
| Air Force | 21.43% (3) | 64.29% (9) | 7.14% (1) | 7.14% (1) | 0% (0) |
| **Total** | **50.00%** **(35)** | **42.85%** **(30)** | **2.86%** **(2)** | **2.86%** **(2)** | **1.43 %** **(1)** |

*Numbers in Table 14.6 between parentheses represent the amount of participants for each case.

Concerning the military training involving low-fidelity computer-based simulations where subjects interacted with a simulated task to learn about, or practice, particular skills or procedures for the task, again 50% of the veterans claimed to never have used computer simulations. Nearly 45% of the veterans responding said that between 10% to 40% of their training utilized simulations in the learning, whereas less than 10% said that the majority of their learning used simulations. Figure 14.5 presents more details about training experience involving low-fidelity computer-based simulations and Table 14.7 presents the results according to each branch of military service.

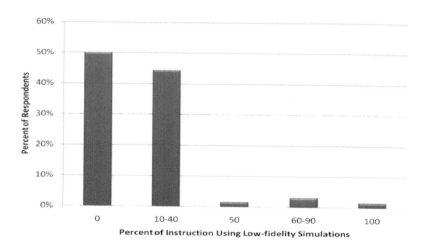

*Figure 14.5*. Percentage of participants whose training involved interaction with low-fidelity computer-based simulations.

14.7. *Percentage of participants whose training involved interaction with a low-fidelity computer-based simulations.*

| Percentage of high-fidelity computer interactions Branch of service | None (0%) | 10%-40% | 50% | 60% - 90% | 100 % |
|---|---|---|---|---|---|
| Army | 54.55% (18) | 45.45% (15) | 0% (0) | 0% (0) | 0% (0) |
| Navy | 57.14% (8) | 35.72% (5) | 0% (0) | 0% (0) | 7.14% (1) |
| Marines | 33.33% (3) | 66.66% (6) | 0% (0) | 0% (0) | 0% (0) |
| Air Force | 42.86% (6) | 35.71% (0) | 7.14% (1) | 14.28% (1) | 0% (0) |
| Total | 50%% (35) | 44.29% (31) | 1.43% (1) | 2.86% (1) | 1.43% (1) |

*Numbers between parentheses represent the amount of participants for each case.

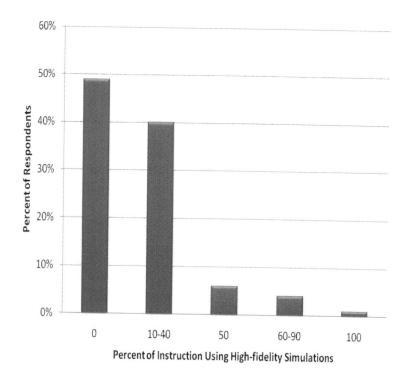

*Figure 14.6.* Percentage of participants whose training involved high-fidelity computer-based interactions.

Training that involved high-fidelity computer-based interactions was also not reported as a common experience by the responding veterans (see Figure 14.6). Air Force veterans reported the greatest amount of experience with such systems and Marine Corps veterans reported the least. Yet almost half of the inquired veterans (48.57%) had claimed to never have had trainings that involved such form of simulations. Table 14.8 presents the results according to each branch of military service.

Table 14.8. *Percentage of participants whose training involved high-fidelity computer-based interactions.*

| Percentage of high-fidelity computer interactions Branch of service | None (0%) | 10%-40% | 50% | 60%-90% | 100% |
|---|---|---|---|---|---|
| Army | 51.52% (17) | 39.39% (13) | 6.06% (2) | 3.03% (1) | 0% (0) |
| Navy | 57.14% (8) | 28.57% (4) | 7.14% (1) | 0% (0) | 7.14% (1) |
| Marines | 33.33% (3) | 66.66% (6) | 0% (0) | 0% (0) | 0% (0) |
| Air Force | 42.86% (6) | 35.71% (5) | 7.14% (1) | 14.29% (2) | 0% (0) |
| **Total** | **48.57% (34)** | **40% (28)** | **5.71% (4)** | **4.29% (3)** | **1.43% (1)** |

*Numbers between parentheses represent the amount of participants for each case.

Qualitative Analysis

As described earlier, as part of an exploratory investigation, open ended questions were presented to participants. For these, participants were requested to type their answers to questions pertaining to some of the curriculum and culture issues faced by veterans on campuses.

1. *When you started college, if you did not have any college preparatory experience, did you feel challenged when starting your education? Why or why not? (If you had college preparatory experience, please skip to the next question).*

The transition from military life to college life can be difficult, as pointed out by Hermann, Hopkins, Wilson and Allen (2009). This way, when asked, "Did you feel challenged when starting your education?", some of the respondents (47%) said that they felt challenged when starting their education. Almost half of these responses (47%) mentioned that the challenges were due to veterans not being use to attending classes or an academic routine. In addition, some responses also mentioned not being used to academic types of people (27% of the veterans who felt challenged) or not being used to academic time-management (13% of the veterans who felt challenged). But, 53% of the veterans did not feel challenged when starting college. Thirty-eight percent of the respondents claimed that the military experience had already provided them with confidence, discipline, and/or motivation for success. Some veterans also reported to have already had previous academic experience or psychological self-preparation, as reasons for not feeling challenged when starting college. Table 14.9 provides a summary of the categorized responses for this first question.

Table 14.9. *Percent of answers for how challenged veterans felt when they started their education.*

| Didn't feel challenged | | 53% |
|---|---|---|
| | Military experience helped; They believed that military experience gave them confidence /discipline/motivation for success. | 38% |
| | Previous academic experience helped; Took college before/ this is their second degree | 23% |
| | Previous psychological self-preparation helped; They planned it in advance and felt "mentally prepared "when entered college | 23% |
| | College was thought to be easy; College started with lower level classes | 17% |
| **Felt challenged** | | **47%** |
| | Not used to classes anymore ; There was a long time since left school and not used to having more free time. | 47% |
| | Not used to academic people; To be in classroom with new people/ work with people and "not try to dictate them". | 27% |
| | Not used to academic time-management; Transition from full-time employment to full-time college | 13% |
| | Others - "Each new experience does present its own set of challenges"/ "Maybe I was not smart enough" | 13% |

*2. Did you seek out assistance for veterans in preparatory instruction in academic skills for college (e.g., note taking techniques, learning/studying approaches, how to participate in laboratories for courses that require them, using study groups outside of class). Why or why not?*

Since veterans have not received college preparatory programs as recently as non-veterans who had just left high-school, it was hypothesized that veterans could lack academic skills when entering college. Thus, they were asked whether they sought out assistance for veterans in preparatory instruction in academic skills for college (e.g., note taking techniques, learning or studying approaches, how to participate in laboratories, or using study groups outside of class). The great majority of the responding veterans (90%) answered that they did not seek out assistance. Forty-five percent of these respondents did not feel they needed assistance and believed they had prior experience already. Some (17%) claimed not to seek out assistance because they did not know if any such veterans' assistance existed on their campus. Others (17%) said they do not like interpersonal experiences and ended up looking for information on their own. Thirteen percent looked for some other sorts of assistance, such as counselors or other veterans. But eight percent of respondents did seek out assistance for veterans. Table 14.10 provides a summary of the categories found for this second question.

Table 14.10: *Percent of answers for veterans who sought or did not seek out assistance and their explanations.*

| Did not seek out assistance | | 90% |
|---|---|---|
| | Did not feel they needed it/ felt they had prior experience already | 45% |
| | Did not know about the assistance to veterans/ their campus does not provide such assistance | 17% |
| | Looked for information on their own/ don't like interpersonal experiences | 17% |
| | Looked for another type of assistance (instructors/counselors/ other veterans/student groups) | 13% |
| | Was not a veteran when they started college | 5% |
| **Sought out assistance** | | **8%** |
| | Wanted to get help from the very beginning, before it was too late: Cites the military saying "Hurry up and wait!" | 50% |
| | Yes, but preferred to study by themselves | 50% |

## 3. What did you think was the most surprising difference about how you were trained in the military versus how you were being taught in the classroom?

When invited to think about the most surprising difference about how the participants were trained in the military versus how they were being taught in the classroom, the most mentioned issue (25% of the answers) was the discipline. According to the responding veterans, military training is more organized, straight forward, whereas higher education is seen as "more relaxed" and unorganized in some aspects. Moreover, military classrooms were described as more tense and lack rapport. Further, some characterized university professors as "weak" with those in higher education generally lacking in "professionalism".

Another remarkable aspect of the differences between training in military and classes at the university is the pragmatic orientation of military training. Twenty-three percent of the participants said that military is practitioner-based, whereas higher education is not (at all or not that much). Some claimed that college cannot be compared to the real world, it was said to be boring, abstract, and to have undefined goals, while in military one can clearly learn a job, "it makes the complete task".

The qualities of the instructors also differ in military and college, according to the opinion of 8 percent of the respondents. In general, they said that instructors are younger in the military, whereas they are more professional and well-versed in their fields in college.

The time issue was also mentioned as a difference between military and college by 5% of the participants. Military is understood as "fast paced", a full time job, and college demands officially "just 3 hours a week" for each course.

Other differences mentioned by 3% of the sample each include the following: 1) Experience and maturity of classmates: The respondents believed that the military experience made them more mature to go to the university in comparison to most of their classmates. 2) Autonomy and individuality also was said to differ between military training and college: Military was characterized as lacking individual thought and involving little (if any) self-teaching. It is believed to be a place where people are told when to do things and they are expected to do what is needed to be done.

On the other hand, in the academic world, it was mentioned that information is not given to students, they have to look for it. 4) Motivation and participation in classes was also mentioned by 7% of the sample as a main difference between military training and college: in the military, people are said to be motivated to participate in activities, and everybody is expected to get involved in the task and ask questions. In college, by contrast, students were characterized as participating only when they are forced to. 7% of the sample still mentioned that there is no difference between the military training and being taught in college. Table 14.11 provides a summary of the categories found for this third question.

Table 14.11. *Differences between military training and classroom education*

| | | |
|---|---|---|
| **Discipline** | Military has more discipline, is more organized, straight forward, whereas higher education lacks professionalism or is more relaxed/ unorganized in some aspects. Military classrooms can be tense and there is no rapport; some professors are weak at the university. | 25% |
| **Pragmatic orientation** | Military is practitioner based, higher education is not (not at all/not that much) "College is not the real world", whereas in military you learn a job. Military learning was structured, fun and unique, whereas classroom in college is abstract, boring, has undefined goals. "Military makes the complete task, and college does not really care". | 23% |
| **Instructors** | Military: young instructors/ different from requirements to be a professor/ College: The instructors are more professional and well-versed in their fields. | 8% |
| **Time** | Military is fast paced, it is treated as a full time job ("not just 3 hours a week") | 5% |
| **Experience/ Maturity** | Going to University after military experience makes one more mature for classes | 3% |
| **Autonomy/ Individuality** | Military lacks individual thought/ military involves little (if any) self-teaching/ . Military: you were told when to do things and exactly what needed to be done. In the academic world there is no second-chance, no re-training. Information is not given to you, you have to look for it. | 3% |
| **Motivation** | Military people are more motivated to participate on activities. Classroom people only participate if forced/ everyone in military was expected to be involved and ask questions | 3% |
| **Nothing/ No surprising differences** | | 8% |

4. *What did you find most challenging about your classroom education when you started college after the military?*

The biggest challenge about classroom education veterans reported was related to the behavior of their younger classmates. According to 33% of the reports, students in academia are perceived as civilians with different life experiences. And some of them are said to be "immature", "naïve", "careless", or "idealistic". Some veterans criticized their civilian classmates as people who sometimes have no idea of what sacrifice, or duty, or respect, or self-discipline is.

Another challenge faced by veterans right after entering higher education programs was related to academic issues and duties. Twenty-seven percent of the sample reported difficulties in dealing with the dynamics of classes, keeping up with homework, writing academic papers. They also mentioned a lack of "clear concise direction" in most of their studies, a lack of "guidance for learning", a lack of structure and discipline in the academic routine. Academics also required a higher level of thought than that in military, and often required working in groups with unfamiliar people.

Adjustments to the civilian life in general was also a topic brought up by 12% of the veterans as challenging when starting college. They mentioned in this category financial difficulties, such as dealing with rent, bills, and work, and balancing studies with a job; commuting issues, such as "the drive to college"; scheduling problems,, since some said they would like to wake up and have classes earlier in the morning. Table 14.12 provides a summary of the categories found for this fourth question.

Table 14.12. *Challenges about classroom education right after the military.*

| Behaviors of young classmates | Students in academy/civilians have different life experiences. Some classmates are immature/naïve/careless/idealistic/slow pace/have no idea what sacrifice or duty or respect or self discipline is. | 33% |
|---|---|---|
| Academic issues/ duties | Dynamics of classes/ more homework to keep up with/ writing academic papers/ lack of clear concise direction in most of my studies/ lack of guidance for learning/ lack of structure and discipline/ Level of thought is higher than that in military/ hard to work in groups of people who they have never worked with/ The relaxed atmosphere | 27% |
| Adjust-ments to "civilian life" | Dealing with rent bills and work/The drive to college/Time schedule (they would like to have classes earlier)/ Balancing studies with job/ Used to work in teams in military | 12% |
| Finding motivation to study | Staying awake, sitting and listening to someone's lecture is boring, lacks motivation to attend classes | 8% |
| Time | Military is fast paced, Treated as a full time job ("not just 3 hours a week")/ | 8% |
| Nothing | No differences | 4% |

5.    *Do you think it's important that a university take into account a veteran's military occupational specialty when providing veterans with advice about what courses to take? Why or why not?*

Almost half of the participants (49%) think that it is important that universities take into account military occupational specialty when providing veterans with advice about what courses to take. More than a half of those who agreed (57%) believed that veterans feel lost, because there are limited specialties or courses available at the universities for the experiences they have. Some others who agreed (14%) took the opportunity to criticize the "pointless" or "unnecessary" classes they are obliged to take instead.

Yet, some of the participants were not so sure about the importance of taking the military specialties into account at the university. Ten percent of them said it would depend on each veteran's career goals. According to these participants, some veterans might want to switch fields; some others might have liked their occupational specialty and wish to continue an education within that field. In sum, veterans should be able to decide. And actually, within the 40% of the participants who declared that it was not important that a university take the military specialty into account, 19% also supported that idea considering that veterans might want to switch fields. The majority of participants who answered "no" (44%), in fact believe that military training is not academically aligned with course catalogs, thus some jobs do not transfer over as college majors. Table 14.13 provides a summary of the categories found for this fifth question.

Table 14.13. *Veteran's opinion on whether universities should take military occupational specialties into account or not.*

| Yes | | 49 % |
|---|---|---|
| | Veterans feel lost because there are limited specialties or courses for experiences they have | 57 % |
| | So time is not wasted on pointless/unnecessary classes | 14 % |
| | If the MOS wasn't technical or academic in nature, it usually takes time to adjust. | 7 % |
| | Would make them more competitive for the market | 7 % |
| **It depends, if they want to switch fields or not/depends on their career goals/If the veteran liked their job/ occupational specialty does not create an advantage for learning, it depends on the individual goals/ should be able to choose the classes that interest them, as well those that meet their degree requirements. They should not be pigeon-holed into taking classes that no longer fit into a life they do not wish to lead (unless they are continuing an education within that field of study, of course)/ the veteran should decide** | | **10 %** |
| No | | 40 % |
| | Some jobs don't transfer over as college majors/The military training is not academically aligned with course catalogs | 44 % |
| | If they want to switch jobs | 19 % |
| | I would suggest no because it is the student's job to adapt to the changes of college from military education/ My experience was valuable but in no way applicable to my course of study | 19 % |
| | MOS already makes a person feel limited upon ETS and suggesting a major may make a vet feel even more limited and just abandon college altogether. | 6 % |
| | You need a well rounded education regardless of MOS. | 6 % |

*6. Do you think veterans would benefit from having*
*support in designing a plan of study and curriculum*
*based upon their experience?*

The great majority (72%) of the participants
believe that veterans would benefit from having support
in designing a plan of study and curriculum based upon
their experience. Yet, half of these respondents remarked
(again) that it should be optional, since some might want
to change their field, and since experiences vary enough
to not making generalizations possible. Fourteen percent
think that this support should be offered especially to
veterans who were in a supervisor, managerial or
leadership role. Of the 20 percent of participants who
said that veterans would not benefit from such support,
33% believed that veterans' experiences have nothing to
do with college subjects; and other 33% think that
veterans do not need these benefits, since they already
know what they want for their careers. Table 14.14
provides a summary of the categories found for this
question.

Table 14.14. *Veteran's opinion on whether there should be offered support in designing a plan of study based upon their experience*

| Yes | | 72% |
|---|---|---|
| | But it should be optional (some might want to change their field/ experiences vary so much) | 50% |
| | Especially for veterans who were in a supervisors/ managerial/ leadership role | 14% |
| | It could cut a number of credit hours for some veterans/it would be complementary | 14% |
| | If the support comes from a veteran fellow/ there should be "veterans only sessions" | 14% |
| | Others (especially if they never went to college before/ some assistance at the university is important) | 9% |
| No | | 20% |
| | Veterans' experiences have nothing to do with college subjects. | 33% |
| | Veterans do not need that, they already know what they want. | 33% |
| | Veterans' experiences are just an advantage they have. | 33% |
| | Veterans should be encouraged to exceed their previous accomplishments and not merely maintain it. | 17% |
| Others | Did not know | 4% |

7. Did you try to transfer credit for military training and experience? If so, did you have any problems?

The experiences concerning transferring of credits seemed to vary considerably among the sample. Most veterans in the survey (60%) tried to transfer credits for military training and experience to their college curriculum. Sixty percent of those reported finding no problems in the transaction. On the other hand, 41% of those who tried to transfer credits reported feeling disappointed because they got fewer credits than they expected. Thirty-five percent of the veterans did not try to transfer the credits, and the reason for not trying of half of them was that credits were not transferable or the fields were different. Twenty-five percent mentioned that they did not even try because their universities automatically entered credits. Table 14.15 provides a summary of the categories found for this seventh question.

Table 14.15. *Veterans who tried or did not try to transfer credits for military training and experience.*

| Percent of veterans who tried to transfer credit | 60% |
|---|---|
| Found no problems | 60% |
| Got just a few credits (felt disappointed about that) | 41% |
| Tried, but got no credits | 14% |
| Other | 9% |
| **Percent of veterans who did NOT try to transfer credit** | 35% |
| Credits unnecessary/ different fields/ there were no transferable credits | 50% |
| Credits automatically entered by the university | 25% |
| Not yet | 13% |
| College did not accept | 12% |
| Did not know they could do it / Was advised not to even try | 12% |

## 8. *Have you experienced any negative reactions by peers or faculty because of your veteran status?*

The majority of the participants (72%) claimed to never have had experienced any negative reaction by peer or faculty because of their veteran status. Further, 19% responded with an answer suggesting "quite the opposite"; that is, that they had gotten a positive response from faculty or peers because of their veteran status (e.g., treated as more mature/responsible). Importantly, though, 60% of them said that they do not even let others know that they are veterans, they prefer not to mention that. From the 28% of the participants who said that they did experience negative reactions, 46% reported experiencing this once or a few limited times by professors or young classmates, whereas 23% said to have had many negative experiences. Table 14.16 provides a summary of the categories found for this question.

Table 14.16. *Participants' experiences of negative reactions by peers or faculty because of their veteran status.*

| Percent of veterans who NEVER had a negative experience | | 72 % |
|---|---|---|
| | Do not mention/do not let anyone know that they are veterans | 60 % |
| | "Quite the opposite" | 19 % |
| Percent of veterans who had a negative experience | | 28 % |
| | A few/limited reactions (by professors or young classmates) | 46 % |
| | Many experiences | 23 % |
| | Once | 8% |

8. *Have you had non-veteran students ask inappropriate questions about hazardous duty or combat experiences?*

More than half of the responding veterans (59%) said that they had not been asked questions about hazardous duty or combat experiences by non-veteran students. Yet, 10% of these respondents reminded that they were probably not asked because they did not mention their veteran status. Forty percent of the veterans were asked such questions often (20%), or were asked such questions and remarked that they do not mind being asked (15%). Fifteen percent of the veterans also manifested some discomfort when being often asked "if they have killed anybody". Table 14.17 provides a summary of the categories found for this question.

Table 14.17. *Inappropriate questions about hazardous duty or combat experiences.*

| Percent of veterans who HAVE NOT been asked | | 59% |
|---|---|---|
| | Because they do not mention they are veterans | 10% |
| Percent of veterans who HAVE been asked | | 40% |
| | "Often" | 20% |
| | "Yes, and I don't mind being asked" | 15% |
| | "Yes, and don't ask me if I have ever killed anybody!" | 15% |

10. *Do you feel that, as a veteran, you are a part of a minority campus group, but one without appropriately recognized help and status?*

Almost half of the responding veterans (46%) reported that they do not feel part of a minority campus group without appropriately recognized help and status. Twenty-two percent of them believed that they have enough support in their campus already, whereas 17% think that they are a minority group but they do have recognition, and 13% mentioned that in the past they felt that way, but not anymore. By contrast, 46% of the responding veterans feel part of a minority group with no recognition, yet 17% of those are positive towards their status and believe they are more and more being

Table 14.18. *Veteran's opinion on whether they are part of a minority that has little or no recognition.*

| Percent of veterans who DO NOT feel part of a minorit no recognition | 46% |
|---|---|
| No, and we have enough support in our campus a | 22% |
| We are part of a minority, but we have recognitio | 17% |
| Not anymore (felt like that in a campus/university) | 13% |
| Percent of veterans who DO feel part of a minority w recognition | 46% |
| Feels that their situation is getting better/ they are more recognized | 17% |
| Feels that they need more support | 13% |
| Percent of veterans who have not thought about it yet | 6% |

recognized. Some (13%) claimed to still feel they need more support. Table 14.18 provides a summary of the categories found for this tenth question.

## Discussion

This chapter set out to provide a preliminary analysis of research issues facing veterans upon their return to college. The goal was to begin examination of issues so as to ensure that veterans enrolling in college have a positive and productive experience. The multifaceted factors impacting upon the veteran experience were classified along three broad categories consisting of Cognition, Curriculum, and Culture.

The analysis of the quantitative indicators shows clearly some differences in "how" teaching takes place in the military training. Yet, strong similarities can still be noticed between military training and the college classroom. Thus, from the surveyed veterans' point of view, military training already provides some sort of preparation.

Traditional methods of learning were oftenexperienced by the veterans during their military training. Such findings could be explained since the average age of this study sample was 32 years old. Yet, as specific observation of the answers did not show that the younger participants had experienced "less traditional" methods, that is, methods that involve distributed learning. In fact, it was observed that training involving simulations was more common to some military branches than others.

Military training was suggested by at least half of the responding veterans as something that provides some preparation for college. This finding is important in that some suggest that the military may not provide adequate preparation for college (see Herrmann et al., 2009). Yet, it remains unknown what sort of "preparation" is really being considered. For example, is it related to tools and techniques used during the training? Or is it merely a developmental issue in that, once veterans enter college, they are more mature?

Some findings are notable and worthy of further consideration. With regard to a student veteran's status, as stated, most claimed to have never experienced any negative reactions by peers or faculty because of their veteran status. This is a non-trivial finding in that, in the views of some, the legacies of the Vietnam conflict still impact how veterans may be treated in college (Herrmann, Raybeck, & Wilson, 2008). Granted, this was a very small sample, so further and broader research is warranted to more closely examine this issue. Further, what is important to note in this regard is that approximately 60% said that they do not let others know of their veteran status. This is particularly important in that Hermann et al. (2009) argued that both faculty and administrators should be made aware that students are veterans and perhaps obtain a special status for this. Of the percentage who had said that they did experience negative reactions, nearly half said it was only one or few times.

Related to the above, though, was what can be referred to as the maturity issue. This was observed in the qualitative data when veterans complained about the behavior of their younger classmates. Moreover, as one of the participants stated "veterans are normal people", suggesting that the investigation should center on whether differences experienced are due veteran status or to their "more mature" status. Thus any differences that emerge may be an artifact of the age of veterans; that is, they enroll in college only after some years in the military, whereas most students enter college directly after high school. As was also noted, another participant mentioned that professors may sometimes include them in different groups because they are older; further providing evidence that reinforces this "maturity" hypothesis. Comparisons between veterans and civilians who are also older than their classmates could answer these questions. This way, educators could direct special attention to veterans or also to "more mature" students, civilians and veterans.

Yet, there is no doubt that veterans can sometimes compose a differentiated group in college and at universities. They themselves noted that differences in discipline and pragmatic orientation were apparent and that they experienced some difficulties adjusting to civilian life. For example, some found it a challenge to be self-motivated to work, given that, when in the military, goals and objectives were set for them. Moreover, the collaborative and team nature of the military was seen as something in stark contrast to life at the university, which, in their view, emphasized individuality even when much of the work is to be done in groups.

In sum, this was a small sample but our findings do suggest that a broader look may be warranted. Veteran's organizations and academic institutions are encouraged to pursue a new and more sophisticated collaboration to understand and address the needs of veterans. This includes more quantifiable methods for systematically analyzing issues so as to better define any problems. And it includes collaborations that allow organizations to strategically coordinate so as to better address problems both top down (at the policy and administrative levels), and bottom up (through direct support of veterans on campus). As noted from the outset, this preliminary research program was different along two important dimensions. First, veterans were directly surveyed so as to gain an understanding of their subjective experiences as veterans enrolled in higher education. This provided an important first-person glimpse of the experiences of veterans in college. Second, rather than anecdotal evidence, quantifiable data was collected. This was meant as a necessary first step for better understanding veterans in higher education – an understanding grounded in data, and not in stories. The guiding vision was that, while anecdotes can be used to move us, it is data that should be used to convince us.

# References

American Council on Education (2009). *Military Service Members and Veterans in Higher Education: What the New GI Bill May Mean For Postsecondary Institutions.* Washington, DC: ACE.

Chickering, A. W., & Reisser , L. (1993). *Education and identity* (2nd Edition). San Francisco: Jossey-Bass.

DiRamio, D., Ackerman, R., & Mitchell, R.L. (2008). From combat to campus: Voices of student-veterans. *NASPA Journal, 45(1),* 73-102.

Elkins, S. A., Braxton, J. M., & James, G. W. (2000). Tinto's separation stage and its influence on first semester college student persistence. *Research in Higher Education, 41,* 251-268.

Herrmann, D., Hopkins, C., Wilson, R. B. & Allen, B. (2009). *Educating Veterans in the 21$^{st.}$ Century.* North Charleston, South Carolina: BookSurge.

Herrmann, D. J., Raybeck, D., & Wilson, R. (2008). College Is for Veterans, Too. *The Chronicle of Higher Education, November 21.*

Saville, B. K., Zinn, T. E., Neef, N. A., Norman, R. V. & Ferreri, S. M. (2006). A comparison of interteaching and lecture in the college classroom.

178

*Journal of Applied Behavior Analysis, 39(1),* 49-61.

Sternberg, M., Wadsworth, S., Vaughan, J., & Carlson, R. (2009). *The higher education landscape for student service members and veterans in Indiana.* Military Family Research Institute at Purdue University: West Lafayette, IN.

Chapter 15

# A Clash of Cultures: Veterans in Academe

## Douglas Raybeck

Emeritus Professor of Anthropology,
Hamilton College

Ninety-seven percent of students, faculty and administrators lack a military background. Some of these individuals are naïve about the military, and can be insensitive, and even offensive to service members and veterans. The problem seems to be largely a cultural one, a clash of cultures between academics, military and non-military members of the academy, all of whom have their own worldviews. The nature of the challenges encountered by student veterans is examined and some means of alleviating these are suggested.

The problems enmeshed in the introduction of service persons to academic environments are both numerous and complex. It is my belief that the principal difficulties involved in resolving these issues stem from different cultural backgrounds, filters, and perceptions. Cultural differences can be particularly intractable because some of their strongest elements are not accessible to the consciousness of the participants. Stated another way, most of us are unaware of at least some of our cultural biases.

A decent definition of culture would read as follows: Culture is an integrated system of learned patterns for behavior characteristic of the members of society. The important element in this definition is that culture consists of learned patterns for behavior (Keesing, 1976). In short, it is a general template that generates behaviors but does not dictate them in detail. Thus, one can accept the templates of Second Lieutenant, or teacher and interpret the cultural scripts in ways that are both individualistic and even in idiosyncratic.

However, our learned cultural patterns are often both subtle and interlocking in ways that the participants fail to appreciate (Shore, 1996). This is due to the manner in which we learn our culture through a process that begins at birth (Munroe & Munroe, 1994; Williams, 1972). Obviously some of our cultural patterns are the result of conscious instruction: "Sit up Straight at the Table." and so forth. The virtue of these elements is that we are conscious of them and can decide to accept them, reject them, or modify them. However, there are many cultural patterns that we acquire by daily interaction with others without any seeming instruction occurring. These elements can be more problematic because we are unaware that we carry them (Mayer, 1970). We can neither reflect on these elements, nor modify them. This gives them a peculiar power to affect our behavior and our beliefs.

For a quick and uncontroversial example of this power, consider what happens when you approach another person. One or both of you will stop before entering something called the intimate zone. For middle-class Americans that is a range of 18 inches best measured between the bridges of two noses (Hall, 1966; Raybeck, 1991). Similarly, reflect on how uncomfortable it is to be in a packed elevator. People are forced within one another's intimate zone and will strive mightily to avoid eye contact. At no point has anyone ever instructed us not to stand closer to another than 18 inches, but we learn this by interacting with others starting in school and continuing throughout life. Although the rule is an unconscious one, it is extremely powerful. Should you doubt this, try to consciously violate it and see what happens.

Our cultural background provides each of us with a worldview, a set of beliefs and predispositions about the nature of others, ethics, and even reality. Between cultures worldviews can differ widely, but it is also the case that some sub-cultures within a culture can produce markedly different worldviews (Osgood, May, & Miron, 1975). This is a major issue with which we must wrestle, if we wish to facilitate the education of our veterans.

## MILITARY CULTURE

For functional reasons, the organization of military structures is necessarily top-down. There are clear relations among components and every step is taken to reduce ambiguity. This is true not only for the definition of roles within a military structure, but, despite the inevitable "fog of war" (Clausewitz, 2006), it is also true for any orders that are directed throughout the ranks. No one wishes to encounter a set of directions capable of several interpretations, nor should there be any confusion about positions of responsibility with respect to tasks assigned.

The cultural values of the military are clear and are inculcated from the beginning: duty, honor, country. This triad, or something very like it is part of the oath that every service person takes and is reinforced in interactions with both peers and superiors. Indeed, the importance of honor among combat personnel can be traced to medieval times (Murray, 1999). The concern with country generally involves a call for patriotism. This in turn exalts bravery and, to some extent, obedience to authority. This last is literally a functional prerequisite for any military.

Unintentionally, but almost ineluctably, the military also elevates the importance of a macho ethic. This is the case irrespective of gender, as women are also expected to be tough, assertive, and physically capable. Indeed, physical prowess is highly valued, partly because it may translate into good fighting skills. A corollary of these concerns is a remarkable bond between those with whom one fights. Loyalty to your buddies is an integral component of any military endeavor. It is, as many have noted, the main reason that individuals fight (Hillen, 1999).

A more problematic issue, given our concerns, is the general attitude of the military services, exempting the Marine Corps, toward education. As Murray has noted,

> Another apparent weakness in the current military cultural climate, and one that certainly did not obtain in the interwar period, is the decline of professional military education, the subject of a devastating House Armed Services Committee report of the late 1980s. To be sure, the Naval War College remains the finest institution of its kind in the world, but unfortunately the navy still resolutely refuses to send its officers to school. Elsewhere, the fact that the National Defense University seriously considered getting rid of its entire civilian faculty so that it could finance the buying of sophisticated computers suggests a general disdain for serious military education among those heading such institutions. In fact, the inclinations within the world of professional military education reflect the attitudes of both the larger military culture and society: profoundly anti-intellectual and ahistorical (1999:146-47).

To the extent that he is accurate, we must be concerned about the degree to which military organizations will be active participants in preparing veterans to enter or reenter institutions of higher education.

The relationship of the military to society has been problematic, literally for thousands of years, even before Caesar first marched his armies into Rome (Clausewitz, 2006). Acknowledging that military cultures differ significantly one from the other, one must still observe that they are even more different from the society they serve. This is true not only in the United States but in the great majority of countries around the world, excepting those that are ruled by their military structures. United States society aspires to a set of liberal values enshrined in its Constitution. Military organizations, in contrast, are functionally required to emphasize a non-egalitarian, non-inclusive set of rules.

At the same time, the military is committed to a service ethic and the protection of the wider society. This is a core element of military culture and one that is seldom acknowledged by the broader society. Although generally conservative, the tight structure of military organizations can be used as a force for change (Murray, 1999). It was largely through the military that both African Americans and women were able to make significant social progress.

The fact that military personnel live in circumstances that estrange them from the wider society only exacerbates some of these differences and tensions. Negative stereotypes can abound in the absence of shared communications and experience. Military personnel can easily view the wider society as hedonistic, materialistic, and weak. At the same time, civilians can view the military as rigid, authoritarian, and narrow. These opposing percepts set the stage for conflictual encounters.

## ACADEMIC CULTURE

The organization of Academe consists of administrators, faculty and students. Administrators generally serve for a limited period of from 5 to 10 years. It is quite common for deans and even presidents to return to the faculty after their period of service. Responsibilities for the operation of the institution are divided among several bodies including the trustees, the administration, and the faculty. The domains and prerogatives of all three bodies are often poorly defined. To further muddy the waters, there are faculty committees, student committees and joint faculty-student committees, often with an administrator in attendance.

The monthly business of the institution is realized at faculty meetings where changes are made to the curriculum and to aspects of community governance. Such faculty meetings are often characterized by a cacophony of voices and a wide variety of positions. It is even possible for faculty to pass a vote of no confidence in the president. This action effectively terminates the individual's presidency. Imagine anything remotely resembling this in the military.

The values and beliefs of academe highlight the importance of free and unfettered inquiry. Indeed, this is the rationale behind tenure. No one should lose their job because they espoused an unpopular position or carried out controversial research. There is supposed to be, and often is, a commitment to general equality and egalitarianism. This is sometimes violated within departments when a chair or full professor uses his or her position to disadvantage an assistant or associate professor. However, the value of egalitarianism is reflected in common academic rhetoric that emphasizes the institution as a "community of learners".

The great majority of faculty believes that authority should be questioned and they take an iconoclastic position regarding many social institutions. One of the benefits of tenure is that it allows faculty to question their own authorities and to participate actively in the governance of the educational institution. As I noted above, this can go to some extreme. Many faculty, in contrast to members of the military, enjoy ambiguity. If that seems difficult to credit, I recommend reading some postmodern philosophy, perhaps Foucault, or one of the more current postmodernists.

There are also many who disparage the macho ethic, and even some who denigrate participation in many sports. Faculty members, like most of us, are leery of those who are different. Not surprisingly, few faculty seriously engaged in sports during their youth. Many also tend to see physical competition as at odds with a life of the mind.

As was the case for the military, the relationship of academe to the wider society can be problematic, but in a very different fashion. Most members of academe do not have a prominent service ethic. Indeed, as suggested above, many are critical of the wider society and often quite vocal in their critiques. While some of these criticisms can be dismissed as simple carping, many are intended to be constructive and a source of progress and improvement. However, society rarely welcomes academic criticisms. Instead, due to the rather marginal position of most academics, their commentaries are usually dismissed as the rantings of pointy-headed intellectuals.

Members of academe are also somewhat removed from interaction with the wider society, though to a much lesser degree than the military. However, many faculty believe it is beneath them to reach out to the wider public. Many faculty disparage efforts to popularize research with the unfortunate consequence of marginalizing those who undertake this endeavor. Often the public lacks an understanding of how grants that enable the study of a variety of obscure subjects might benefit society at large and, in the absence of good communication, we once again encounter faculty stereotypes such as the one described above. Finally, with notable exceptions, both politically and socially members tend to be quite liberal. (These problems and many more have been very well described by Douglas Herrmann and colleagues, 2009).

THE CULTURE CLASH

It seems obvious that even with goodwill on both sides, conflict between members of these two institutions is likely. I will argue later that the difficulties I am about to describe can be reduced and perhaps even resolved. However, many differences are in direct opposition to one another (Table 15.1). This makes the social and cultural task of integrating service persons into academe correspondingly more difficult, but it paradoxically may facilitate educating both sides about the problems at hand.

Table 15.1
**Issues of Difference and Conflict**

| Military | Academe |
|---|---|
| **Organization** | **Organization** |
| Strong Structure | Weak Structure |
| Clear Relationships among Components | Fuzzy Relationships among Components |
| **Values & Beliefs** | **Values & Beliefs** |
| Duty, Honor, Country | Freedom of Inquiry |
| Service | Education |
| Bravery | Intellect |
| Obedience | Questioning |
| Intolerance of Ambiguity | Tolerance of Ambiguity |
| **Relation to Wider Society** | **Relation to Wider Society** |
| Service Ethic | Iconoclastic |
| Quite Removed | Somewhat Removed |
| Conservative | Liberal |

It is likely that service persons who enter academe will be older and have more experience than the typical undergraduate. Paradoxically, the typical veteran may experience swings between self-assurance and insecurity depending on the context. In circumstances where there is respect shown for the person's accomplishments and sacrifices, self-assurance and even a degree of social acceptance can be anticipated.

However, the educational environment will be novel and even strange. That can lead to uncertainty about the nature of present expectations and acceptable, even approved behavior. For instance, the better professors, and often the more popular ones, enjoy being challenged in the classroom. Disagreeing with or challenging authority may not initially be an easy undertaking for most former service persons.

It is also quite possible that veterans will harbor stereotypes of academe, the typical student, and professors. These can color and interfere with the nature of the educational experience.

There are a variety of other interpersonal factors that can create friction between former military personnel and other students. Prior service persons may well be resentful of those who haven't served and done their duty. They may also find them both naïve and inexperienced. Many military persons are likely to take a very pragmatic attitude toward their education, viewing it mainly as a means to employment, and eschewing abstractions and courses that do not seem directed toward a practical goal. To the extent that this attitude is visible to professors, they may be expected to respond unenthusiastically or even negatively.

The problems confronting healthy entering military personnel are significant, as we shall see below. The main issue is one of cultural and perceptual differences. However, many entering former service persons will have a degree of mental trauma such as PTSD or related problems with which they must deal. Obviously, these issues complicate an already difficult situation. Finally, there are those service persons who enter with significant and visible physical trauma. In addition to managing the situational difficulties they encounter, they must also manage the attitudes and behaviors of those around them (Goffman, 1959, 1963).

The existing students that the service person will encounter range from privileged to poor. The precise mix will depend upon the nature of the institution, but one commonality is that nearly all of these other students will be ignorant of military life and of the experiences it promotes. Students may be admiring of, or resentful toward, the service person depending on a variety of factors such as class, comportment, and even appearance. While some will be curious about the experiences of the military personnel, many, perhaps most will harbor a variety of inaccurate stereotypes. It may also be anticipated that many of these will be negative. Ex-service people may be seen as unintelligent, unoriginal and even in favor of killing (Herrmann et al., 2009).

Most faculty and administrators are also likely to be less than wholly cognizant of the transition problems facing veterans. Many may well possess the same negative and ignorant stereotypes held by many students (Herrmann et al., 2009). The issue here, like many of the ones described above, is largely one of culture. Many faculty view the military as a dangerous and unfortunate necessity. Historically however, there have been significant exceptions. During World War II numerous well-known anthropologists contributed their expertise to understanding the enemy. Benedict's flawed, yet useful and extremely influential work on the Japanese is an excellent example. Despite the liberal and academic nature of the profession, many well-known anthropologists not only served in WWII, they employed their expertise in covert activities. More than two dozen of them worked with the OSS including such luminaries as Gregory Bateson, Carleton Coon, Cora DuBois, Felix Keesing, and George Murdock (Price, 1998). Now, however, many anthropologists harbor reservations concerning the present participation of some colleagues in some military efforts in Iraq and in Afghanistan, particularly those involving tribal relationships. http://www.aaanet.org/issues/policyadvocacy/Anthropolg y-and-the-Military.cfm. Even those administrator and faculty members who are well disposed toward veterans may well unintentionally and insensitively estrange and discourage these new entering students. The problem seems to involve both cultural misperceptions and a lack of adequate communication.


TOWARD A RESOLUTION

The first step to addressing the problems described above is to recognize that they exist. This is the responsibility of the administration. They must take steps to educate their faculty and staff concerning these matters. This education should be of an experiential rather than literary nature. Nothing works better than interaction, because it increases communication and diffuses stereotypes. Communication is key to easing the entry of veterans and to making others aware of the complex nature of the problems at hand.

Many entering veterans may need, and certainly are likely to benefit from, remedial training in academic skills. Educational institutions are discovering that this is also true of many of the usual students. Thus, where possible, it would be desirable to place both sorts in joint classes designed to address reading, writing and quantitative deficiencies.

Public forums, including veterans, students, and faculty, could be directed specifically to these problems. In addition to serving as educational vehicles for the wider community, these forums would greatly deepen mutual understanding for the participants. Other public forums such as those that address current events could also fold in veterans as well as the typical student. Finally, every educational institution has a series of joint social and educational endeavors, such as community outreach programs, where veterans could be encouraged to play a role. Indeed, given what will often be their less privileged background, they may be extremely well suited to be helpful with the disadvantaged.

Much work clearly needs to be done on support services. Most counseling centers are not prepared for, nor experienced with, the mental traumas that may accompany the entry of many veterans. It would also be very helpful if the educational institution were to provide facilities for physical therapy. This need not be enormously expensive as most institutions have elaborate gyms and many have excellent trainers and physical therapists. The nature of the disabilities that some veterans will have may require further training on the part of physical therapists. Educational institutions should encourage this and underwrite the cost of it. Obviously, steps should also be taken to improve physical access both to dormitories and to classrooms.

A less obvious, yet important, concern is the enforcement of social rules and norms. This is something that administrators often do not handle well. Fear of bad publicity, lawsuits, and a series of other negative possibilities often leads administrators to deal very leniently with bad behavior. Nonetheless, virtually every campus possesses a behavior code, even though it may be poorly enforced. I am recommending that enforcement be prompt and strict. It should be obvious that this is the case whether the offender is a typical student or a veteran. Similarly, physical violence and intimidation should be punished firmly. Most campuses have rules about harassment and insults, but those are typically directed to the issues of race, gender, and sexual orientation. Educational institutions need to become sensitive to the manner in which former military personnel can be mistreated and insulted.

The military itself could play a much greater role than it presently does in preparing those who plan to leave the military and enter academe. The services could hold seminars and role-playing exercises that could offer a glimpse of some of the problems that may well be encountered. At the very least, brochures or even relevant books such as Educating Veterans in the 21st Century (Herrmann et al., 2009) could be provided to veterans to help them anticipate some of the difficulties they will encounter.

Finally, the objective of successfully integrating and educating veterans in an academic environment can be greatly facilitated by better communication within the various components of the academy and between the academy and the military. At the present time, the relationship between these two vital institutions is more conflictual than cooperative. Each needs to be able to see the other as a complementary component of the wider society. Both have missions to accomplish and both benefit the society at large. That they do so in very different ways should not be a cause of friction, particularly if it is realized that each need, perhaps even require, the other.

## References

Clausewitz, C. v. (2006). On War (C. J. J. Graham, Trans.). London: Project Gutenberg EBook.

Goffman, E. (1959). The Presentation of Self in Everyday Life. New York: Doubleday Anchor Books.

Goffman, E. (1963). Stigma: Notes on the Management of Spoiled Identity. Englewood Cliffs, NJ: Prentice-Hall.

Hall, E. T. (1966). The Hidden Dimension. Garden City, NY: DoubledayAnchor.

Herrmann, D., Hopkins, C., Wilson, R. B., & Allen, B. (2009). Educating Veterans in the 21st Century. North Charleston, South Carolina: BookSurge.

Hillen, J. (1999). Must U.S. Military Culture Reform? OrbisPhiladelphia, 43(1), 43-58.

Keesing, R. (1976). Cultural Anthropology: A Contemporary Perspective. New York: Holt, Rinehart and Winston.

Mayer,P. (1970). Socialization: The Approach from Social Anthropology. London: Tavistock publications.

Munroe, R. L., & Munroe, R. H. (1994). Cross Cultural Human Development. Prospect Heights, IL: Waveland Press.

Murray, W. (1999). Does Military Culture Matter? OrbisPhiladelphia, 43(1), 27-42.

Osgood, C. E., May, W. H., & Miron, M. S. (1975). Cross-Cultural Universals of Affective Meaning. Urbana: University of Illinois Press.

Price, D. H. (1998). Gregory Bateson and the OSS: World War II and Bateson's Assessment of Applied Anthropology. Human Organization, Winter.

Raybeck, D. (1991). Proxemics and Privacy: Managing the Problems of Life in Confined Environments. In A. A. Harrison, Y. A. Clearwater & C. P. McKay (Eds.), From Antarctica to Outer Space: B. Life in Isolation and Confinement (pp 317 330). New York: Springer -Verlag.

Shore, B. (1996). Culture in Mind: Cognition, Culture, and the Problem of Meaning.: Oxford University Press.

Williams, T. R. (1972). Introduction to Socialization. St. Louis: C.V. Mosby Company.

Chapter 16

# Neurorehabiliation for Veterans Returning to Academia

## Dr. Rick Parente', PhD
Towson University

## Ms. Ariane Burns
Towson University

Combat can result in brain damage in different ways through penetrating and non-penetrating wounds as well as concussive head injury. This brain damage interferes with cognitive functioning and makes completion of college more difficult, and sometimes impossible. This would have been possible to a veteran prior to his or her military service. This chapter discusses what educators can do to help veterans with brain damage as they seek a college degree.

With the influx of military personnel returning from foreign wars, colleges and universities, vocational training programs, community colleges and state vocational rehabilitation agencies will soon be inundated with young men and women who are trying to reintegrate into an academic environment (Kodak, 2008). These students face a host of unique problems secondary to their experience in the military that set them apart from the usual student populations who are transitioning from high school. For example, most have been under severe stress during their war-time experience and many suffer from Post-Traumatic Stress Disorder (PTSD). Most have experienced different life experiences in their military training and deployments relative to the general student population many of whom have never been out of the country. Many veterans are still struggling with the emotional, physical, social, and domestic after effects of their deployments. In addition, many of the veterans will have suffered traumatic brain injuries which create a host of cognitive problems that can interfere with their academic performance, their cognitive functioning, and their overall ability to adjust (Millike, Auchterlonie, & Hoge, 2007; Seal, Bertenthal, Miner, Saunak, & Marmar, 2007; Whealin, 2004).

Traumatic brain injury occurs whenever the brain is shaken violently or impacts with another object, pierced with a projectile, or lacks oxygen for an extended period. It also occurs because of extended medication use, long-term alcohol use, or any combination of the above. Each of these causes can occur during war; the more deployments the veteran undergoes, the more likely he or she will experience a brain injury. The usual symptoms of brain injury include poor memory, inability to remain focused, emotional volatility, poor planning and executive skills, and personality change. Veterans who demonstrate these symptoms are often at risk for other problems including poor academic performance, family turmoil, and inability to integrate into a new social environment.

Returning veterans are also more likely to have emotional challenges. Statistically, although most do not have severe post-traumatic stress, many (13 to 25%, compared to 3.5- 7% in general population) will have been diagnosed with PTSD. Between 5-13% will enter college with diagnoses of depression, 6% will have anxiety Disorder diagnosis, 15% have had mild traumatic brain injuries, 5 15% have substance abuse issues (Burns, Lambert, & Powers, 2009). However, these statistics likely underestimate the problems the veteran experiences upon return. Most experience severe psychosocial problems including family stress, problems getting employment, and financial issues. Emotionally, they may experience an exaggerated startle response, sleep disturbance, distractibility, flattened affect, and social awkwardness. They might also have persistent intrusive thoughts, nightmares, problems with anger management, social avoidance, fear of crowds and driving. They might also experience limited cognitive flexibility, emotional volatility, lack of awareness, increased disinhibition and problems with memory and attention.

Returning veterans are also more likely to have additional responsibilities, which are not part of the usual student's lifestyle. For example, they may have families, children, ongoing military duties and full-time jobs. They may also have serious physical injuries and chronic medical conditions that require ongoing treatment. They may be older than the average college student and having just returned from the life and death struggles of a warzone, it may be hard for them to accept the perceived frivolities of the college environment.

To make matters worse, returning veterans report a host of problems related to the process of registering for coursework. For example, Herrmann et al. (2009) indicated that veterans often report that a college or university does not provide appropriate information about the school or the problems they are likely to encounter before they begin their coursework. There is limited information concerning the campus culture, information about financial aid, procedures to transfer academic credit, specific health care for veterans, or assistance with job placement after graduation. Herrmann (2007a) reported that although the reports of problems varied from school to school, most schools he surveyed reported that between 8-60% of veterans experience problems in one or more of the above categories.

The situation described above suggests a general lack of preparation for the coming tidal wave of returning veterans who will soon descend on America's colleges and universities. There are so many potential problems that a book like this one is necessary to address them in categories. This chapter addresses only one of a multitude of problems that will likely affect a returning veteran's ability to adjust to college life. Specifically, the chapter describes the challenges faced by those veterans who have had brain injuries secondary to their deployment. This type of veteran will have specific needs that colleges and universities are ill-equipped to address. Along these lines, our goal is not to describe the neurophysiology that underlies these problems but, more so, to make practical suggestions for dealing with them.

General suggestions for structuring the veteran's college experience

Return to academia can be a confusing and frustrating time for veterans who are only recently returned from a war-zone. The confusion is amplified for those veterans who have had even mild brain injuries during their deployment. The following are suggestions that the veteran and the academic institution should implement when they return to school.

Limit the course load. Any student who returns to school after sustaining a brain injury should not attempt a full complement of coursework during the first year. They will require more time than the average student will need to assimilate the materials that are required for each course. As a rule, they should begin with a six or nine hour load and not add to that course load unless they have a 3.0 or better grade-point average (GPA) in the courses they are taking.

Providing instructor notes. Instructors should make available their notes to veterans to help them organize the materials effectively. This is less of a problem in recent years as instructors have begun putting notes on a university's computerized\ blackboard systems and using visual displays of their notes as talking points during lectures.

Regular office hour visits. Veterans should schedule regular office visits with instructors and teaching assistants to answer questions about the materials. The veterans should also use other means of communications such as email and text messages.

Recorded lectures. Memory problems often result from even mild head injury. One way to ensure adequate processing of lectures is to record them and listen to them later. Although tape recorders have been largely replaced by digital recorders, they have the advantage of being multi-speed so that the veteran can record and then listen to the lecture quicker the second time around. Recording lectures is like seeing a movie for the second time. The veteran will hear things he or she did not hear the first time, which will greatly improve memory for the material.

Medications. Drugs affect cognition, more or less depending on the dosage and the type. Some drugs, like mood stabilizers may be necessary to maintain emotional stability whereas others like those who control ADHD help to focus the person. Regardless, a well thought out and balanced regimen of medication may be necessary to perform well in a college atmosphere. If the veteran requires medication then it is necessary to monitor him or her.

Earplugs when taking tests. Ideally, the veteran could take tests in a quiet room, away from the rest of the class, to screen out noise. In lieu of this, the veteran should use earplugs to provide a quiet environment in which he or she can think.

Suggestions for creating a positive academic environment for veterans - Study groups provide an argosy of information about specific course content and the college environment in general. They are especially helpful for veterans who are used to working in teams. A study group can be extremely helpful for providing tips about courses, professors, and unique study habits that may be beneficial in their courses, making new friends, and for providing feedback about what is necessary to succeed socially.

Mnemonic training – All students benefit from using mnemonics. Mnemonics for learning course related information improves acquisition of the material although many veterans may not have learned how to create them. Training the veterans to create their own mnemonics is especially useful. Excellent sources for this type of training are the Memory Works CDs, which are available from Memoryzine.com.

Record verbal note summaries from books - A person can speak approximately 11 times faster than he or she can write. Taking handwritten notes is a slow process whereas taking notes using a digital recorder can greatly speed up the processing of textbook materials. If the veteran prefers written notes, then using a laptop and a speech-to-text device like Dragon Naturally Speaking can be quite useful.

Relating the abstract to the concrete - The best way to learn novel information is to find concrete, everyday examples of the concept. Training veterans to generate these types of examples greatly improves their understanding of the material.

Structured study skills training - Veterans may not have been in school for several years before returning to college. The veteran may not have developed good study skills or may have forgotten them. Either way, it is a good idea to take any non-credit course that will refresh the skills that are either non-existent or rusty.

Behavioral issues may also be a problem for returning veterans. Although many colleges and universities have counseling services available for students, few are prepared to provide services that are tailored uniquely to the needs of veterans. The staff is not trained to deal with issues like PTSD, explosive behavior, or family pressures that may arise after a return from deployment. However, several things can be done to help the veteran adjust.

Providing neurorehabilitation services and support groups for veterans and their families

Neurorehabilitation services are provided by a variety of different therapists. Neuropsychologists, speech/language therapists, occupational therapists are the usual professions that provide these services. Often, this type of therapy is best delivered in group setting, which may be especially useful with veterans because they are used to working with one another in teams. These groups are not difficult to lead and require a minimum of support. Even a support group that allows the person to vent frustrations can be extremely helpful. Veterans and their families often become friends and share information about other services that are available in the community. Regardless of the format, the critical factor that determines the success of these groups is their content. Several areas of training are pointed out that neurorehabiliation therapists should address.

Identify inappropriate behaviors. Brain injury often precipitates disinhibited behaviors that are socially unacceptable. The often Spartan nature of a veteran's deployment requires behaviors that may be inappropriate in civilian culture. Pointing out these behaviors can help to reduce their frequency. For example, one veteran would urinate in his backyard when doing yardwork rather than go into his house and use the bathroom. His wife would interrupt him when she observed this behavior which eventually eliminated it. Another veteran reported that he and his wife would use a code word that signaled to each that it was a good time to separate until they both calmed down during a family altercation. When one or the other said the word "watermelon" then they would separate and later return to the conversation after a minimum of 1/2 hour which would give each time to collect their thoughts. A person may not accept the fact that certain of their behaviors are offensive unless others point them out when they occur.

Training cognitive flexibility. Therapy that teaches cognitive flexibility is especially important for veterans who have had brain injuries. Damage to the frontal lobes can cause problems shifting focus and breaking set. As a result, the veteran will often seem rigid and inflexible in their approach to social interaction. Therapy to teach the veteran different ways of looking at situations is one way to teach this ability. The authors provide clients with scenarios that can be interpreted in a variety of different ways and the client is require to give as many different interpretations as possible. For example: "A young attractive woman in a mini-skirt is standing on a street corner at 2am." Some possibilities are: "She is waiting for a ride." "Her car broke down and she has just called a cab or AAA." "She is a waitress in a night club and has just gotten off work." Any of these is a reasonable alternative to the possibility that the young woman is a prostitute.

Role-playing appropriate behaviors. Many returning veterans have never been on a college campus before and are unaware of the social structures of campus life. They might not have had much of any social life outside of their high school experience or the military. Teaching behavioral scripts can help the veteran to learn the rules of engagement in an academic social setting. In a group therapy setting it is often helpful to have coeds come to the group and explain their likes and dislikes to the group members. For male veterans, it may be helpful to have women role play a social setting where he can practice approaching a woman and initiating a conversation. For either gender, training in non-verbal communication will usually help the person interpret correctly the social signals that others give off during conversation an in group settings.

Non-verbal perception training. About a quarter of what we experience comes via the verbal content of our conversations. The rest conveys via non-verbal sources such as facial expressions, body language, and tone of voice. Providing the veteran with training to interpret these messages can improve his or her ability to adjust in any social setting.

Video training. Several videos are available for teaching social skills. These are especially useful for demonstrating appropriate social behavior. Once the person has viewed these video training programs, then videos of his or her responses in different role-playing situations can also be used as a training technique for teaching appropriate social behavior.

## A Crash Course in Social Skills Training for Veterans

Neurorehabilitation professionals should emphasize specific skills in their therapy with brain injured veterans. These social skills have a major impact on the veterans acceptance into the academic social environment. Many of these skills may seem like common sense however, they may not be social skills that the veteran demonstrates unconsciously. To that extent, it may be necessary to train the person to do them consciously until they become second nature. For many of these skills we recommend specific training mnemonics that have been suggested by Parente and Herrmann (2009). The reader is referred to this source for a more elaborate account of these and other techniques for training social skills after brain injury.

Eye contact. Maintaining eye contact has a strong affect on social interactions. Lack of eye contact suggests lack of confidence in the message, low self-esteem, or social awkwardness. Training veterans to maintain eye contact may prove to be important in their social adjustment.

Remembering names. Persons with brain injuries often have problems associating names and faces. Forgetting a person's name is often a social slight that few will mention but also seldom will go unnoticed. Training the person to remember names is therefore an important social skill. Parente & Herrmann (2009) have used the NAME mnemonic for this type of training. The mnemonic reminds the person of the necessary steps to recall a name. The N means "notice the person's – maintain eye contact. The A stands for "ask the person to repeat his or her name." The M stands for "mention the name while conversing and looking at the person's face." The E stands for "Exaggerate some special feature about the face." Using this technique can greatly enhance memory for names and faces. The veteran must first memorize the mnemonic then practice using it. Video training can be useful in this regard. Video recording the person during an introduction then reviewing the video shows the person what aspects of the NAME mnemonic still need work.

Listening skill training. Another important social skill is listening. As a rule, everyone wants to be heard, but few want to listen. Training veterans to listen can improve not only their adjustment to campus life but also their grades and interactions with family members. Parente & Herrmann (2009) suggest the LISTEN mnemonic for teaching listening skills. L = Look at the person, I = maintain interest in the conversation, S = speak less than half the time, T = try not to interrupt or change the topic, E = evaluate what is said – ask questions, and N = notice body language.

Controlling anger – many veterans are angry about different aspects of their lives in the military and their difficulties adjusting to their civilian life. However, the anger they display, although a necessary part of the adjustment process, can interfere with their ability interact with others in the civilian world. Traumatic brain injuries worsen the situation because they typically decrease the person's ability to inhibit their behavior. Therapy to teach anger management skills can improve the person's ability to adjust to the stresses of civilian life. Parente & Herrmann (2009) suggest the ANGER – CALM mnemonic as a starting point for helping veterans to deal with anger. The A stands for "Anticipate the signs of anger", i.e., teach the veteran the physiological signs of anger like rapid heartbeat and feeling warm. The N stands for "Never act in anger." The G stands for "Go through the CALM sequence." The E stands for "Evaluate the situation in retrospect." The R stands for review the situation and remember how you coped.

The CALM sequence works together with the ANGER mnemonic. The C stands for "Call someone for help" who you can trust and who understands the veteran's history. The A stands for "Allow yourself to emote." Teach the veteran to let out his or her emotions but only in the presence of a person of trust. The L stands for "Leave the situation that is causing the anger". The M stands for "Move about" or walk around and do not sit down. Physical movement will help to decrease the anxiety resulting from the anger. This mnemonic will help the veteran to control anger in most social situations.

Solving Problems – Problems are situations that are annoying in some way but that have no obvious or rapid solution. Veterans experience a diverse set of problems after deployment and their emotional stability is often determined by their ability to solve the problems. We suggest the SOLVE mnemonic for dealing with problems. The S stands for "Specify the problem." that is, define it. We recommend spending at least 60% of time spent thinking about the problem, defining it. The O stands for "Options – what are they?" which emphasizes the goal of defining what the person is physically, emotionally, economically, etc. capable of doing about the problem. The L stands for "Listen to others' advice." Parente & Herrmann (2009) recommend explaining the problem to at least seven persons who are willing to offer unbiased advice. At a minimum, if the person simply behaves according the consensus of this group, then he or she will solve the problem more often than not. The V refers to value clarification. The veteran should ask questions such as: "What would I have to do to make the problem worse?" This contradiction strategy forces him or her to assess the extent to which their behavior is actually worsening the problem. The E stands for "Evaluate the results." The veteran should not simply assume that the problem has been solved. It is necessary to evaluate in some way that that the problem has been solved. If not, then the veteran should go through the problem solving sequence again.

Making decisions – Decisions are situations where the problem is to decide among several alternative options. A person with brain injury often has difficulty making decisions because they lack a mechanism that can be used to select the most feasible options. Parente and Herrmann (2009) suggest the following mnemonic to help with the decision-making process: D – decide to begin. Do not procrastinate. Evaluate several options. Create options when none of the existing ones is acceptable. Investigate all possible alternatives. Discuss he decision with others and look for consensus in their advise. E valuate your intuitions and include them in the decision making process but do not let them dominate the process.

Interpreting tone of voice – tone of voice is a crucial component of communication. One way to train this skill is to play recordings of the same sentence with different words inflected. The person then interprets differences in the meaning of the sentences when the inflections change. Below are examples of a sentence modified in this fashion. The capitalization in each sentence represents a word that is emphasized in the various versions of the sentence. For example, the sentence "I never said that he did that" can be easily modified to say: "I never said that he did that!" to imply that the speaker never said it. "I never said that he did that" to imply that the speaker flatly denies making the sentence. "I never said that he did that" implies that the person did not make that specific statement but could have said something else. These types of statements are easy to generate and to make into a therapeutic activity.

Understanding body language – Most people unconsciously interpret body positions. For example, most of us know what it means when another frequently looks at his or her watch during a conversation. However, persons with brain trauma often misinterpret or fail to interpret different aspects of body language. This type of non-verbal communication may be especially important in social settings. There are several excellent books that are useful for training body language (Pease and Pease, 2004). The therapist should use this book or one like it to train the veteran to interpret meaning from body positions of other students.

Facial expression – Facial expression is another avenue of communication that a veteran with brain trauma may misinterpret. One way to train facial expression interpretation is to ask the person to find magazine photos of people who are expressing different emotions such as anger, joy, or pleasure. These are easy to combine into a collage that then can be used to exemplify the various facial expressions.

Personal space – Our comfort level with others is often determined by how close a person is from us. In western cultures, the zone of discomfort begins at six feet. It is therefore necessary to train the veteran to stand more than six feet apart from others unless he or she is already acquainted with the person.

Being on time – lack of punctuality is seldom forgiven more than once. Being perpetually late gives others the sense that the meeting is not important enough for the person to be on time.

Organizing output - Other people evaluate us based on our ability to organize our thoughts. Training the person to study in groups by teaching the material to others is one way to teach organization. Training the veteran to take notes using a recorder to summarize what he or she is studying is another. As a rule, the person should not go onto the next section of text until he or she can summarize the paragraph in their own words.

Compliments – Part of social competence involves pointing out things about other s that are unique. People are attracted to those who recognize their uniqueness. Being complimentary will seldom have a negative effect.

Smiling – is a social skill that determines how others react to us. This is especially important when one person approaches another because it sets the tone for the impending social exchange.

Topics to avoid – knowing what to say to others is as important as knowing what not to say. The old saying "Avoid discussion of religion and politics" captures only part of the picture. Knowing what a person likes and does not like can determine how well a person is accepted into a social group.

Knowing when and how to exit – It is important to recognize the social signals that suggest an end to a social exchange. Most of these signals are subtle and non-verbal. Training the person to recognize the signals like a person glancing at a wristwatch when talking, will allow the person to make socially appropriate exits.

These suggestions are useful therapeutic techniques for anyone who has had a brain injury. For veterans, the suggestions may be especially helpful when the person tries to reintegrate into an academic environment. The authors recommend that neurorehabilitation therapists integrate these treatment suggestions into an overall program of therapy with veterans.

References

Herrmann, D., Hopkins, C., Wilson, R. B., & Allen, B. (2009). Educating veterans in the 21st century, North Charleston, South Carolina: Booksurge.

Kotok, A., (2008). Student-Veterans Come Marching Home: Their Return to Studies, http://sciencecareers.sciencemag.org/career_develo pment/previous_issues/articles/2008

Milliken, C.S., Auchterlonie, J.L., & Hoge, C.W. (November 14, 2007). Longitudinal Assessment of Mental Health Problems among Active and Reserve Component Solders Returning from the Iraq War. JAMA, 298 (18), 2141-2148.

Pease, B. & Pease, A. (2004). The Definitive Book of Body Language, New York: Bantam/Dell.

Seal, K.H., Bertenthal, D., Miner, C.R., Saunak, S., & Marmar, C. (2007). Bringing the War Back Home, Archives of Internal Medicine, 167, 476-482.

Parente, R., & Herrmann, D. (2009). Retraining cognition: Techniques and applications, Austin Tx: ProEd Publishers.

Whealin, J.M. (2004). Warzone-related stress reactions: What veterans need to know. A National Center for PTSD Fact Sheet. Iraq War Clinician Guide. Department of Veteran's Affairs, National Center for PTSD.

Chapter 17

# PTSD and Other Psychological Issues of Veterans

## Dr. Stacey Pollack
Department of Veterans Affairs

Hazardous duty and combat sometimes induces stress that emerges after the traumatic experience. Sometimes the post traumatic stress disorder (PTSD) and other psychological issues emerge while a veteran seeks a degree. This chapter discusses what professors and administrators can do in order to help these veterans.

Traumatic events can impact an individual across a wide variety of domains to include: psychological, physical, cognitive, emotional, behavioral, interpersonal and spiritual. This chapter focuses on veterans who have recently returned from combat and focuses on how being exposed to trauma in a combat zone may impact an individual. Additionally, this chapter will address ways that educators can work with returning veterans to help assist in their transition from military to civilian life. This chapter will also address ways educators can assist returning veterans to assure that they are successful in their academic pursuits.

## How Educators Can Partner with the VA

### Become Aware of Benefits

As an educator, it is important to be aware of some of the services offered through the VA healthcare system. While no educator is expected to become an "expert" on the VA system, knowing a few basic facts that can be provided to veteran students may prove to be worthwhile in assisting a returning veteran reintegrate. All veterans who are deployed to Operation Iraqi Freedom (OIF) or Operation Enduring Freedom (OEF) and have received an honorable discharge from the military are eligible for VA healthcare. This is important to note, as many returning soldiers do not view themselves as "veterans" and may not be aware of their entitlements (both health care and other benefits). If veterans have questions about what benefits they are eligible for, much of that information is accessible via the VA website – www.va.gov. Once an individual has accessed that website, he or she can enroll in the VA online, however, if a veteran does not wish to utilize the online system, he/she can come into any VA medical center and enroll in person (as an educator, it may be useful to know the location of the closest VA Medical Center).

Additionally, educators may want to be aware of the closest VA Community Based Outpatient Clinic (CBOC). Community Based Outpatient Clinics are outpatient clinics where veterans can receive care. These clinics are typically closer to a veteran's home. While CBOCs do not typically have the same array of services as a larger medical center, they do offer both primary care and mental health treatment – (either by a provider at the CBOC or by the utilization of tele-health technology). In addition to knowing the location of the local VA, it may be beneficial for educators to be aware that currently every VA medical center employs an OEF/OIF program manager. This individual may be a useful point of contact for veterans enrolled in the VA system (or for veterans thinking of enrolling in the VA system). Educators may want to find out who the local OEF/OIF program manager is in order to be able to provide students with a VA contact person if the student has any questions about VA healthcare.

Once an Operation Enduring Freedom/Operation Iraqi Freedom (OEF/OIF) veteran is enrolled in the VA, he/she is eligible for free health care related to their combat service (for five years after their date of military separation). Mental health conditions (such as PTSD) are considered to be related to combat service. Thus, if an individual presented himself/herself to the VA for care for PTSD within this five year eligibility period, he/she would not be billed for services. It is important to note, that during this eligibility period, not all VA healthcare is free of charge (i.e. if a veteran was being treated for a sinus infection not related to combat – that veteran may be charged a co-pay for such treatment). This benefit (free health care related to combat service) is extremely important to many returning veterans and is much deserved. Often, returning veterans are young men and women who do not have health insurance and thus may refrain from seeking health care due to financial concerns. It is important for educators to be aware of this benefit and to encourage returning soldiers to enroll in the VA within this five year eligibility window.

Individuals are to facilitate health screenings of service members for combat related conditions (including PTSD) as well as to assure that Returning Service members are offered enrollment into the VA (they can often enroll in the VA at the PDHRA). Types of outreach that could occur within a college community include: identifying students who have served in OEF/OIF; having special programs for returning veterans and creating opportunities where returning veterans can become acquainted with one another as they may feel as if they can relate to each other and provide support to each other in a manner in which those who did not serve in the military can not.

What Can A Veteran Expect if Receiving VA Healthcare?

OEF/OIF veterans who come to the VA for healthcare are often seen in Post-Deployment clinics. These post-deployment clinics are comprised of staff members who are well aware of some of the unique needs of treating a returning veteran population. These post-deployment clinics were developed in order to assure that veterans receive a thorough comprehensive evaluation. As part of this standard assessment, veterans are not only evaluated for any physical concerns that they may have secondary to their deployment but also are evaluated for any mental health concerns. By standardizing this practice (all veterans seen in post-deployment clinics get evaluated by primary care as well as mental health), individuals do not have to be asked if they would like to see a mental health provider, instead mental health screening has become part of standard care. This is very important as individuals with mental health issues are often more likely to seek primary care (as opposed to mental health care).

If an individual decides to access VA healthcare, that individual can expect to be seen within 30 days for routine care (although typically much sooner than that). The VA has made access to care for OEF/OIF veterans (as well as all veterans) a priority. A national VA mandate exists that assures that if an individual presents at a medical center, that a mental health screening must occur within 24 hours, and that a more comprehensive appointment must be scheduled within 14 days. If for some reason, the VA is not able to provide an appointment within this time period, fee basis services may be utilized. (Fee basis is utilized when the VA cannot provide care for some reason. This may be due to distance, i.e. if the closest VA medical center is over a certain distance from a veteran, he/she may be able to have the VA pay for his/her services with a private provider that is closer to his/her home, or due to the fact that the VA does not provide that particular service (i.e. maternity care).

Demographics of Returning Veterans Utilizing VA
Healthcare

In terms of demographics of the returning veteran
population that are currently utilizing VA health care,
there are both men and women veterans accessing care
(88% male; 12 % female). It is important as an educator
to remember that there are many more women serving in
the military and to remember this fact when working with
students and not make assumptions based on gender (the
female in your class may have just returned from Iraq).
The ages of returning veterans presenting for VA care are
as follows: 9% under age 20; 49% between ages 20-29;
22% between ages 30-39 and 17% over age 40. As an
educator this is important because the age group of
individuals seeking via healthcare is similar to the age
group of students attending college. It is also important to
note that 49% of individuals seeking VA care are former
active duty service members, while 51% are Reserve or
National Guard.

The fact that many Guard and Reserve troops are
serving in combat is important to note, as issues that face
returning Guard and Reserve service members may be
slightly different than issues that are facing individuals
who return to an active duty military environment. For
example, individuals who are in the National Guard or
Reserves may be more likely to return from a deployment
and enroll in college (or return back to college). These
individuals may be returning to communities where there
is not a large military presence and where the community
may not be aware of common issues that individuals may
face when reintegrating back into civilian life.
Additionally, it is important to recognize that given the

number of deployments that individuals are often facing, it may become somewhat difficult to engage in school fully if there is concern that another deployment may be looming. While many individuals have returned to school after serving in the Armed Services, there also may be unique issues facing an individual who has returned from an active duty deployment and has now separated from military service due to medical issues (perhaps having been wounded). Returning service members may have never thought that they would be attending a traditional college and may have thought that their entire career would be spent in the military. An individual may have a difficult time engaging in academic pursuits when not sure what to do as a career and may have a difficult time accepting that a military career is no longer feasible.

Common Reactions to Deployment and Post-Deployment

There are many common reactions that one may experience after serving in combat. It is important to note that these common reactions usually decrease and normalize after an individual comes home (this typically occurs within three months). Typical reactions include thoughts such as: "the world isn't safe", "the government betrayed me", "others may want to harm me", I must be ready for danger at all times", "civilian life is boring and meaningless", and "I had a sense of purpose in war, now what?". While some of these thoughts may have been adaptive while serving in a combat zone (it is adaptive to be prepared for danger at all times), if these reactions do not dissipate over time, these reactions may start to interfere with an individual's education, relationships and overall quality of life. For example, if one does not feel as if "anything matters" this can certainly impact an individual's academic performance. If a returning veteran believes that the world isn't safe, this may impact his/her ability to feel comfortable in a classroom setting. If an individual believes the government betrayed me – that individual may have a difficult time trusting the staff at the university (especially if it is a public university).

Other common challenges that occur after returning home from a combat zone are that a veteran may miss the excitement of deployment and engage in risky behavior. It may be difficult for an individual to accept that others have advanced in their education while the veteran did not. Additionally, a returning veteran may be struggling with reintegration with his/her family. For example, roles for other family members may have changed to manage daily living (i.e. the wife had to pay the bills for the year even if it was the husband's job previously) and the veteran may then struggle with thoughts such as "where do I fit in now" and how do I resume my role in the family?." Additionally, the veteran's priorities and outlook on life may have changed "how do I cope with adjusting to my disability and how will it impact my ability to attend school and have a relationship". Other challenges may include a veteran student now trying to cope with a disability that they may not have had when they enrolled in school (prior to deployment) and are now trying to determine how this disability may impact their academic pursuits. Educators and advisors can assist veteran students in helping to answer difficult reintegration questions, such as "where do I go from here?".

Mental Health and Returning Soldiers

Approximately 20% of individuals returning from Iraq or Afghanistan are presenting with mental health problems. This is consistent with the National Vietnam Readjustment study which found that there was a lifetime rate of 30% of PTSD in Vietnam veterans (30% of Vietnam Veterans had PTSD at some point in their life) and a current rate of PTSD of 15%.

When screening OEF/OIF veterans for Mental Health issues, the VA standardly screens for PTSD, depression and substance abuse as these are common difficulties that present in a returning veteran population. Each of these disorders will be briefly discussed.

PTSD develops following exposure to a situation that is perceived by an individual to be threatening to his or her well being or to the well being of another. Those individuals with PTSD stay constantly aroused as if they are emotionally prepared to flight or flee at all times and this chronic arousal can become a source of distress – impacting that individual's physical and emotional being.

PTSD has three clusters of symptoms – intrusive symptoms (i.e. finding oneself thinking about one's combat experiences when one does not wish to); avoidance symptoms (feeling disconnected and numb) and hyperarousal symptoms (i.e. extreme startle response, hypervigilance, difficulty with sleep). Four questions are asked about PTSD in the VA screening: have you had any experience that was so frightening horrible or upsetting that in the past month you (1) have had any nightmares about it or thought about it when you did not want to (intrusive symptoms) (2) tried hard not to think about it or went out of your way to avoid situations that remind you of it (avoidance symptoms) (3) were constantly on guard, watchful or easily startled? (hyperarousal symptoms) (4) felt numb or detached from others, activities or your surroundings (avoidance symptoms). If individuals answer this screen positively – they are typically referred onward for additional assessments. It is not known why one individual develops PTSD and someone else does not, however, there are certain factors that contribute to the development of PTSD such as the level of trauma one is exposed to and one's perceived social support.

The questions that are asked to screen for depression screen are: during the past month, (1) have you often been bothered by feeling down, depressed or hopeless? (2) have you been bothered by little interest or pleasure in doing things. Veterans are also screened for alcohol abuse (which is also quite common on a college campus). The alcohol screen asks - (1) have you consumed alcohol in the last 12 months? (2) How often did you have a drink containing alcohol in the past year? (3)How many drinks containing alcohol did you have on a typical day when you were drinking in the past year? and (4) how often did you have six or more drinks on one occasion during the past year? If someone screens positive on any of these screens, it is not diagnostic in and of itself – but does suggest that someone may need additional screening.

It is important to note, that if an individual is depressed, has a substance abuse problem or has PTSD, that individual's academic performance may be impacted. Some examples of how academic performance may be impacted are as follows: (1) an individual may not be able to concentrate on school work (symptom of PTSD and depression) (2) an individual may miss classes in the morning due to an inability to sleep (symptom of PTSD and depression); (3) a veteran student may not interact with classmates due to social isolation (symptom of PTSD) which may prevent that individual from engaging in activities that may be beneficial to academic success such as studying with a group; (4) an individual may be hypervigilant (PTSD symptom) and only be able to sit in a certain part of the classroom – typically the back of the room where one has a better viewpoint; and (5) a veteran may have difficulty with the professor as individual's with combat PTSD often struggle with dealing with someone in a position of authority.

It is imperative to remember that in a returning veteran population, that while some individuals have symptoms of depression, PTSD or alcohol abuse soon after their return from combat, in other individuals, these difficulties may develop over time. As an educator it is important to recognize that even if a student returned from combat many years ago, it does not mean that individual is still not being impacted by his/her deployment. As an educator it is also important to keep in mind that in Iraq and Afghanistan there are not "front lines" and that all soldiers may be at risk. If an individual indicates that he/she served as a cook in Iraq – that does not imply that individual was not exposed to combat. While educators are not expected to be able to screen for PTSD, depression or alcohol use, there is much useful information on-line that might help educators in helping returning veterans (www.ncptsd.va.gov).

Common Treatment Themes

Common treatment themes in working clinically with returning veterans include disruption in relationships, difficulty discussing experiences with friends and family; anger and road rage; re-deployment ambivalence and difficulty with sleep. It is important for all university staff to advocate for veterans. It may be important to assure that clinicians at the University Health Center or Counseling Center are trained to work with veterans with PTSD. This may be assuring that providers are versed in the evidence based therapies for PTSD (Cognitive Processing Therapy, Exposure therapy) or even being aware if there are enough veterans presenting for care to potentially develop a support group. Health center clinicians may be encouraged to speak to VA providers who specialize in PTSD who may be able to provide trainings to university providers. When providing treatment to a returning veteran, treatment should be based on the recovery model of getting an individual back to his or her optimal level of functioning. It should be emphasized that most individuals do not need long term treatment, they may just need assistance readjusting.

It may be beneficial for treatment to take a non-stigmatizing approach and perhaps focus on post-traumatic growth. Post-traumatic growth focuses on how we can help these men and women build on their strengths? how we can help them see themselves as more self-reliant, and more capable? And how they can be aware of their positive contributions? All educators can remind a veteran that he/she learned a set of survival skills from the military and that these skills and strengths have allowed him/her to survive the war. Veterans can be encouraged to figure out what those strengths were and how to continue to utilize them in an academic setting.

Challenges

There are many challenges in terms of veterans accessing treatment for mental health conditions related to combat. Individuals are often working (in addition to school) and may believe that they do not have the time to attend treatment. VA clinics often have either evening hours or weekend hours to address this need. Additionally, the potential for re-deployment certainly may impact a veteran's treatment. An individual may not want to seek treatment if a redeployment is looming. Additionally, it may be difficult to plan for one's future if a re-deployment is looming.

There is still a large stigma attached to mental health treatment. Individuals may be worried about their professors or classmates "finding out". An individual may struggle with when he/she may need to disclose mental health concerns – i.e. "do I want to tell my professors that my concentration may not be so great due to my PTSD?". Some individuals feel as if they are the only one with these problems and hope that "these difficulties will go away on their own". Of active duty soldiers who met criteria for mental disorders, only 38% - 45% expressed interest in getting help through the military system and only 23% - 40% had gotten any professional help in the past year.

Importance of Partnerships

The VA can not do it alone. There is a need for partnerships to be developed. Partnerships between the VA and educators as well as partnerships with disability services on campus as well as the veteran representative are imperative.

Chapter 18

# How Can Institutions of Higher Education Support Citizen Service Members, Veterans and their Families?

## Ms. Lynn M. Malley, JD. MA. LLM
### Creative Conflict Engagement Services

Service members, veterans and their families (spouses, partners, parents, children) and communities are all impacted by repeated military deployments, whether to a combat zone or not. Communities must step up to support our service members in the reintegration/reconnection process. Colleges and universities are well positioned to lead this support effort.

## Background

Since 9/11, the US military force has undergone a number of staggering changes. Just one is that National Guard and Reserve service members make up about 50% of the fighting force.[i] Unlike their active duty counterparts, these continually redeploying service members (over 80,000 at the height of the surge in Iraq) and their families are not living on military installations but in civilian communities. These service members generally hold regular civilian jobs or attend institutions of higher education, meet and train for weekend drills monthly and for two weeks each summer. As forces under the command of the governor of their state, prior to 9/11, National Guard members expected to be activated to meet domestic emergencies like the Katrina cleanup. As forces under the command of the President, prior to 9/11, Reservists expected to be activated should the need arise for someone with their military job (MOS or military operation specialty). Since 9/11, however, like active duty forces, both groups have been facing and continue to face repeated deployments. While the duration and frequency of the deployments generally differs by branch of the service,[ii] all are impacted, both service members and family members. Because they do not live in proximity to other service members and their families, these Citizen Soldiers and their families do not have the support and information, before, during and after their deployments, which their installation-based colleagues have.[iii] Although similar to their active duty and retired (Veteran)[iv] colleagues in many ways, these groups present both unique challenges and unparalleled opportunities for institutions of higher education to be of service. Because of their unique attributes and needs, unlike the other chapters in this book, this essay focuses primarily on these Citizen Soldier (National Guard and Reserve) groups and their families, though when there are similarities with other groups, they will be pointed out.

With respect then to National Guard and Reserve service members and their families, this essay looks at the landscape they encounter in higher education through the lens of re-integration. It briefly introduces two pieces of legislation (*Yellow Ribbon* as it applies to the new GI Bill and as it applies to the deployment cycle). It then briefly sets out characteristics of nontraditional students and their retention, in general, then turns to the concept of a veteran or service member-friendly campus and what that means. Finally, it makes the argument that the creation of a service member and family-friendly campus is more than a campus with links to supports for veterans on its website and a room for veterans to gather in. Indeed, it is a campus that has made efforts to learn about military culture and to build bridges to that culture by building on what we know about characteristics and retention of nontraditional students generally to clearly/conspicuously support not only the service member but the family member, whether enrolled as student or employed as staff, administration, or faculty.

## Re-integration

Although seldom the word we use, re-integration is a common life experience with common challenges. Most people can identify with the feelings of frustration that can come on return from a week-long business meeting or vacation. Leaving the desk clean, the inbox cleared out, and the house and family in order does not preclude the sense of flailing upon return from either. There is always more work piled up than expected at the office and frequently problems that have arisen in the household during an absence of a week or two. How many times have you heard someone say that they should not have gone away, that the price of catching up is just too steep? It's always a challenge to get back in step, to re-integrate.

A less common experience, but one most are familiar with, is that of the high school or college student who participates in a study abroad program. Especially those who live with a local family and study abroad for a full academic year in another culture come back changed. Mostly proud of themselves for their success in adapting to that other culture and having a successful school year in a different type of system, they come back excited to share their experiences with their friends. To their dismay, these now bi-cultural young people may find themselves a little out of touch. The friends they left behind may not be as eager to listen to their exploits as they had expected because, of course, the friends have had their own experiences over the year. Eventually, the youthful world travelers shake off the sense of dislocation and re-integrate into the school setting they left or move on to a new one.

Many higher education faculty members have experiences similar to their students who study abroad when they live in another culture to teach or do research. While in most cases, they remain closely in touch with colleagues from their home school during such sabbatical years, in others, their work abroad is more isolated. For the second group, the return home can be more than a bit disconcerting. Colleagues who were there before the sabbatical may have moved on, the structure and leadership of the institution may have changed, there may have been serious financial cutbacks due to the downturn in the economy, etc. All of these things are in addition to the differences in culture.[v]

Given the normal feelings of dislocation following these common and positive experiences, it is not difficult to see that those service members who are periodically deployed might come back disconcerted. Not only have they been away from family, friends, work, and/or school for extended and perhaps repeated periods of time, they have been in stressful and/or[vi] dangerous situations that may have strained their abilities to cope easily. Not only have they changed, but the families they left behind have changed, as well, having rebalanced the family to handle life without the service member. A clash within the family should not be unexpected upon the return of the service member. Re-integration is seldom easy.

## Yellow Ribbon Legislation

To support this relatively new group in our fighting force, Congress has recently passed multiple pieces of legislation. Two are often referred to as *Yellow Ribbon* legislation, one designed to support these service members and their families and communities throughout the deployment cycle, and the other providing more educational funding designed to allow more service members to be able to afford to attend private colleges and universities. Administration and staff at institutions of higher education are likely to be aware of the provisions of the latter only. The former has as a primary purpose the support of service members and their families before, during, and after deployments, particularly re-integration of service members into their communities.[vii] While this *Yellow Ribbon* legislation reads as if it aims to include community members as part of the network supporting the service members and families, the reality is that it is difficult for the *military* to provide *community* support. Communities must step up and do that on their own. Numerous individuals and professional groups (i.e. therapists through the Veterans Families United Foundation at www.veteransfamiliesunited.org and Give an Hour at www.giveanhour.org, lawyers through the National Veterans Legal Services Program at www.nvlsp.org) have stepped forward to offer services at no charge to service members and their families.

Institutions of higher education, especially those with a large number of service members attending due to the provisions of the new GI Bill, have an unparalleled opportunity to step up and support these Citizen Soldier service members and their families. Schools are uniquely situated to do this because they are a gathering place for a significant portion of this group in a way that military installations are not. Family members of deployed National Guard and Reserve typically do not have the support of a group outside of their own extended families. Although the military has taken numerous steps to address this issue,[viii] those efforts are still not meeting the needs of those not living on or around installations.

By providing not only services for service members but support groups for their family members, institutions of higher education could go far toward meeting the support needs of those family members.

Because of the generous provisions of the new GI Bill and because of the ongoing economic slowdown, institutions of higher education will be seeing and perhaps recruiting increasing numbers of service members and their family members on campus, both in the classroom and in the staff and administration. While all legislation has snags in implementation, this bill promises to be challenging to implement and has already resulted in delays in funding. It is important, but not enough, that campuses make the transition from service members to student a financially smooth one; campus administrators can and must do more.

## Adult Learners/Nontraditional Student Characteristics and Approaches to Retention

Although we do not have much data yet about any special needs of service members as they return to campus, there is extensive data about adult learners and how/whether they even spend time on campus. These service members, whether they are 19 or 39, are nontraditional students.[ix] Nontraditional students are typically older, have some post-secondary credits, often have dependents, generally work to support their family, want to take classes that are connected with their current or desired work, may need flexible leave policies to allow them to care for aging family members (or kids while the service members spouse is deployed). Perhaps they are going back to school and juggling a family and a job. Perhaps they are just beginning their college education and look like all the other teens. Either way, they are different and, as a group, have different needs than the traditional student, no matter whether they want to fit in and not be noticed or whether they wish to self-identify.

## Veteran-Friendly Campus v Service Member and Family-Friendly Campus

Where are the service members and family members on your campus? *They are not just in the student body but throughout the system.* How can you best support service members? *You can offer them and their families your support.* But, why do the families of service members need support; and, how does that support, or the lack thereof, impact service members?

Many schools, communities, professionals, and the military itself have worked hard to provide services for those who are wounded most seriously in combat, whether by physical or psychological injuries.[x] This help may come in the form of Wounded Warrior Programs or enhanced training for and services from the physical and behavioral health clinicians, particularly for service members suffering from Post Traumatic Stress Disorder (PTSD) or Combat Stress as it is more recently called.

Whether one takes the number of service members suffering from PTSD (between 5 and 15 %) from the Rand study[xi] or from the Center for Deployment Psychology[xii] (between 4% and 22%, depending on length of deployment and number of fire fights), it is clear that most service members do not fall into this group; yet, they do face increased re-integration challenges when returning to their families and communities in the US. According to Brigadier General Rhonda Cornum, we have been overlooking the rest of the service members.[xiii] It is this group, the other 80% who are facing the challenges of re-integrating into the civilian lifestyle through returning to school for job skills, that institutions of higher education have the opportunity to help most.

Turning to the earlier question of the importance of supporting the families of service members who have been subjected to repeated deployments, recent studies have begun to confirm what behavioral health providers have known for a while: the effects of trauma are not limited to combat veterans. They can affect anyone who has witnessed a trauma or who has treated or lived with a trauma survivor. The question of how to attend to the needs of service providers of those suffering from PTSD is currently being addressed by a small handful of researchers and service programs like The Coming Home Project.[xiv] There is national legislation pending that would provide support for home/family caregivers of Wounded Warriors.[xv] But who is providing support for those who support service members on a day-to-day basis and do not live on an installation? This is where schools can step up.

Inviting and supporting the service members on campus to form a Student Veterans' Organization (SVO) is a place to start but not an end in itself. If the SVO is expected to act like other student organizations and come out for the games and do raffles at Halloween, it may not last long, especially if its leaders are struggling with re-integration or preparing for a coming deployment. Training counselors on campus to treat PTSD without training faculty and staff to recognize the signs of PTSD may be an exercise in frustration. Providing mental health services for service member students but not their families may not be effective. Allowing students who are deployed before the end of a semester to take an incomplete and finish the class later may seem like an appropriate accommodation, but having to complete a class that was begun two years earlier does not often result in a good grade or a good learning experience for the service member.

What more can be done? The Iraq and Afghanistan Veterans of America (IAVA) suggest that the following areas are basic places to begin making simple changes that can make a school more veteran-friendly:

1. School Websites
2. The Application process
3. Student Orientation
4. Credits transfers
5. Tuition, Fees & Scholarships
6. Veteran Groups
7. Veterans Day

The IAVA website details the changes it suggests in each of these areas. [xvi]

Inviting family members of service members to attend informational meetings or form support groups on campus may be an effective way not only to support these individuals but the service members they support.

## Summary

Military culture is strikingly different from civilian culture in significant ways. Where civilian culture sometimes requires critical thinking, at most levels, military culture always requires doing what you are told, instantly. Where civilian culture encourages emotional relationships among family members, military culture encourages emotional stoicism. Where service in a combat zone requires offensive driving, living in a neighborhood requires defensive driving. Targeted aggression in the combat zone may come out as domestic violence in the home or may result in behaviors that create a hostile work or school environment. Giving orders in the combat zone may not transfer well to the home front, whether at home or work or school. Hyper-vigilance may keep a service member alive in the field, but it may get a civilian employee fired or a student reprimanded.

Effective re-integration into civilian society requires flexibility and adaptation, not only from the service member, but from those in the community. Institutions of higher education certainly have their own, often bureaucratic challenges. Changes must be made to more than the school's website and psychological services. A new culture must be created on campus. The whole campus must become more service member friendly. If retention is a goal, there must be support for service members and their families whether they are found in the student body, administration, faculty, or staff. If educating students so that they can take a leadership role in society is a goal, service members bring discipline and drive with them. It is up to each educational institution to help them channel that discipline and drive and to provide assistance with the challenges of re-integration.

## Footnotes

[i] According to Sandra Dye, PhD, SMSgt AFR, Interim Director of the AFR Yellow Ribbon Program, the following National Guard and Reserve Forces were deployed in December of 2008: ANG (Air Nat'l Guard)-2911, ARNG (Army Nat'l Guard)- 26,709, USAFR (Air Force Reserve)-2192, USAR (Army Reserve)-14,874, USCGR (Coast Guard Reserve)-3, USMCR (Marine Corps Reserve)-3377, and USNR (Navy Reserve)-4325, for a total of 54,391 Guard and Reserve, down from about 80,000 at the time of the surge in Iraq in 2008. Members of this group returned to their homes, and perhaps to your campus, in 2009.

ii For example, Army National Guard troops typically train for six months, then deploy for twelve, with a twelve month break between deployments while Air Force Reservists typically train for one month, then deploy for three, also on a repeating cycle.

[iii] As the recent tragic deaths at Ft. Hood, TX illustrate, it is easier to provide support to those living on or near an installation. According to reports from national news agencies, on the day after the mass shooting at Ft. Hood on November 5, 2009, all installations had a moment of silence the following day and psychological support and suicide prevention services were prominently advertised. For the half of the armed forces who live far from an installation in a civilian community, no such supports were apparent and were perhaps not available.

[iv] Make no mistake, words matter in this situation, and they are not easily defined, or rather they are differently defined in legislation, by armed service, and by generation. What is important is not only that you understand what you mean when you use a particular word, but what the hearer understands. For example, many NG&R families often do not think of themselves as military families and may not respond to surveys of opportunities for military families.

Similarly, those who have retired after 20 or more years of active duty are veterans, and they may tell you that as soon as one signs up for the military, they are a veteran. Those who served as an active duty service member for one term of enlistment may have radically different needs than veterans of twenty years. And certainly, airmen do not consider themselves to be soldiers and will not respond to materials for soldiers (hence the term used in this essay – service member).

This footnote is expanded upon in the chapter *Words, as Well as Facts, Do Matter*, later in this book.

v My own experiences as a faculty member abroad in a developing country for two years left me floundering when I returned to the US. My time as a Civic Education Faculty Fellow and a Fulbright Scholar came back to back. I spent two years in Serbia shortly after the end of the civil wars that dismantled Yugoslavia. In these two years, I lived in four small apartments in a big city, used public transportation or walked where ever I went, used the back and front of every piece of paper, copied articles and parts of textbooks so my students could have materials to read. I had gotten used to soldiers walking four abreast toting machine guns on the city streets and sporting events often being the scene of political violence. I had not gotten used to the violence that was taking place in Kosovo and that touched both my colleagues and my students. When I returned to a small town in the Midwest, there was no public transportation but every student had textbooks and most had cars. Real estate prices had soared and reality TV shows had taken over evening viewing options; I was not prepared to discuss either. No one was prepared to hear me talk about my experiences for long. When the American Embassy in Belgrade was set a fire in 2008 (see http://www.nytimes.com/2008/02/22/world/europe/22kos ovo.html last visited 12/30/2009), after Kosovo declared independence, I was not surprised. But I still could not talk about my experiences related to these things, even though several years had passed. I just did not think that anyone who had not been in a similar situation could understand.

vi "Experiences in the military and during deployment have helped make your service member more responsible, a better leader, and team player. He or she may have received incoming fire. Or witnessed the death or injury of friends or other military personnel, civilians, or enemy combatants. Your loved one may have received very serious injuries as a result of a bombing, mine blast, improvised explosive device (IED), or accident.violence. I had not gotten used to the violence that was taking place in Kosovo and that touched both my colleagues and my students.

When I returned to a small town in the Midwest, there was no public transportation but every student had textbooks and most had cars. Real estate prices had soared and reality TV shows had taken over evening viewing options; I was not prepared to discuss either. No one was prepared to hear me talk about my experiences for long. When the American Embassy in Belgrade was set a fire in 2008 (see http://www.nytimes.com/2008/02/22/world/europe/22kos ovo.html last visited 12/30/2009), after Kosovo declared independence, I was not surprised. But I still could not talk about my experiences related to these things, even though several years had passed. I just did not think that anyone who had not been in a similar situation could understand.

Being in an unfamiliar setting and an unfamiliar culture may have complicated these experiences. All the while, your loved one was in full military mindset. It can be difficult to change back to a "civilian" mindset upon returning home." From *Returning from the War Zone: A Guide for Families of Military Members*, http://www.ptsd.va.gov/public/reintegration/returning-war-zone-guide-families.asp, last visited 12/21/2009.

[vii] *Yellow Ribbon Reintegration Program* legislation is found at Section 582 of National Defense Authorization Act FY 2008. A website with more information about its purpose and the activities it funds is www.dodyrrp.mil. *The Yellow Ribbon GI Education Enhancement Program,* on the other hand, provides that institutions of higher education may provide support greater than required, matched by the VA, to service members. A website with more information about this program is http://www.gibill.va.gov/School_Info/yellow_ribbon/ind ex.htm.

[viii] For example, the Department of Defense has funded the Red Cross to design and offer brief courses in Coping with Deployment. These courses have currently been offered in about one third of all states but according to the trainers who offered the first such course in Oklahoma in October of 2009, few are taking them and many of those who are the service providers for families, not the family members themselves. The National Guard is offering training for leaders of Family Readiness Groups (FRGs) for NG&R. At least at the training offered in OK, the materials were prepared for FRGs situated on bases and did not take into account that the members of NG&R FRGs are geographically dispersed and do not have the same understanding of military culture and command structure that installation-based AD families have.

[ix] Adapted from *Changing Demographics: Why Nontraditional Students Should Matter to Enrollment Managers and What They Can Do to Attract Them,* http://consulting.aacrao.org/2009/02/27/changing-demographics-why-nontraditional-students-should-

matter-to-enrollment-managers-and-what-they-can-do-to-attract-them/, last visited 12/21/2009.

[x] "We're devoting a great deal of effort to treating pathology, but 99 percent of people in the Army have normal reactions to fear and trauma. And we have done nothing for these people." Gail Sheehy, quoting Brigadier General Rhonda Cornum, in *The Sensitive Soldier*, November 11, 2009, 11:09pm, The Daily Beast, www.thedailybeast.com/.

[xi] *Invisible Wounds of War: Psychological and Cognitive Injuries, Their Consequences, and Services to Assist Recovery*, Rand Center for Military Health Policy Research, http://www.rand.org/pubs/monographs/2008/RAND_MG 720.pdf, last visited 12/30/2009.

[xii] From a presentation given by David Riggs, Ph.D., Director of the Center for Deployment Psychology, on July 15, 2009, in Stillwater, OK, on file with this author.

[xiii] *The Sensitive Soldier*, November 11, 2009, 11:09pm, The Daily Beast, www.thedailybeast.com/.

[xiv] For example, The Coming Home Project (www.cominghomeproject.net) provides support for service members and family members and service providers at no charge.

[xv] http://www.govtrack.us/congress/bill.xpd?bill=s111-801, last visited 12/21/09.

[xvi] IAVA suggests specific ways for schools to be more veteran friendly.  A few are excerpted here and the rest can be found on their website at http://newgibill.org/ways_schools_be_more_vetfriendly. School websites are hard to navigate for veterans which gives them the impression that veterans are not welcome. This can be addressed by providing clear links to a veteran page on the website, having contact information for the schools VA certifying official listed, and providing links to other veteran resources such as the VA, IAVA, VFW and other veteran websites. Many veterans are not being identified when they start school therefore they are having a difficult time getting their benefits because they do not know where to go or what to do. This can be addressed by identifying veterans from the beginning - Have a box for veterans to check on the application which will send the veterans contact information to the VA certifying official at the school, then have the VA certifying official contact the veteran to make sure the veteran knows the process to receive the education benefits the veteran has earned. The author would suggest taking this or a similar step for family members of veterans.

Chapter 19

# Operation Diploma
## Supporting Higher Education Institutions in Promoting the Academic Success of Student Service Members and Veterans

### Dr. Stacie F. Hitt
Director, Operation Diploma
Military Family Research Institute
at Purdue University

Operation Diploma's primary goal is to help institutions of higher education in Indiana strengthen their efforts to support academic persistence and success among student service members and veterans. Operation Diploma's major activities are outreach, regarding the needs of student service members and veterans and promoting strategies to meet them.

The mission of Operation Diploma is to support institutions of higher education in Indiana as they strengthen efforts to support academic persistence and success among student service members and veterans. Support is provided in a number of ways including outreach, consultation, and other resources, awareness raising, training, and grants to institutions and Student Veterans' Organizations (SVOs) for programs and practices that show promise based upon available evidence.

Historically, 70% of Vietnam-era veterans sought VA educational benefits (Iraq and Afghanistan Veterans of America). Of this number, only a fraction actually earned a degree (www.gibill.va.gov). There are a number of reasons for the failure of schools to retain these students and the lack of persistence on the part of the students themselves, but key among them are the challenges associated with financing school expenses beyond tuition. The benefits provided under Chapter 33 (Post 9/11 GI Bill), which went into effect on August 1, 2009, are intended to address these barriers by paying not only all or nearly all tuition, but also books, some fees, and living expenses for eligible student service member and veterans, and their primary family members. The enactment of Chapter 33 represents an opportunity to transcend many of the financial barriers to achieving academic success and, ultimately, meaningful employment. A secondary gain for campuses and the communities in which they reside are tuition revenue and cost of living stipends. With the anticipated record numbers of student service members and veterans expected to make use of these and other VA educational benefits, institutions of higher education have a unique opportunity to re-examine educational policies, practices, and procedures to ensure the needs of all students, including student service members and veterans, are adequately met.

In addition to financial challenges, student service members and veterans returning to or attending college for the first time often find campus to be a puzzling maze (Ackerman, DiRamio & Mitchell, 2009). They may have difficulty integrating into the academic and social fabric of the campus community (A.C.E., 2008) and often discover that inconsistent or incomplete information is provided by various academic, financial aid, and other administrative offices on campus (Williamson, 2008). Further, faculty and staff are often described as lacking awareness of the unique needs and attributes of the student service member and veteran (DiRamio, Ackerman & Mitchell, 2008). Our own limited survey of policies, programs, and services on Indiana's campuses seems to support this (The Higher Education Landscape, 2009).

With the generous support and vision of the Lilly Endowment, Inc., Operation Diploma was established under the auspices of the Military Family Research Institute (MFRI) in December 2008. The strategic goals of Operation Diploma are to educate institutions about the needs and attributes of student service members and veterans; engage campuses in identifying gaps between existing and needed programs; enrich campus-affiliated SVOs as a means of promoting successful "boots to books" transition and engagement with the campus; and generate new knowledge about evidence-based promising practices. Guided by the answers to the following questions, Operation Diploma strives to achieve its goals in a number of ways:

- What are the campus experiences of student service members and veterans?
- How well are colleges and universities prepared to meet the needs of student service?
- What evidence-based success strategies are being used on Indiana campuses?
- On campuses throughout the country?

In the first year of funding, nearly 25% of Indiana 2- and 4-year campuses were awarded grants totaling more than $270,000. While Year 1 schools implement the proposed initiatives for which they were funded, Operation Diploma will shortly be releasing the RFP for Year 2 awards of more than $1.1 million. Concurrently, outreach activities extend throughout Indiana allowing us to reach all interested schools, regardless of whether they were awarded an Operation Diploma grant. Outreach activities can take many forms depending upon the needs of the institution, but generally include providing information, resources, training, and/or consultation. Using a combination of on-site campus visits, regional and statewide meetings, conference calls, virtual meetings, and social media, Operation Diploma creates a statewide network of support for the institutions of higher education.

To address the strategic goal of enriching SVOs, Operation Diploma convenes semi-annual organizational plan competitions, which to date have resulted in $25,000 being awarded to SVOs. Similar to business plan competitions, SVO representatives present organizational plans that include mission, goals, and plans for leadership and financial sustainability. These competitions are organized in collaboration with the Burton D. Morgan Center for Entrepreneurship at Purdue University and are judged by representatives of our corporate partners, student veteran peers, and business/entrepreneurship faculty. In addition to awarding funds to SVOs, Operation Diploma hosts monthly conference calls and a Facebook page to encourage information sharing and networking. Participation in the calls has grown by more than 300% in 7 months, suggesting these calls are perceived as a valuable forum.

It is customary for MFRI to achieve its missions through partnerships and collaborations among individuals and programs best able to respond to the need. As a program within MFRI, Operation Diploma has established a number of relationships that enhance its ability to respond to needs and create synergies by coordinating the efforts of multiple constituencies. In addition to benefiting from our corporate partners during SVO competitions, corporate volunteers mentor individual SVOs, support various events to benefit student service members and veterans and their families, and consult as needed.

The response to these efforts from campuses and organizations around the state has been extremely encouraging and suggests the interest and will to put forth supportive initiatives was waiting to be tapped. In the first year of Operation Diploma the following initiatives have been initiated:

• In collaboration with a faculty partner, a longitudinal, e-survey of institutional and community supports and barriers to academic success was launched among 357 military, R.O.T.C., and civilian students.
• Consultation was provided to the Indiana community college system on a system-wide assessment of programs, policies and procedures.
• Geographically close public and private institutions share SVO space and a consultant for their Operation Diploma initiatives.
• A consortium of public and private, 2-year and 4-year institutions meets regularly to share promising practices. Only 2 of these schools received awards from Operation Diploma funds in Year 1.
• A network of public and private institutions has formed a work group to explore the unique experiences of female student service members and veterans on Indiana campuses.
• A 2-day annual meeting to explore promising practices, hear national experts, and learn from each other was hosted by Operation Diploma and attended by 84 campuses in the state.

Clearly there is much work to be done. The data that will guide us toward promising practices is just beginning to be collected and analyzed, but the message seems clear. Higher education is at a crossroads at which it can continue the status quo and risk losing substantial human capital and financial resources or seize the opportunity to make enhancements that will benefit all students. The colleges and universities in the state of Indiana have made it clear they intend to seize the opportunity, and Operation Diploma stands ready to support their commendable efforts. Our dream is that every school in Indiana:

- Is a grantee or an affiliate of Operation Diploma.
- Is a member of Servicemembers Opportunity Colleges.
- Has highly visible points of contact and web pages for student
  service members and veterans.
- Gives specific credit for military training and experience.
- Has implemented successful support and transition programs.
- Enacts and enforces supportive campus policies.
- Engages in dialogue about promising practices.
- Attracts, retains, graduates, and places a significantly larger number of student service members and veterans

## References

ACE Center for Lifelong Learning. (2008). Serving those who serve: Higher Education and America's veterans.Retrievedfrom from http://www.acenet.edu/Content/NavigationMenu/ProgramsServices/Military Programs/serving/Veterans_Issue_Brief_1108.pdf

Ackerman, R., DiRamio, D. & Mitchell, R.L. (2009). Transitions: Combat veterans as colleges students. New Directives for Student Services, 125, 5-14

DiRamio, D., Ackerman, R., & Mitchell, R.L. (2008). From combat to campus: Voices of student veterans. NASPA Journal, 45(1), 73-102.

Military Family Research Institute. (2009). The higher education landscape for student service members and veterans in Indiana. Retrieved from http://www.mfri.purdue.edu/content.asp?tid=4&id=38.

Williamson, J. (2008). How non-traditional students are changing education. Retrieved from http://www.distance-education.org/Articles

# Section IV. The Future Resolution of the Veterans Higher Education Problem

## Chapter 20

# Campus Strategies for Improving Veteran Education

### Dr. Kathryn M. Snead
#### President, Servicemembers Opportunity Colleges

> Conference attendees identify existing challenges campus veterans experience. Recommendations may be made for prioritizing the veteran challenges and developing local and national action plans to address critical issues. These recommendations are summarized here.

I want to share information from a national campus survey effort recently completed to determine what programs and services are available on college campuses. My remarks will summarize key findings from a report,

From Soldier to Student: Easing the Transition of Service Members on Campus, that offers a first-of-its-kind national snapshot of the programs, services and policies in place on campuses to serve veterans and military personnel, as well as areas in which campuses need to improve their offerings. It is the product of a collaboration between the American Council on Education (ACE), the Servicemembers Opportunity Colleges (SOC), the American Association of State Colleges and Universities (AASCU), NASPA - Student Affairs Administrators in Higher Education, and the National Association of Veterans' Program Administrators (NAVPA), and was produced with the generous support of Lumina Foundation for Education.

The plan for this segment of the program is that I will highlight the key findings of the campus survey to be followed by group discussions among conference attendees to identify existing challenges and successes that today's campus veterans experience. As we discuss strategies for improving the educational opportunities for veterans, we may also prioritize our perceptions of the challenges facing veterans and develop recommendations and suggestions for addressing those obstacles and challenges. Developing local and national action plans to address critical issues for veterans would be a laudable goal for the College Educators for Veterans Higher Education (CEVHE).

The report based on data from 723 institutions of higher education finds that 57 percent of responding institutions currently provide programs and services specifically for servicemembers and veterans. Public four-year institutions account for an overwhelming majority of the institutions with veteran and military student programs in the national survey (72% of responding 4-year public institutions indicate they have established services or programs). Sixty-five (65) percent of institutions that offer services to veterans and military personnel reported that they have increased emphasis on these services since September 11, 2001.

It was interesting to note as well that sixty (60) percent of respondent colleges indicated the programs/services for military student population were part of the institution's long-term strategic plan. A majority of the responding campuses reported that they were considering veteran-friendly changes or enhancements in the next five years; general consensus was that veteran student population programs was an essential component in strategic plans for the institution. When queried on the types of veteran related support program or initiatives under consideration, below are the most frequently listed items:

1) Professional development for faculty and staff on meeting needs of service members and veterans (57 %),
2) Exploring state or federal funding or private grant proposals to fund campus programs (52 %),
3) Increasing number of veteran services/programs on campus (43 %),
4) Training counseling staff to assist students with health issues including post-traumatic stress disorder (PTSD) and brain injuries (42 %).

For a more thorough description of the campus enhancements under consideration, please refer to the report, From Soldier to Student: Easing the Transition of Service Members on Campus, in its entirety.

The research study highlights the great diversity in how institutions have addressed the needs of the veteran student population on their individual campuses. Great variety exists in the type of services and programs offered as well as where the services/programs are housed within the administrative infrastructure of institutions. Results of the survey identified the most commonly veteran-specific services offered by the respondents to be: VA education benefit counseling (82 percent), financial aid/tuition assistance counseling (57 percent), employment counseling(49 percent), and academic advising (48 percent).

Among the areas where higher education is meeting the needs of military students are:

- Recognizing prior military experience. Eighty-one percent of institutions with services for military personnel and veterans award college credit for military training.
- Assisting military students with finding appropriate counseling services. Eighty-five percent of campus counseling centers at institutions with services for military students coordinate and refer students to off-campus services when necessary.
- Providing financial accommodations for military students

who are called to active duty. Seventy-nine percent of colleges and universities with military services have an established policy for refunding tuition for military activations and deployments.
• Assisting military veterans with their education benefits. Eighty-two percent of postsecondary institutions provide Department of Veterans Affairs education benefits counseling for military students.

Among the areas in which higher education generally can improve their efforts to serve military students and veterans are:

• Assisting military students with their transition to the college environment. Only 22 percent of postsecondary institutions with services for military students and veterans provide transition assistance.
• Providing professional development for faculty and staff on the transitional needs of military students. Approximately two out of five schools that serve military students and veterans provide training opportunities for faculty and staff to be better able to assist these students with their transitional issues.
• Training staff to meet the needs of military students with brain injuries

and other disabilities. Twenty-three percent of colleges and universities that serve military students and veterans have staff who are trained to assist veterans with brain injuries, and 33 percent have staff trained to assist veterans with other physical disabilities.

• Streamlining campus administrative procedures for veterans returning from military deployments. Only twenty-two percent of institutions with programs and services for military personnel have developed an expedited re-enrollment process to help student restart their academic efforts. Sixty-two percent of the surveyed institutions require students returning from deployment to complete the standard re-enrollment process, while 16 percent require students to reapply and be readmitted.

• Providing opportunities for veterans to connect with their peers. Only 32 percent of institutions with services for veterans and military personnel have a club or other organization for these students.

The report, intended to provide a benchmark for institutions by which to measure their current veteran-specific practices and services with a national standard, is available electronically on the web sites of each collaborating association and Lumina Foundation for

Education. I encourage you to read the report as it includes far greater detail and granularity than I summarized for this overview.

So, where do we go from here in formulating an "issues" priority list? What are the key veteran concerns that the higher education community should seek to improve? As initially conceived, this portion of the conference is for attendees to identify the key veteran challenges in post-secondary education, to prioritize challenges, and develop successful strategies at local and national levels to address these critical issues. Throughout the last course of the conference we have had subject matter experts share their knowledge, apprise us of new and updated veteran initiatives, and share their observations and views on us policy and program. Now it's your turn to participate in open discussions and share what you feel at the most important veteran challenges on college campuses today. I propose that we work in small working groups to highlight develop priority lists of the most critical issues.

Once we have reached some consensus on the issues, in the time remaining we will focus on generating action plans. Clearly some issues need to be elevated to national, regional, and state levels for discussion and remedy; others may be more localized to individual campuses or college systems. For purposes of this conference, I would ask you to focus on the broader, more pervasive issues that veteran students encounter in post-secondary education. To have the greatest impact on veteran students, we need to identify those roadblocks or challenges that impede their access and success in higher education. Once we've identified the most common or onerous obstacles, we can begin to develop strategies to minimize or remove the roadblocks. To get us started in the discussions among your colleagues, I've generated a list of six issues or challenges that veterans identify as barriers to college entry. From your perspective, which of these issues should be our top priority for improving educational opportunities for our veterans?

- Access and Informational Challenges
- Academic Practices/Policy Challenges
- Administration Issues/Policies within institutions
- Campus Culture/Veteran Acculturation (creating a veteran-friendly environment)
- Injury and/or Trauma Related Challenges
- Legislative Changes

Chapter 21

# Scaling the Ivory Towers: Making College Work for Veterans and Servicemembers

## Dr. Carol Y. Yoder, Ph.D.
Trinity University

Veterans face particular challenges in adapting to university life. Creating a strong support structure to advance incoming students' acculturation is especially important for those entering college after having served in the military. Some key strategies for smoothing this transition will be described. While institutions of higher education will have different ways of interpreting and implementing support, a multipronged approach focused on strategic career planning, tailored orientation, special advising, study-skill training and campus-wide education, can dramatically improve veterans' adjustment to the college-culture.

Transitions into college way-lay many incoming students, but servicemembers and veterans face particular challenges in adjusting to university life. Creating a strong support structure to advance incoming students' acculturation is especially important for those entering after military service. In 2007 and 2008, 660,000 undergraduates were veterans (accounting for 3% of all undergraduates) and 215,000 students (another 1%) were military service members in either the reserves or on active duty (Radford & Wun, 2009). These beginning military undergraduates sought out institutions, first based on location (75%), although program of study was also an important factor (52%) as was cost (47%).

The average amount of financial aid used for this group in 2007-2008 was $9900 and the new GI Bill is likely to increase possible financial support (Radford & Wun, 2009). In this summary, strategies for smoothing this transition will be described. While institutions of higher education will use different methods to support military undergraduate learning, a multipronged approach which includes campus-wide education, specialized advising, and enhanced study skill supports, will improve the transition to college life.

I. Creating Appropriate Expectations for the Campus Community.

For the most part, universities are insufficiently aware that military undergraduates have different needs and experiences from traditional and even non-traditional college students. Often university staff simply are unprepared for mid-semester deployments or other complications of military service. On the one hand, stereotypes about military personnel, may leave some faculty members wondering whether veterans are adequately prepared for college. On the other hand, many faculty members have experienced positive interactions, finding military backgrounds foster a disciplined attitude towards classwork and the learning process. Indeed some of us have often relied on veterans' dependability to provide good role models for other less motivated students. However, some key facts about aspects of this relationship, require updating.

While seriousness and strong performances are still an important part of military personnel's learning, today there is a higher ratio of injury to death in war. For example, in Vietnam, the ratio was 3:1 whereas in Iraq, the ratio is 16:1 (DiRamio & Spires, 2009). This means that many more soldiers survive to find themselves coping with physical and emotional injuries. Colleges need to consider these new circumstances and provide additional support for these students, as we have for many other veterans with different types of special needs. And even when military undergraduates side-step these challenges, the experience of war inevitably changes one's thinking and approach to life. Because veterans and servicemembers may physically blend in, these differences require educating universities about the diversities military experience brings to campus.

Initial Setup and Training. At the outset, university presidents or their board of directors should charge a dean or vice-president with the responsibility for creating policy, coordinating procedures, and developing programs to accommodate the special needs of military undergraduates. In all likelihood, this individual would appoint a task force to deal with these issues.

Next, workshops should be developed for faculty members, staff and administrators to improve awareness of the particular challenges faced by veterans. While these workshops would be mandatory for counseling center staff, advisors and other key personnel, efforts should be made to encourage faculty who teach General Education classes to commit time to understanding veterans' specific needs. Since certain majors are routinely selected as preferred programs of study, at least one faculty member or the department chair should be recruited to attend. The newly created task force, should organize a well-designed workshop, based on advice provided by military, medical, mental health and cognitive/memory function professionals to highlight veteran and servicemember issues.

Training should highlight biopsychosocial factors that may impact class performances. For example, people who work with veterans should be aware that exposure to war often results in a lost sense of safety. That may mean that veterans prefer small classes, sitting near doors and windows, to maintain a sense of physical control over the environment (Hudson, 2009). Veterans may re-experience trauma in many ways, through ongoing physiological problems (see Parente and see Pollack for a more in-depth treatment, this volume). This may include nightmares which interfere with sleep or intrusive thoughts and flashbacks that break ability to concentrate. Inadequate sleep is associated with a host of learning and other problems in daily living including irritability, difficulty tracking sequenced information, and ability to grasp consequences and implications. Of course, when sleep loss is chronic, mental and physical health suffer, including hippocampal damage which results in memory storage and retrieval impairments.

Veterans may over generalize from their role in the military to their role at college. Veterans may avoid any situation that cues those memories. To cope, they may detach from others, avoid situations or simply decide not to allow themselves to think. Even content that is seemingly innocuous can trigger a chain of associations that interferes with learning and memory. We all experience these distractions from time to time, but veterans' challenges are substantially greater, given their recent life-changing experiences. Maintaining an awareness of these biopsychosocial involvements can help faculty members and administrators refrain from inappropriate attributions or comments in and outside of classrooms. Also some faculty members may benefit from being reminded that it is unprofessional and unproductive for classroom climate to make comments that target the military as a means of protesting government policy.

Zoroya (2007) estimates that between 11 and 28 percent of combat soldiers suffer from some level of traumatic brain injury (TBI), typically due to explosion. Emmons (2006) calls TBI the signature injury for this soldier cohort. TBI escapes diagnosis because the symptoms of headaches, dizziness, blurred vision, memory and attention problems, depression, anxiety, and irritability are common and non-distinctive, appearing gradually over time. Each symptom complicates college performance, given the high demands for abstract and reflective thinking. Features of TBI, like headaches and dizziness, also affect attendance, which can contribute to faculty making negative evaluations of students; in the absence of other information, other kinds of inferences are likely to be drawn regarding the students' assessment of the course, its content, or the instructor. And when classes are large, not all instructors take the time to even track, much less follow-up on students who don't attend.

Workshop content should also describe skill sets typical in military assignments which should facilitate the award of transfer credit and selection of appropriately challenging coursework. Making certain that veterans are enrolled in stimulating classes significantly improves the likelihood of a meaningful college experience.

To improve learning efficacy, workshops should encourage faculty members to offer specific guidelines for optimizing learning in their classrooms (which will benefit all but the most effective who already use these strategies). The university's Teaching and Learning Center or Academic Dean should provide a range of resources to help instructors effectively teach and support student learning. Instructors, who undergo this veteran-oriented training, should be preferentially recommended to military undergraduates and ideally receive verbal and monetary acknowledgements for successes in facilitating these students' success. Since it involves acknowledging our soldiers' contributions, local businesses might willingly underwrite workshop costs, by providing meals or nominal gift cards to participants and presenters.

Educating the Broader Community. With the lead from a chief academic administrative officer and task force the campus community needs to better understand veterans' experiences. Despite curricular foci on international affairs, diversity, and globalization, this information remains an abstraction on college campuses; many students are unaware of the realities of our world. Getting military undergraduates involved in these conversations will encourage a better grasp of global issues and realities. Acknowledging this contingent might take the form of recruiting veterans with appropriate expertise to serve as student participant on panels focusing on political, government, or cultural issues that invariably populate university schedules. Also encouraging campus organizations (e.g., student veteran groups, or student discipline-oriented groups with many veteran members like computer science) to take the lead in spotlighting experiences of military personnel would improve campus awareness. Identifying appropriate military students who will benefit from these teaching experiences will probably fall to individual advisors, who have access to application materials and have personal knowledge of their advisees although chairpersons and key instructors may help. Advisors could inform campus newspaper reporters about veterans' activities so that interviews might focus on veterans sharing their experiences. Increasing awareness of veterans' special skills and understandings will help educate the college campus about veterans' nontraditional involvements.


II. Creating appropriate expectations for military undergraduates.

The dream of going to college to pursue a particular career is highly motivating to many veterans and can provide the impetus for rebuilding a life that war has changed. After completing their tour of duty, a common next step military undergraduates face is realigning one's priorities. Carefully considering career options and matching skills acquired in the military to career choices is time well spent. A number of websites are available to help service members translate military skills to civilian careers.

Initial selections. Making a positive transition into civilian living is partially dependent on making appropriate choices in pursuit of one's goals. For veterans interested in furthering their education, finding the right school environment is critical (see Miller, this volume). Part of this decision will rest on one's desires and expectations for college and whether the selected schools offer strong curricula in the area of interest. Admittedly, sorting out the latter is difficult although national program rankings may be available or program accreditation depending on discipline. Scholarly publication provides additional information about program quality although perhaps more importantly, it suggests better networking opportunities for highly motivated students interested in jobs/placements. Knowing what recent graduates are doing can also quickly pinpoint program effectiveness.

Before matriculation, opening up university's career or counseling centers to veterans by providing career assessments/testing and making counseling staff available to help veterans realistically assess abilities should also minimize false and ineffective starts. Counselors on-site at universities know what works well and what is less effective at their institution. Encourage veterans to create a reasonable plan, while making it clear that what happens in college may cause one to reconsider goals. Down the road, maintaining relationships with the career center, one's advisor, and developing connections with key personnel in the program of study will provide additional focus and career development advice.

Recognizing the college culture. After carefully selecting a school and program of study, developing an appropriate set of expectations about college will help veterans understand what they can reasonably accomplish in their time on campus. Given the contrasts in their military work with university work, it may be helpful to underscore differences. To make the environment demands more transparent, special orientation sessions for veterans could describe this culture shift (see Raybeck for another perspective, this volume).

Few military undergraduates come to college with a nuanced understanding of the academy. Universities see themselves as creators and disseminators of knowledge, which come about through teaching and through research in laboratories. How these two goals are balanced depends on the type of institution. Content is often abstract and conceptual, with no immediately discernable application. Indeed, teaching in science and technology often require much basic information learning, such that students wanting to find practical, problem-oriented approaches will have to shoulder through a series of pre-requisites before getting to the kind of information they came to college seeking. Curiously, purer forms of knowledge are often viewed as more important than applied work in the academy. When application is a particular interest, realize that basic classes must be tackled first. However, universities sponsor a host of hands-on experiences such as service learning, practicum/placements, and project-oriented labs for advanced students.

While group projects are part of college experiences, a key skill-set, that college experiences should include, is training people to be autonomous thinkers and effective communicators though faculty-student interactions. Developing these one-on-one relationships takes extra time and commitment, but many faculty members are interested in fostering individual students' development. These faculty-student mentorships are weighted more significantly at schools with smaller faculty-to-student ratios and where teaching is emphasized. In contrast, larger schools are likely to offer a greater variety of classes and programs of study. And while similar relationships can happen, the student will have to be much more active when seeking a mentor.

Whereas the military is highly ordered, academic environments can seem chaotic and unstructured. While the military is often about following orders and team work, universities require initiative and independent thinking. Universities aim to produce knowledge and doubt; in their best incarnations deep and provocative questions are raised and explored. In that vein, realities must be constructed, with careful detailing of evidence, logic, and rationale created by personal quest. There often are no 'right' answers or singular authorities, just different ways to construct arguments, of better or worse quality. One practical application of this, in how universities work, is that rules and stated requirements may be waived with the right arguments in the presence of the right individuals. In contrast to military decisions, university policies may be negotiable.

Academic cultures routinely emphasize individual contributions, in the form of testing, papers, and presentations. Whereas the military promotes meeting specified standards, academia may reward few with marks of excellence. Further, defining those standards of excellence, may seem elusive and arbitrary. While military obligations structure minutes and hours daily, college students must decide how to allocate their time and investments among a myriad of tasks with consequences and outcomes often seemingly temporally distant. Tasks may be intentionally ambiguous with the expectations that students will work through them to develop new structural representations of their knowledge. Embracing that freedom and responsibility can be quite unsettling, particularly if one is accustomed to following someone else's rules and being part of a team. In addition, the faculty and peer leaders in charge of this chaos may seem unworthy, disrespectful and unresponsive by military standards. As in most fields, some individual faculty members may have an overblown sense of personal importance or the meaningfulness of their course content. And like the military, there are ranks and different statuses between faculty members, largely based on research productivity and subject expertise. Recognizing these cultural differences can help one manage campus environments.

Where Group Work Helps. Nevertheless, while individual achievements are the rule, sometimes group support from others is essential. While many classes have projects requiring teamwork, more effective performance in other courses simply benefit from pooling resources. Becoming familiar with the available resources (e.g., tutors, skills centers, faculty office hours) and recognizing that seeking help is appropriately responsible (and not remedial) also promotes efficacy and self-sufficiency. In short, transitioning into a campus routinely involves adjustment. While college offers freedom, knowledge, competing experts, and the right and obligation to choose life paths, this transition is eased by understanding these sometimes bewildering rules of engagement.

Advisor assignments. While orientation and admissions staff can help veterans develop appropriate expectations and skills, a knowledgeable advisor is key (Council on Education, 2008). Advisors should be well versed in military issues, know the 'ins and outs' of GI bills, be familiar with relevant health concerns, and know how universities work. Proactive advising may require contacting program chairs, for best recommendations to maximize military undergraduates' fit with programs. The advisor should be an effective coach/ advocate, knowledgeable about transfer credit and ACE credit assessments for military experiences (see Wilson on transfer in this book). This advisor should make certain curricular choices appropriate and consistent with the veteran's career selection, and be ready to interface with instructors if necessary. This would involve developing a group of quality introduction-to-subject classes (e.g., history, math, biology) that met common curricular requirements, taught by instructors committed to student education.

Advising support is especially critical before and in the opening weeks of the school semester. Consequently, advisors should have a limited number of beginning military undergraduates in any given semester so that attention is focused on getting things started well. Research on first-year transitions into college suggest that when things go badly, much was presaged by what occurred in the first few weeks of class. If an advisor is attuned and alert, many problems can be averted or tackled by appropriate adds/withdrawals or other early interventions. Having a successful first semester is critical. A secondary advisor might be assigned to family members to help them understand the particular demands of school or a specific course of study, to provide support, and to network them to other resources, including counseling, if needed. The military spouse may be enrolled in school or simply trying to support a servicemember in school. While universities may not initially see this as their responsibility, if the goal is to improve retention of military experienced students, investing in their families' adjustments will sometimes be necessary (see Malley for another perspective, this book).

Advisors must also be prepared to serve as liaisons to other on-and-off campus services. Recognizing there may be serious concerns about confidentiality, additional psychological, financial, and religious resources should be identified to supplement military sources.
III. Applying skill sets that contribute to success.

Veterans have demonstrated their abilities to succeed under challenging circumstances. While understanding campus culture is useful, it is important to realize college may require more self-imposed discipline and more conceptual learning, relative to previous experiences.

Disciplined job-like approach to school. One key part of success is to prioritize study. Like a paid job, it is important to consistently affirm through actions one's seriousness of purpose with family and friends. This requires good time management. That may mean a strictly adhered to 8 to 6 schedule. Many students will benefit from using an array of scheduling devices and reminders to ensure good daily progression through goals. While product features and availability changes rapidly (LoPresti, Mihailidis & Kirsch, 2004), research clearly indicates that cueing increases alertness and executive functioning (Manly et al., 2004) and devices can be selected to compensate for specific deficiencies. Although the Veterans Administration (VA) currently provides reminding devices to veterans with TBI, colleges or veteran service organizations could provide computers, organizational tools, and software to lend strategic support. Consistently spreading out one's responsibilities throughout the day also strengthens memory, by improving encoding and retrieval. Additionally, better time management provides the option to search out supplemental information and provides time to revise/edit thoughts and communications.

Strategy use and support. Although many students come to college ill prepared for college work, applying a range of learning and retrieval strategies can substantially improve performances. Counseling service personnel, peer-tutors, and tutoring services teach students useful techniques. Introductory psychology and memory classes routinely cover some of these techniques and libraries house supporting materials on mnemonics. In addition, writing centers provide advice for improving written communications whereas speech/communication departments often have programs designed to improve speaking. Taking advantage of these resources can make the difference in whether students learn to be effective or not.

However, not all study skills are created equal. To be useful, strategies have to fit with content, projects, and assessments. For content that needs to be remembered, making it meaningful is one of the most important ways to aid learning. Reading assigned material before class makes lectures more useful and informative. Many students rely on multiple readings, and/or extensive note taking. Others apply the more involved SQ3R approach (survey questions read recite review). A recent comparative study found these were all effective in improving learning (McDaniel, Howard & Einstein, 2009). Interestingly, McDaniel et al.'s research provided clear support that a simpler read-recite-review method (RRR) was actually more effective for learning and more efficient for time than other methods tested. RRR is relatively fast and can be implemented while driving, waiting, or exercising, akin to the popular choice of re-reading, except before re-reading, materials are verbalized. The simple task of saying information aloud strongly affects both short- and long-term memory retention and helps represent concepts in one's own words and associations.

Study groups. Learning is also facilitated by creating study groups for individual classes especially when content has broad principles and systematic organization. A key element to making this effective is to get learners to explain material to others. The process of describing often results in discovery of relationships and connections between ideas and helps with identifying structures and the implications of these relations.

Anxiety and managing arousal. Even when students have learned material well, evaluation anxiety can adversely affect educational performances. This is a common problem even for traditional students, but especially for those who have not been in a classroom for many years. Counseling staff are well prepared to help. Test anxiety has both cognitive and affective elements. Our beliefs and judgments about testing organize our affective response and that in turn, influences how we approach learning. Problem-focused coping, where material and assignments are subdivided and treated as issues needing resolution, is generally more adaptive than emotion-focused coping.

In preparing especially for first exams, veterans should be encouraged to over prepare to lessen the likelihood of 'going blank.' When feeling anxious while test-taking, it is usually best to concentrate on easy items first. Focus internal talk on strategies like managing time, mining test items for information, and keeping focused on the task. While unpleasant emotions can cause us to attend more to detail and the task, this can backfire if anxiety keeps us from being able to focus.

Learning to channel arousal effectively is a problem for everyone occasionally, but veterans may grapple with this more. With more than 50,000 cases of

Karn —

David Byne & I
spoke at the conference
of which this book is
an outcome.

See tab for my article.


For the library. Thanks.

post traumatic stress disorder (PTSD) diagnosed during Operation Iraqi Freedom and Operation Enduring Freedom (Ephron, 2007), coupled with TBI and normal responses to war, all of these challenges increase arousal. While higher arousal can motivate us to work harder and study in more focused ways, we can also become too stimulated to be able to concentrate on the task at hand. One key management strategy is to focus on more or less valued tasks to up or down regulate emotions. Matching tasks to arousal levels can be effective, such that high levels of arousal might be best put to use on one's most challenging tasks. While it can be difficult to focus when highly aroused, if you can make yourself begin a demanding task, you may be able to harness that energy to good effect. Once focused, much can often be achieved before fatigue occurs. Similarly, when one is not feeling particularly motivated or aroused, chipping away at simpler tasks can be fruitful. Increasing the difficulty of tasks can also be used to increase arousal. Switching between items on an organized to-do list may help manage arousal while creating a sense that work is proceeding toward completion.

Concluding Remarks. Colleges must better recognize the diversities veterans bring to campus life. Relative to other incoming students, servicemembers and veterans face different, and usually more challenging circumstances when transitioning to university life. The higher education community can and should do more to help military undergraduates be successful (see Kime, this book). While many veterans will develop into stellar ambassadors for universities, others will benefit from programs targeting their particular needs. Part of this effort should involve training staff, which should include learning about the effects of combat on individual learning ability. Other efforts need to involve special policy development which can accommodate delayed government tuition payments, deployments, or other military-influenced disruptions with reasonable flexibility. These elements should not continue to create the kind of interference, distraction, and stress that they currently generate. It is also important to improve campus awareness of military undergraduates' contributions, so that all members of university communities have a better appreciation of veterans' and servicemembers' experiences, skills and commitments.

After choosing a school and program of study, learning about the college environment will help establish expectations. Having a knowledgeable advisor is key. It is also critical to apply the right tools and learning skills that will enable one to put forward best performances. Realizing the importance of taking advantage of the available supports (e.g., tutors, study groups, centers for learning, faculty office hours) will also improve learning efficacy. Given all the contributions veterans and servicemembers make for our safety and security, universities need to provide appropriate support for scaling the ivory towers.

## References

American Council on Education (2008). Severely injured military veterans: Fulfilling their dream. http://www.acenet.edu/Content/NavigationMenu/P rogramsServices/MilitaryPrograms/veterans/index. htm. 2008a. Retrieved Oct. 10, 2009.

DiRamio, D. & Spires, M. (2009) Partnering to assist disabled veterans in transitions. New Directions for Student Services, 126, Published online in Wiley InterScience (www.interscience.wiley.com) • DOI: 10.1002/ss.319

Emmons, M. (2006). Traumatic brain injury: The 'Signature wound' of wars in Iraq and Afghanistan. Oakland Tribune. [http://nl.newsbank.com/nlsearch/we/Archives=11 3840p]. Dec. 26, 2006. Retrieved Sept. 14, 2009.

Ephron, D. (2007). Forgotten heroes. Newsweek, Mar. 5, 2007, pp. 29–37.

Hudson, J. (2009, May). Personal communication.

LoPresti, E. F., Mihailidis, A. & Kirsch, N. (2004). Assistive technology for cognitive rehabilitation: State of the art. Neuropsychological Rehabilitation, 14, 5-39.

Manly, T. et al. (2004). An electronic knot in the handkerchief: "Context free cueing" and the maintenance of attentive control. Neuropsychological Rehabilitation, 14, 89 116.

McDaniel, M. Howard, D. & Einstein, G. (2009). The read-recite-review study strategy: Effective and portable. Psychological Science, 20, 516 522.

Radford, A. W. and Wun, J. (2009). Issues tables: A Profile of military servicemembers and veterans enrolled in post-secondary education from 2008-9. Retrieved December 15, 2009, from http://nces.ed.gov/pubs2009/2009182.pdf

Zoroya, G. (2007). Military prodded on brain injuries. USA Today, http://www.usatoday.com/news/washi

Chapter 22

# Demands on Veterans Entering Higher Education

## Dr. Bert Allen
### Milligan College

This chapter gives consideration of those factors that interfere with the adjustment of veterans to academic settings and demands. Examining how the cognitive, educational, social and familial issues affect a veteran's academic performance and the perceptions held by members of academe when confronting a veteran student.

When entering the academic land of higher education, the ambassadors who the young GI Joes and GI Janes will meet are the troops' professors. Many of these know little about these new invaders. In fact, some of the invading troops will meet hostility from these ambassadors. Many professors are products of the 1960's era of radicalizing US politics from the campus outward, - the genesis of an extended era during which the armed forces have been held in suspicion and low regard. Senior professors and the administrators, who employ these professors who will be ambassadors to the troops, are educational products of the 1960's and '70's - the epitome of anti-US sentiment which was focused on a number of vital issues; one of most divisive was the war in Vietnam and those who fought there. This sentiment has continued on college and university campuses. The senior professors now were the students and demonstrators then. Our senior legislative leaders and policy makers are also products of that era. Powerful and negative attitudes in academe about the military and its veterans remain, though less conspicuously.

These biases rise at times and places in subtle ways in which political discussions occur, e.g., classrooms and other academic settings. Colored terms like "military minds" or "military intelligence" are used in pejorative ways. When representatives of the military services enter institutions of higher education, they are greeted in a quiet, distant way. For example, efforts of the military services for nursing and officer recruitment are ignored; not mocked, not harassed, but deliberately ignored as something foreign to the academic culture. Or, when as a part of a formal exercise, a graduate becomes a commissioned officer, faculty members complain that ceremony is improper, but are silent about pinning or acknowledging the successes of other graduates.

Veterans are foreign to academe. Those in higher education do not know the military experiences of veterans. Few in higher education care to know the traditions, history and culture of the military services through firsthand study or from the inside experience. Throughout the education and careers of those in higher education now, the academic culture has displayed contempt for those in the services and toward those whose career plans include military service. Many of our nation's top tier educational institutions have attempted through a variety of methods to prevent the recruitment of officer candidates on their campuses and have not allowed the inclusion of the Reserve Officer Training Corps (ROTC) programs in their curricula or on their campuses under the auspices of any collegiate office. Among these are Harvard, Yale, Columbia, Brown, Tufts, Stanford and Chicago. As an example, the recruitment of potential officers and enlisted personnel by the US Marines in Berkley, CA, has led to demonstrations by members of the largely university-related community to evict the entire recruitment effort from the city. During times of conflict from Vietnam to Iraq and Afghanistan, our nation's college and university campuses have been the sites of protests of the government's policies and the military action which has resulted from those policies. Veterans who choose to study in these collegiate settings are confronted with hostility and targeted as undesirable. Although colleges and universities profess openness, incidents suggest otherwise. Noted by The Wall Street Journal, two students at Harvard who were interested in officer training while at Harvard were forced to participate in the ROTC program at Massachusetts Institute of Technology. The students, Marine lieutenants Joseph Kristol and Daniel West, said to the WSJ reporter, "Cadets begin every semester seeking to avoid professors known to exhibit hostility towards students who wear uniforms to class." Recently, a young soldier briefly home from combat in Iraq attended a class with his wife, who was a student at a university in this region. The professor whom the young man had never met greeted the soldier with derision. The young man was told that he is an example of those returning from combat who think they deserve favors and benefits resulting from their service in Iraq. Without comment, the young man exited. Although the soldier was planning to enter this university, he has chosen to enter another.

A vast socioeconomic chasm separates troops and academic leaders on campus. The two are from two vastly different economic worlds. The academic professionals have found resources for gaining their educations, while few with experience in the military services have had any access. At the economic table of life, the academics are seated among the haves; those who are veterans are among those seated among the have not's and scrapping for the crumbs falling from above. Those who have, gain access to family and group resources which include human and social capital. These family, business and community traditions provide the economic resources, awareness of professional and educational routes, as well as funds for academic pursuits and beyond. Those have not's at the table of life lack mentors. Fewer have funds with which to pursue learning through wide travel, tutorial instruction or to provide musical or athletic activities. And among those above the salt, this inability of their lesser fellows to take advantage of these opportunities is misperceived as a lack of qualification cognitively as well.

Ron Liebowitz, President of Middlebury College, stated in 2007 via the Middlebury campus blogspot on

November 21, concerning military (USMC) recruiting on the campus:

> preventing recruiting on campuses like Middlebury is likely to widen the divide between civilians and the military. It would also contribute to the sense of elitism that surrounds campuses like ours and accentuate an already class-based division in our armed forces. The less educated and less well-off socioeconomic groups are widely overrepresented in our volunteer military service branches and therefore suffer the disproportionate casualties defending our country and its interests. The successful recruitment of students from places like Middlebury would bring (different) values to the armed forces . . . Preventing the recruiting of these voices, in the long-term, will prove to be counter-productive.

I say to President Liebowitz, "Preach it, Brother!" You and your colleagues might find that the veterans and other military folk are more similar to you than you realize, and might teach you something about life from their own experience. Education, when permitted to be such, can be reciprocal and bilateral. Also, I would suggest to those of Middlebury and other institutions that increasing the diversity of the student body to include those who are under-represented for economic and other issues might be informative to the entire community, not only to students.

Paul Fussell, a professor emeritus of Classics from the University of Pennsylvania, describes his own assistance to those students of the upper classes during the Vietnam era: stay in school. Others from the lower economic classes without capital were sent to Ft. Polk, Ft. Bragg, Great Lakes or Parris Island. Academic professionals and their students have access to both human and social capital which has provided access to educational resources of a nature those outside the academic "fraternity" do not have. Perhaps those of us in the academic realm of our nation's colleges and universities would do well to spend some thought on the writings of Paul Fussell. Fussell noted in Doing Battle: The making of a skeptic, his professorial protection of his students at Rutgers during the 1960's:

"While we devoted ourselves to swimming and gourmandizing and sporting our espadrilles in Greece and France, fancying ourselves the heirs of the writers and artists of the twenties, on the other side of the world working-class American youths were, uselessly, dying in agony, and by the thousands. If you thought about it, it seemed gravely unfair, and it was. How unfair I didn't fully appreciate until, returning to Rutgers, I learned that attending college, any college, for any purpose, was a sufficient reason for a draft deferment. The class system was doing its dirty little work quite openly, and nobody seemed to care. Nor were the rest of us morally clean. Early in the war, I had written disingenuous letters testifying to the deep religious convictions of sons of middle-class friends of mine to keep them out of the army, and later I was perfectly happy to see many of my students flee to Canada, leaving the less fortunate boys, those emanating from Trenton and Camden instead of

Bernardsville, the job of pursuing America's misbegotten course in southeast Asia. I never knew anyone whose son had been killed, wounded, or even badly inconvenienced by the war. It now seems hard to believe that any of us emerged from the years of the Vietnam debacle entirely guiltless. I think that my objections to the Vietnam War stemmed less from humanitarian impulses, as I pretended, than from my simple hatred of the army and all it works."

Paul Fussell is a Purple Heart recipient for wounds received as an infantry officer during World War II.

Dave, a veteran of Iraq who served with the 101st Airborne Division has just entered a course toward ministry at Milligan College. As a teen, he entered the military service after a less than stellar high school career. His dreams were to make the military service his career. Yet, even the military was a stretch for him. School had been a place of absenteeism, numerous suspensions, and several assaults by Dave on students and staff members. He left high school following junior year and with those who watched him go feeling as much or more relief than he. Dave had to detour through a route other than the traditional high school graduation to enter the service. He gained his GED through an alternative education program, was given some breaks in the recruitment process and from the judicial officials of his community and entered the Army as soon as he was permitted, without having anyone divulge his delinquency. Dave did well in his training and as an infantry scout for four and a half years. He excelled during that time and loved the military. With a tour in Iraq behind him, he was doing well stateside. He would not face another deployment to the wars for some months, so he could breathe a sigh of relief. Or, so he thought. An injury while training severely damaged his knee, forcing an abrupt end to his military career.

Yet, Dave had seen beyond the horizon of his teens. He, like some, used the military experience and benefits as the foundation for an education beyond the GED. The young man took advantage of educational opportunities and grants to complete training to become an airframe and power-plant aircraft mechanic. After being employed at this for two years, Dave realized that the injuries to his leg and knee suffered at Ft. Campbell would be a hindrance to his work and mobility in the confined spaces in aircraft. So, this fall he entered the world of higher education. What will Dave and others like him find as they enter this new arena?

First, Dave and those like him have been given little foundation to meet the expectations of higher education. Research throughout the $20^{th}$ century and the current era of war in Iraq and Afghanistan, has shown that those who have provided the corps of US troops have been from the lowest strata of income and education. In their families and in their culture, little coaching or guiding has led them to the academic courses and behaviors which are required in higher education. The human capital in their worlds has limited them to goals demanding little training in the literature, languages, arts, politics, and economies of societies. The collegiate study of history for these troops is beyond the levels to which they were introduced in the grades and courses through they traveled toward their high school diplomas. These who defend our nation have had little or no contact with courses which would provide a deeper, fuller awareness of the nation's history or government, the economic or political systems, the sociologic and psychological understanding of groups and the individuals who compose societies. Yet, those who compose the military ranks in the enlisted and noncommissioned officer ranks can perform the tasks of moving materials and personnel, firing sophisticated weapons and maintaining aircraft and their avionics with confidence and skills. But these skills and competencies do not offer a broad foundation on which to base study of the humanities, the arts, and collegiate subjects and courses foreign to the troops. These troops and their counterparts come to college from radically different routes. Yet both routes demand rigor and focus to succeed. Dave, the infantry veteran and mechanic, passed examinations of significant bodies of knowledge in technical and mechanical areas. His counterparts who are academically aware travelled a route which required awareness and appreciation of dynamic relationships in history, application of arithmetic and physical laws and abstractions unlike Dave's. Many veterans know little of what they will encounter as they enter colleges and universities. Veterans in general have never seen college as a destination or a means to get to a destination. Never in their educational career have they focused on the array of courses and gaining the skills which would prepare them for higher education. Academically, these veterans lack both knowledge and skill sets which enhance success in college. Yet, to assume that they possess less than the innate cognitive abilities to succeed in collegiate studies is erroneous. They lack and have lacked the resources with which to build on their cognitive foundations.

These resources, which they lack, include possessing the awareness of   study, e.g.,

- the needs and means for taking in information,

- processes of remembering that which is read or seen or heard,

- methods of developing compartments of the mind in which to store information,

- the processes to retrieve, and

- how to report verbally and/or on paper/disk/video what has been presented to him or her.

Also, the veteran must develop quickly the realization of:

- what things are important and what is informational , etc.,

- an appreciation of the abstractions,

- underlying theories and pieces of knowledge of events and facts,

- the development of methods of study, retention, expression of what one learns.

This adaptation to a new method of learning and display of learning is overwhelming, more for the troops than others who are entering college directly from high school and who have had recent coursework which had prepared them for college.

Facilities in our nation's communities and in the military services which teach vocational skills utilize training methods which espouse thinking within the box, drill work, memorization, rote learning of basics, i.e., employing the standard methods and routes toward solution and rapid completion or resolution of a problem or project. In military training for the masses focuses on how to do a task, complete a task, get from point A to point B. The lessons are how not why, with the how being drilled over and over. This training is laid on the foundation of the classes into which the have not's are directed in secondary schools. Students are in rows and columns at benches and tables, learning the steps A to B and beyond, one brick on top of another. Not valued for those who staff the military services' occupations and which are products of the K-12 educational systems which lead to these vocations are skills and practice in innovation, diverse modes of thinking and thinking outside the box, moving deliberately to developing many routes toward solution(s) are. Throughout veterans' education, they have relied on an accumulation of facts, formulae and methods of rapidly responding to known and new problems with the development of solutions, routes of processing and answering to questions in proscribed ways. Taking the road less traveled results in penalty; it is not the way taught although it might be more expedient, more elegant, or less costly. These are not in the book, however, so we cannot allow them.

Valued is arrival at the result and completing the desired fix/mission/assignment rapidly. Significant and demanded by the person making the order or request is expedient delivery. Employees and service personnel in the trades or in combat are taught to act quickly, to follow directions, to do tasks in an efficient, tried-and-true manner, without considering alternative methods, innovative tools and equipment, or routes less traveled. Veterans and technicians in all of the services and trades have heard, perhaps many times, "you're not paid to think, you're paid to act. When an officer, NCO or supervisor says 'jump', all you need to know is how to jump, not the mechanics or the kinetics." Firing a weapon when demanded requires precise and rapid responding; laying an azimuth or guiding an aircraft to a carrier landing demands quick thinking/consideration of a myriad of details without considering alternative demands. Yet, these are focused, unwavering, stressful occupations guiding, using and caring about/for protecting sophisticated equipment and guarding people's safety. Although very different than the demands of a collegiate campus, these environments demand skills and thinking at very high levels and very rapidly. We in the academic realm appreciate the display of these skills when we are approaching Dulles or Hartsfield-Jackson or LAX in a 767, or wanting our meal served quickly or correctly or ensuring that the bone scan surveys the correct area of our child's body. Skills here are vital but differ from those valued on campuses.

Colleges and universities primarily cater to a population which is in late adolescence, coming out of their teen years. Those who are entering college following a span of time in the military service are some years older than the traditional students are. Developmental needs and those related behaviors, thinking, and wants of the two groups differ, e.g., in types of housing, employment opportunities, child-care services, shopping availability, financial aid programs, activities for the student and family members, study sites, computer access, transportation.

Following a span of time outside of the academic arena, students need academic support services which differ from those needed by students coming directly from high school. These services might include study-skills development or renewal, computer skills development or renewal, tutorial services, assessment services in academic abilities and achievement, modes of learning and use of memory and senses, one's attitudes and vocational interests. Veterans might utilize counseling services in general or specifically for acclimation to the civilian life and academic life as a part of a collegiate setting. The spouses and/or children might also need counseling support after having the spouse/parent absent for some time and the family members becoming independent during that absence and now adjusting to re-entry of that spouse/parent.

Colleges and universities receiving veterans might provide to the administrators, professors and other employees an orientation to the culture of the military, the mission of the military and the experiences of the returning veterans. These veterans who are returning are like students from other minority groups. They cannot be, should not be expected to be spokespersons for anyone beyond themselves. As with any individual, some areas of their experience are very personal and private.

One would do well to drop from one's repertoire of questions for veterans, such inquiries as, "News video shows people like you kicking in the doors of homes in Baghdad of innocent Iraqis. How powerful does that make you feel?", "When you killed someone, what kind of rush did you feel?", "Is war like a sexual thing?", "How did you and other black troops feel about fighting against other people of color?" "How many of the guys you were with were killed?" Unless we in the collegiate community orient one another and sensitize one another to this minority group, the veterans who are coming our way, the orientation will be incomplete and the field of play, i.e., the classroom and its surrounding facilities and campus, will be a foreign duty station to the veteran. The faculty and those other collegiate leaders who support students' learning endeavors must become sensitive to the wishes and needs of the veterans to continue their education. As for any other arriving student, the collegiate environment should meet these new veteran students by providing a welcoming, empowering environment.

We in collegiate settings should be aware that although these men and women fought in war(s), they did so not as a lark of their own making; they did so because our government, that is we, who through our proxies, the legislators and our president, sent them. And many troops saw combat, with all the grotesqueness of war, which is the expedient tool, selected by us through our government, by which to implement our nation's foreign policy. Veterans who are coming our way are the tools of war who have been guarding our nation in the manner in which we, through our agents in the federal government, ordered them to. Now, these men and women are at our gate seeking to turn their individual swords into plowshares. We can help them to do that, if we choose. We also might hear a veteran who tells his or her fellow citizen-students that, "no one desires peace more than the veteran, for he must pay the greatest price in war."

We need our defense and we need educated citizens, including those who have guarded, and who are guarding, our freedom. Without that defense, in a perfect world, we would be fine, healthy and safe. But our world is unhealthy; our world is unsafe; our world requires those who choose to be our guards to protect our freedom of speech and academic freedom in our classrooms, to ensure that both liberals and conservatives have the right to speak and say what they wish to, in spite of what each says being perhaps ugly to others. We need those guards to ensure that we can travel freely without undue restraint. And we need to guard our freedom to be educated, and to have equal access to an education in a setting where all are honored, where all can enter without regard to their class or whether or not they served the ugly tasks as our nation's guards.

"The willingness with which our young people are likely to serve in any war, no matter how justified, shall be directly proportional to how they perceive the veterans of earlier wars were treated and appreciated by their nation."

—George Washington

Chapter 23

# Consequences of Not Eliminating the Veterans Education Problem

Dr. Doug Herrmann

Mr. Dan Hopkins
College Educators for Veterans Higher Education

Veterans, higher education, American society and the regard for our nation in the world can benefit in various ways if the difficulties of veterans in higher education are corrected. Veterans, higher education, American society and the regard for our nation in the world will suffer in various ways if the problems of veterans in higher education are NOT corrected. This chapter reviews these consequences.

Americans have great respect for veterans. Consequently, professors and administrators, in colleges and universities also may be assumed to be as patriotic as any other occupational group. There is no reason to presume otherwise. Even educators who participate in protest activity do so in order to steer their country in the direction of an appropriate military policy. Nevertheless, there is considerable evidence presented in this book and in previous publications (e.g. Creating a veteran-friendly campus: Strategies for transition and success, Akerman & DiRamio, 2009; Educating Veterans in the 21st Century, Herrmann et al., 2009) that some members of higher education sometimes mistreat veterans or fail to help them (Fiore, this book; Sternberg, MacDermid Wadsworth, Vaughan, & Carlson, 2009; Herrmann, 2007).

Collective action of individuals with similar concern for veterans can also demonstrate significant awareness of mistreatment. Each chapter, reported in this book, advances unique viewpoints on how to help veterans obtain a college degree. Additionally, this conference has revealed that there are presently at least four kinds of such collective action occurring or in the offing. First, industry and educational institutions have developed grants to reward higher educational institutions for programs that ensure improved treatment of veterans on campus (ACE/Walmart Grants; 2009; Lily Grants for Operation Diploma, Hitt, this book). Second, educators themselves have proposed a program of education for professors, college administrators, and college staff about the best practices to engage in when interacting with servicemembers and veterans (see Indiana Educators Best Practices Program reported by Gibbens this book; ACE's Best Practices program).

Third, just as the Servicemembers Opportunity Colleges rewards higher educational institutions for treating servicemembers well, a Veterans Opportunity Colleges has been proposed to be led by the Veterans Administration (VA) to reward higher educational institutions that treat veterans fairly (Kime, endnote, 2009). Fourth, there are those who believe none of the aforementioned programs would put an end to discrimination against veterans and instead propose that veterans be provided protected Class Status for Veterans. Just as other protected classes (women, minority races, minority sexual-preferences) cannot be discriminated against by law, it is proposed that veterans be given legal protected class status as well (Gordon, this book). The four kinds of collective action are shown in Table 23.1.

Table 23.1
Programs Designed to Stop Widespread Mistreatment of Veterans by College and University Educators

Grants to Higher Educational Institutions that Design Veteran-Friendly Programs
Programs to Educate Professors and College Administrators about how to treat veterans fairly
A governmental program in the VA to Reward Higher Educational Institutions for treating veterans fairly
Awarding veterans legal status that protects them from discrimination in higher education

Origins of Poor Treatment of Veterans

The chapters presented in this text have examined the veterans higher education problem, its origins, proposals to resolve it, and as mentioned above evidence of mistreatment of veterans. Different speakers have explained different aspects of the Veterans Higher Education Problem. Different difficulties require slightly different approaches [1]

The origins of these aspects seem to fall into at least four categories. Table 23.1 lists four origins. An assessment of the possible consequences of eliminating or not eliminating the veterans education problem presumably vary across these origins. These origins are addressed in a more detail in Table 23.2.

Table 23.2
The Origins of Problems Encountered by Veterans in College

Economic forces separate the upper and lower classes in American society while shrinking the middle class but does not indicate what part of society veterans can make a contribution

Department for Veterans Affairs and other parts of the government do not always address the higher educational problems of veterans, making college more difficult for veterans

Federal and state bureaucracies do not inform veterans of opportunities to apply for loans and grants,

Some higher educational institutions employ administrative practices unfriendly to veterans

Some professors and administrators engage in bad practices that impact on the education of veterans and the lives of their families

[1] A footnote at the end of the chapter addresses approaches to resolving the different kinds of difficulties of veterans and servicemembers.


## Economic Forces

Veterans sometimes encounter problems in college because there are societal forces that lead the difference in the wealth of the upper and lower classes to increase. Moreover, economic facts force the wealth of the middle class to decrease and to be absorbed by the lower class, or far less frequently force the wealth of middle class to increase and become part of the upper class. Each force leads to the disappearance of the middle class.

As a result of economic pressure on the middle class, American society needs people trained in a variety of technologies. However, technologically able persons are usually not found in the lower class and if found in the upper class, these individuals do not want to take work that once was done by the middle class. Veterans represent a pool of individuals with technological skill that can do the work that once was done by the middle class. However, American society does not make its need for veterans clear to them and the rest of society (Gomez, this book).


## Department of Veterans Affairs

Veterans sometimes encounter difficulties in college because the Department for Veterans Affairs does not address some of their problems. While the VA classifies schools according to whether a veteran can get GI Bill at a particular school, the VA does not classify schools according to how friendly they are to veterans (Kime, this book).

## Federal and state bureaucracies

Veterans sometimes encounter problems in college because they are not aware of federal and state requirements for bureaucratic practices that affect college loans. Some bureaucracies do not inform veterans of opportunities to apply for loans and grants, making college harder for veterans (raised by conference attendees).

## College Administration

A veteran sometimes encounters problems in college because schools employ administrative practices that are unfriendly to a veteran. For example, some schools do not have a policy on how veterans should be educated. There are rarely committees concerned with veteran education. There are no officials at many higher educational institutions designated to assist veterans with problems unique to them (Herrmann, Hopkins, Wilson, & Allen, 2009) and several chapters reported in this book. Some schools make an effort to help the families brought by some veterans to schools, whereas other schools make no such effort.

Statistics demonstrate a greater percentage of veterans attend and complete college. The Military

Family Research Institute from Purdue University conducted a research project that demonstrated the administrators at a substantial number of Indiana schools overlook or fail to perform various services for veterans (Sternberg, MacDermid Wadsworth, Vaughan, & Carlson, 2009). A research project done for the Indiana Employer Support for Guard and Reserve found that some guard and reserve members at Indiana Schools complained that they did not receive transfer credits to which they were entitled and encountered a less than friendly classroom climate (Herrmann, 2007). Fiore (this book) reported survey results that again indicate that veterans are sometimes not well treated in college. Seven other survey results have been reported both by veterans and college administrators, these sources are described in footnote [2].

## Professors and College Administrators

Gibbens (this book) reported on a comprehensive program developed by higher educators in Indiana to persuade other educators in the state to adopt the very best practices in their interactions with servicemembers and veterans. The American Council on Education created a similar set of best practices by surveying college CEOs about the current problems that veterans face in college or that discourage them from going to college. When corrected, the same or similar percentage of veterans as non-veterans could receive a college education. If the percentage of veterans receiving a college degree were the same as the percentage received by non-veterans and a fair job-search system is established, then veterans will finally have the same opportunity to achieve career success in spite of the span of time the veterans have spent outside of the academic realm while in the military.

The Need for Change

The chapters in this book show that one important reason that veterans are not educated at an acceptable rate is that American higher education is not equipped, administratively, academically or attitudinally to help veterans get the education that they could receive (Kime, introduction and concluding chapter in this text; Wilson, this book). Academia, no doubt, is as patriotic as any other sector of American society. Many authors of the chapters in the book believe that once higher education comes to understand the difficulties that many American veterans encounter in college, higher education will make changes needed.

However, some of Academia's most brilliant scholars will be needed to improve educational opportunity for veterans. Economists and political scientists the end of the chapter discusses other surveys pertinent to veterans in college. They will be needed to determine ways that increases and decreases in the upper, middle, and lower classes can be used to influence government to invest more in veterans education problems. Legislators and bureaucrats can create changes in the Department for Veterans Affairs that will provide better support of veterans in higher education.

Federal and state bureaucracies can be required to inform veterans of opportunities to apply for loans and grants. College administrators may be guided to drop bad practices and adopt good practices that facilitate administrative practices that involve veterans. Higher education, in general, as discussed in some of the chapters in this book and in Educating Veterans in the 21st Century (Herrmann, Hopkins, Wilson, & Allen, 2009), can develop ways to encourage professors and administrators to engage in practices that impact on the education of veterans and the lives of their families.

Assessment and Correction of Learning Disabilities. Some veterans have service-connected disabilities that interfere with the ability of veterans to learn in college. The Department of Veterans Affairs (DVA) provides treatment for these disabilities and programs for vocational rehabilitation. However, the DVA does not directly treat the cognitive impairments that may come with service connected disabilities. One thing academia could do to help veterans would be to develop procedures for training veterans to compensate for the cognitive impairments caused by service-connected disabilities (Herrmann, Gruneberg, & Raybeck, 2003).

Undiagnosed Service-Connected Disabilities. Some veterans have service- connected disabilities that have not been diagnosed by the DVA. Thus one thing academia could do to help veterans would be to develop procedures to diagnose possible service-connected disabilities and then provide training for these veterans to compensate for the cognitive impairments caused by service-connected disabilities.

Preexisting Educational Disabilities. Some veterans have educational disabilities that they acquired before they joined the military (Section 504 of the Rehabilitation Act of 1973; Americans with Disabilities Act of 1990; Federal Tax Incentives to Encourage the Employment of People with Disabilities and to Promote the Accessibility of Public Accommodations; the Individuals with Disabilities Education Act Amendments of 1997). Currently most adults with educational disabilities are not subjected to diagnostic procedures that would reveal these disabilities. One thing academia could do to help veterans would be to develop procedures to diagnose educational disabilities and then provide training for these veterans to compensate for the cognitive impairments caused by educational disabilities.

Some veterans are assessed as educationally disadvantaged and given training through the Upward Bound program. However, only a small proportion of veterans are given an assessment for educational disabilities. If higher education is intent on preparing those veterans for college who might complete a degree program, then higher education (probably with the assistance of the Department of Education) will need to play a major role in giving veterans a good preparation for college [3]. The footnote [3] at the end of the chapter discusses federal educational regulations pertinent to veterans in college.

## The Purpose of this Chapter

This chapter addresses consequences if colleges and universities do or do not follow the recommendations presented above and in the previous chapters. These consequences include those that affect four groups: the veterans themselves; academia; American Society; and America itself. The authors of this chapter consider the effects on these four groups as a result of efforts by higher education to eliminate the veterans higher education problem by helping veterans succeed in college.

## The Positive Consequences of Improving the College Education of Veterans

Improvement of the college education provided to veterans has more than one consequence. It is important to acknowledge what these consequences might be.

### The Positive Consequences for Veterans

Many good things will happen to veterans if American higher education chooses to treat veterans in the same manner as it treats non-veterans. Table 23.3 lists some of these good consequences. Good and fair treatment of veterans will yield positive outcomes.

Table 23.3
If Academia Helps Veterans Get Educated
Veterans Will Experience Positive Consequences

More veterans will apply for and enroll in college
Fewer veterans will drop out
More veterans will obtain one or more college degrees
More veterans would become employed in civilian
    occupations because of the knowledge they gained
    from their college education and experiences in the
    military
More veterans will achieve more productive and fuller
    lives

## The Positive Consequences for Academia

Americans who value veterans will learn about the good treatment given to veterans. As a result, veterans will come to respect higher education more than before. These positive consequences are shown in Table 23.4.

Table 23.4
If Academia Helps Veterans Get Educated
Academia Will Experience Positive Consequences

Education enrollments of veterans will increase
Veterans who graduate will increasingly
        become employed
Educational programs for veterans will be better
        funded
Lectures that involve anti-veteran comments in
        class discussions will decrease

## The Positive Consequences for American Society

It is in the best interests of our nation and society if veterans obtain college degrees and achieve more productive and fuller lives (Herrmann, Hopkins, Wilson, & Allen, 2009). These positive consequences are presented in Table 23.5.

Table 23.5
Positive Consequences for Veterans

Our nation will benefit more from the knowledge that veterans have acquired in the military and is extended in college.

Our nation will benefit more from the skills that veterans have acquired in the military as they become educated.

Our nation will benefit more from the management skills that veterans have in acquired in the military are utilized in their education.

America's prosperity will increase because different sectors of society will have more knowledge and skills available to them

Society itself will function better because academia would be increasingly integrated with other components of society: e.g., business, medicine, law, and religion.

## The Positive Consequences for America

It is in the best interests of our nation if veterans obtain college degrees and achieve more productive and fuller lives. Other countries will respect our nation for doing what it should for veterans. Table 23.6 presents the positive consequences for America.

Table 23.6
Worldwide Support for Academia

If our nation needs to become involved in warfare,
Other nations will be inclined to support our war efforts
Our servicemembers will perform their duties better
    because they will know that after the war they will be
    able to get an education like that acquired by non-
    veterans

The consequences of failing to eliminate the Veterans Higher Education Problem are clearly negative and occur to veterans, academia, American society, and America. These negative consequences are as follows.

The Negative Consequences for Veterans

Inadequate and unfair treatment of veterans will yield negative outcomes for them. These negative consequences are listed in Table 23.7.

Table 23.7
Negative Consequences for Veterans

Fewer veterans will apply for and enroll in college.
More veterans will drop out.
Fewer veterans will obtain one or more degrees.
Fewer veterans would be employed in civilian occupations
    because they did not learn enough knowledge in
    college
Fewer veterans will achieve productive and full lives.

## The Negative Consequences for Academia

Americans who value veterans will lose respect for higher education. Lectures that involve anti-veteran discussion in courses unrelated to the military will make it harder for veterans to succeed in class. Table 23.8 presents the negative consequences for Academia if it fails to give veterans the good education they deserve.

Table 23.8
Negative Consequences for Academia

Education enrollments of veterans will decrease
Veterans who graduate will have difficulty finding a job
Educational programs for veterans will not be funded or
  supported with fewer funds
Lectures that involve anti-veteran comments in class
  discussions will increase
Americans who valued veterans will come to dislike
  higher education
Society itself will function less well because academia
  would be increasingly isolated from other
  components of society: business, medicine, law,
    and religion.

## The Negative Consequences for American Society

If veterans do not obtain college degrees, they will fail to achieve more productive and fuller lives. It is not in the best interests of our nation and society if our nation does not help veterans succeed in college. The negative consequences to American society of not providing veterans the education they deserve are summarized in Table 23.9.

Table 23.9
Negative Consequences for American Society

Our nation will benefit less from the knowledge that
veterans have acquired in the military.
Our nation will benefit less from the skills that veterans
have in acquired in the military
Our nation will benefit less from the management skills
that veterans have in acquired in the military
America's prosperity will decrease because different
sectors of society will have more knowledge
and skills available to them.

## The Negative Consequences for America

If fewer veterans obtain college degrees, this will
be apparent to other countries. As a result, these
countries will hold our nation in lower regard for not
doing what it should for veterans. The negative
consequences of other nations perceiving us as weaker
and more vulnerable as summarized in Table 23.10.

Table 23.10
Negative Consequences for America

If our nation needs to become involved in warfare,
other nations will not be inclined to support our
war efforts
If our nation needs to become involved in a war, our
servicemembers will perform their wartime
duties poorly because they know that after the
war they may not get the education as promised
to them.

What Colleges and Universities Can Do About the Possible Negative Consequences of Their Treatment of Veterans

Colleges and universities can avoid the possible negative consequences of failing to educate veterans (Yoder, this book). College presidents can resolve some of these consequences by changing policies that give rise to the problems of veterans, such as those involving how veterans finance their education. Other college administrators can make changes also such as altering the ways that veterans get college credits for military credits. Faculty governance can change policies as well, such as by creating grievance procedures for veterans that are comparable to those for non-veterans. Professors can adopt the practices discussed in this book about how to treat veteran students.

## Summary

The manner by which a nation educates or fails to educate its veterans does certain damage to the lives of veterans. Success in educating veterans has consequences that extend well beyond veterans themselves.

Good treatment of veterans by higher education will yield positive results. More veterans will apply for and enroll in college and fewer veterans will drop out, and many more veterans will obtain one or more degrees. Treating veterans well in higher education will lead to positive consequences for academia itself, American society, and America. Americans who value veterans will respect higher education more than in the past.

American society will benefit from the significant amounts of its annual budgets invested into the training and maintaining of our military troops and their support. America itself will be respected by other nations for treating veterans well. It is to the advantage of our nation's efficiency and possible survival for academia to help as many veterans as possible.

If veterans are treated poorly by higher education, academia itself, our society, and even the perception of our nation in the world will experience negative consequences. Americans who value veterans will have less respect for higher education than was the case in the past. American society will be defended less well because our nation will have invested less amounts in the training and maintaining of our military troops and their support. Other nations will perceive America as less able to defend itself if it is does not eliminate the Veterans Higher Education Problem.

Footnotes

[1] This chapter by Herrmann and Hopkins addresses differences in college problems of servicemembers and college problems of veterans.

Servicemembers: individuals who have raised their right hand to swear to defend the Constitution of the US and who currently serve in the active duty military of the US. Servicemembers are veterans of military service for as long as they have been in the military but they are not identified as "veterans" by the Department of Veterans Affairs until they are discharged in an honorable manner.

[Someone who has raised his or her right hand to defend the Constitution of the US but who has been discharged dishonorably from active duty is just that: a person who has been discharged dishonorably from active military service]. The term 'servicemember' has a specific meaning in a particular context. The use of 'servicemember' in different contexts is presented below.

College Problems of Servicemembers

• College Selection: Some servicemembers are directed by the Department of Defense (DoD) to obtain a certain degree. Often they are told to attend a certain school and, if not, they are told to attend a "Servicemen's Opportunity College" (SOC) school.

• Transitioning: Some schools offer servicemembers a course on how to make a transition to college life. These courses usually not on par with other courses offered for new students at these schools. The vast majority of schools do not offer these programs for servicemembers.

• Campus Culture: Adjustment to campus culture can be difficult for servicemembers because some members of the campus population know that a student is a servicemember and harass them.

• Academic Skills: Servicemembers at SOC schools may be advised to take training to improve their academic study skills.

• Financial Assistance: Servicemembers usually do not use the GI Bill while in service because they have most tuition and fees paid by their branch of the service (tuition assistance). If this does not apply or tuition assistance funding has stopped for that fiscal year, a servicemember, he or she can obtain support through their GI Bill

• Credit Transfer: Servicemembers are likely to get transfer credits for military training and military experience at SOC schools. The amount of transfer varies widely and sometimes depends on whether the school has someone qualified that knows how to look at the servicemembers military training, schools and experience

• Health care: Servicemembers can maintain their health while in school because of their access to military medicine through the Tricare System, which pays 100% of active duty medical costs.

• Employment Search: Servicemembers may not need help in finding a job if they remain in the service because they will be assigned to a job by their branch of the military. Even if they plan on leaving the service, they can easily get instruction on job searching. In general, servicemembers have the immediate support of SOC. However, servicemembers usually do not get as much help from their college or university as non veterans at finding a job on graduation.


College Problems of Veterans

Someone who has raised his or her right hand to defend the Constitution of the US and who has been discharged honorably from active duty. The meaning of the term 'veteran' varies with the context in which this term is used.

• College Selection: Veterans are not directed to attend a certain school. Some colleges do not receive GI Bill payments. Veterans can find out from the VA whether an institution accepts GI Bill payments and has additional benefits such as the Yellow Ribbon Program. If a veteran participates in VA vocational rehabilitation (Voc-Rehab) program, the VA will pay the costs of college and their VA Rep will have to approve the program and college they attend.

• Transitioning: Some schools do offer a course for veterans on how to make a transition to college life.

• Campus Culture: If a veteran served in the military for a long period of time and has disabilities, noticeable or not, the adjustment can be extremely difficult. Servicemembers attend schools that have agreed to eliminate prejudicial treatment for them but, unfortunately, veterans have no such program to protect them from discriminatory treatment.

• Academic Skills: A small percentage of veterans who are in the upward bound program will also be advised similarly. However, no system exists for the remaining veterans to be advised to improve their study skills.

• Financial Assistance: Veterans can use the GI Bill but their use of it is dependent on the amount of service they had in the military and when they were discharged from service. Combat veterans will very likely receive the new GI Bill but veterans with less active duty time may not.

320

Colleges have a variety of scholarships, grants and even stipends for various groups of students on campus, but few are offered to veterans because they are not regarded as a special class or interest group at most schools.

• Credit Transfer: Veterans may receive transfer credits for their past military training, schools and experience, if they still have their records and if their school has a staff member qualified and motivated to help.

• Health care:  Most veterans do not have access to VA health care. The   VA gives veterans health care if they have a disability. If they do not have a disability adjudicated through the VA, the VA will usually not see them. Disabled or not, many veterans must wait months for a VA medical appointment at some VA hospitals and clinics. If a veteran retired from the military, they will have retired Tricare benefits to use with civilian doctors.

• Employment Search: Veterans, unless they are under a VA program, usually do not have help finding employment, and must depend on the unemployment office,  which is not geared to help the needs of veterans. Veterans usually do not get as much help from their college or university as non-veterans at finding a job on graduation.

[2] This chapter by Herrmann and Hopkins addresses surveys pertinent to college experience of servicemembers and veterans.

I.  Three survey studies asked staff members of colleges and universities about whether they  provided certain services for veterans and non-veterans (Cook, B. J. & Kim, Y. (2008; Indiana Employer Support of the Guard and Reserve, 2007; Sternberg, MacDermid, Wadsworth, Vaughan, & Carlson, 2009).

Cook, B. J. & Kim, Y. (2008) From Soldier to Student: Easing the Transition of Service Members on Campus. Lumina Foundation. [A survey investigation of colleges; Statistics of college services for veterans].

Indiana Employer Support of the Guard and Reserve (INESGR) (2007) Investigations into Services of Indiana Higher Education to Members of the of Guard and Reservists. [A survey investigation of colleges; Statistics of college services for veterans.]

Sternberg, M., MacDermid Wadsworth, S., Vaughan, J., & Carlson, R. (2009). The higher education landscape for student service members and veterans in Indiana. West Lafayette: Military Family Research Institute at Purdue. [A survey investigation of colleges; Statistics of college services for veterans.]

II. In addition to the survey research reported in this book by Fiore, three other surveys asked veterans and non-veterans about attitudes and psychological issues experienced in college (DiRamio, Ackerman, & Mitchell, 2008; Minnesota State Colleges and Universities, 2008; Pryor, Hurtado, DeAngelo, Palucki Blake, & Tran, 2009).

DiRamio, D., Ackerman, R., & Mitchell R. L. (2008). From combat to campus: Voices of student-veterans. NASPA Journal, 45(1), 73-94.

Minnesota State Colleges and Universities (2008) HEALTH AND HEALTH-RELATED BEHAVIORS survey: Minnesota Postsecondary Student Veterans. Boyton Health Service. [A survey of veterans and non-veteran students; Results from the 2008 College Student Health Survey presented in this report document the health and health-related behaviors of veterans enrolled in the participating institutions.].

Pryor, J. H. Hurtado, S. DeAngelo, L., Palucki Blake, L., & Tran, S. (2009), The American Freshman: National Norms Fall 2009. The Cooperative Institutional Research Program (CIRP) Higher Education Research Institute, UCLA.
www.heri.ucla.edu.

III. The National Center for Educational Statistics (2008) compiles data on the college attendance of veterans and non-veterans

Digest of Education Statistics (2008) Table 231. Number and percentage of attendance: 2003–04 for veterans and non-veterans. National Center for Education Statistics.

[3] This chapter by Herrmann and Hopkins addresses federal educational regulations pertinent to veterans in college.

Federal Regulations that may pertain to the higher education of some veterans include: Section 504 of the Rehabilitation Act of 1973; Americans with Disabilities Act of 1990; Federal Tax Incentives to Encourage the Employment of People with Disabilities and to Promote the Accessibility of Public Accommodations; the Individuals with Disabilities Education Act Amendments of 1997.

# References

American Council on Education (ACE), American Association of Small Colleges and Universities (AASCU), National Association of Student Affairs, Administrators in Higher Education (NASPA), and the National Association of Veterans Program Administrators (2009) From Soldier to Student. American Council on Published by the American Council on Education for Military Programs: Washington D.C.

American Council on Education (2008) A TrAnsfer Guide: Understanding Your Military Transcript and ACE Credit Recommendations. Published by the American Council on Education for Military Programs: Washington D.C.

Herrmann, D.J. (2007) Investigations into the Treatment of Servicemembers by Indiana Higher Educational Institutions. Terre Haute, IN: Veterans Higher Educational Group.

Herrmann, D., Raybeck, & Gutman, D. (1993). Improving student memory. Toronto: Hogrefe and Huber.

Herrmann, D., Hopkins, C., Wilson, R. B., & Allen, B. (2009). Educating veterans in the 21st century, North Charleston, South Carolina: Booksurge.

Sternberg, M., MacDermid Wadsworth, S., Vaughan, J., & Carlson, R. (2009). The higher education landscape for student Servicemembers and Veterans in  Indiana. West Lafayette: Military Family Research Institute at Purdue.

# Chapter 24

# Words, as Well as Facts, Do Matter

## Lynn Malley, JD, MA, LLM
### Creative Conflict Engagement Services

Over the last three years, it has been my pleasure and honor to work with many different kinds of people who are or have been in the military service, as well as their family members and the communities and educational institutions which support them. Coming to the field as a novice as I did, all has been new. This is not to say that I did not have my own subtle and not so subtle biases. I was in high school and college during the Vietnam war. In the 1980's I was married to an Army Reservist. My son was recently in the active duty Army for five years. In spite of all these military connections, I knew that I did not know much, so when I followed my passion to assist those having re-integration challenges, I knew that I had much to learn.

My desire to find a place where I could be most of service has taken me many places. Here are some things that I have learned along the way...

- It truly is NOT your father's army.
  - o About 20% of our forces are currently female.
  - o Almost half of our current force is not active duty but activated National Guard and Reserve service members.
- These things matter because
  - o These forces may not answer to the word 'soldier.'
  - o They may not consider themselves to be veterans because they still have a military obligation.
  - o Since about half of them do not live on or around a military installation, they do not have the day-to-day support of others like themselves.

To put it another way, it is likely that those on your campus who are leading the way in supporting current student service members/veterans are assuming that those students face the same problems they faced when they returned from military service. As well-meaning as such people are, it is simply not the case that current service members / veterans are returning to the same world that those who came before them did. One of the primary distinguishing characteristics is that nearly half of our force faces continuing military obligations. That means that many of our student service members know that they may face additional deployment orders at any time.

If that is not complex enough, it is further complicated by the fact that many terms are used to mean different things in different situations. Let me give a few examples. A first example is Yellow Ribbon. It's the name of a program that all higher education staff members who deal with veterans know as a financial aid program. On the other hand, Yellow Ribbon is also the name of the program which provides for pre and post deployment services for National Guard & Reservists and their families. Both are big programs and each is independent of the other. If you have a poster up about a Yellow Ribbon program on your campus, a service member who has just been through the post-deployment part of that Yellow Ribbon program may not even read the poster as s/he may assume that s/he knows what it's about or that s/he has already met its requirements.

A second example is the term Veteran. An organization labeled a Veterans' Service Organization (VSO) may draw no National Guard or Reserve service members as they may not think of themselves as Veterans. And if you call it a Service Members' organization, that may draw no veterans, as in the active duty context, a service member is one who is still active duty and who is being sent to school at the direction of his branch of the service, as the term is used in the context of Servicemembers Opportunity Colleges.

Another important distinction in terms is that Soldiers are not Marines are not Airmen. Yes, the military is not unlike academia. There are silos and branches if not disciplines. Above all, there is a history that colors how things are seen and indeed how things work today. Since 9/11, National Guard and Reserve have served as an operational force without the supports that the active duty receives. This lack of support remains as they return to schools and employers.

There are many more important distinctions and nuances. Military women may choose not to be in activities for the military generally, but may well join in activities for military women. Service members generally may not want their families to be part of any groups formed on campus, yet family members may also need support in the transition back to civilian life or back and forth between civilian and military life.

If we want to reach them and keep them on our campuses, we have to help find solutions to this problem. Certainly it is not possible to be culturally sensitive enough to always use the correct term or to use all the possible terms so as to include everyone you want to reach. What is possible is to be aware of the history and culture of those on your campus who are working with today's military or former military student or family member and to work to broaden not just the perspective of that person but of the materials that they produce to reach out to those they are trying to assist on the campus.

Here are a few examples to help you evaluate whether that is happening on your campus.

If you have an organization called Student Veterans Organization or a location called the Veterans Resource Center or specially designated Veterans' Advisors, you may think you are providing the needed services and you may be, but National Guard and Reserve members may not recognize those services. Changing the names or adding a subtitle may help. If you have trained your student counselors to identify and treat PTSD and TBI but no one is using the service, you may need to reach out to the families of those who have served as they are the ones more willing to speak.

The bottom line is simply being sensitive to the ambiguities that our student military members bring with them and recognizing that when they say they are having trouble with the transition from the military to school, that they may really be having difficulty with the transition from the military to the civilian culture.

# Chapter 25

Endnote Address

# Improving College Education of Veterans

## Dr. Steve F. Kime
Past President, Servicemembers Opportunity Colleges
Vice President of the American Association of State Colleges and Universities
Former Chair of the Veterans Advisory Committee on Education

> This chapter describes where we are now and what we can do to make the education of veterans the best it can be.

First, it is important to recognize that veterans' education is emerging from a poisonous environment that lasted more than a generation. Some of the past still haunts policy for the college education of veterans.

It has been a rough road. Forty years ago this author was a student working in the ROTC building at Harvard under threat of bombing. Veterans were spit upon and slept in the streets. Political opportunists made hay by throwing away combat medals. The Professoriate, already dominated by academics skeptical about the use of force, became infused with "students" who judged that smart people lingered in college and lesser boys could do the fighting and dying. Such students were welcome in academe where they dominated a generation or two of college and university faculties by outshouting and intimidating legitimate objectors to war and the Vietnam debacle. It was a terrible time to go to college if you were a veteran.

There were GI Bills, but they were grudging, almost laughable, efforts of legislators to assuage their own, and the public, conscience. The Montgomery GI Bill, for example, was passed only after a compromise that caused veterans that could not afford to go to college on the meager stipends in the Bill to fund veterans with additional resources who could!

When this writer joined the Veteran Advisory Committee on Education in the early Nineties, the $1,200 paid by recruits in their first year of service added up to more than was being paid out for Montgomery GI Bill benefits. This travesty was attenuated somewhat as the Vietnam Stigma faded, but the Department of Defense (DoD) and legislators clung shamelessly to the concept that military recruits should provide funding for veteran education.

Once a three-star officer, accurately and shamefully representing DoD, testified that there was danger of making the GI Bill too good. The Partnership for Veterans Education had proposed that the nation fulfill its education promise to new military recruits by providing a GI Bill that would cover the cost of a four-year public college. It was a modest proposal, but DoD's position was that it would reduce military retention and be harmful to the country. The Armed Forces Committees accepted this unprincipled nonsense for years without a scintilla of evidence.

Eliminating the draft partially defused the draft evaders in academe, and it helped rehabilitate and legitimize the warrior. After all, even if a War is a colossal error, the warrior remains a volunteer who is doing the duty of those who will not serve. This less than heroic perspective, shared by a Congress increasingly populated by politicians that had never served, helped to erode resistance to increasing veterans' benefits.

The passage of time helped. The hated Vietnam War receded in memory. More important were the passing of veteran-loathing professors and the emergence of generations of students and teachers who did not confuse their own attitudes about service with their academic identity. Gradually, dignity and respect returned to veterans, and some of this began to be reflected on campuses.

National Military Strategy shifted. Regardless how one views the kind of wars policymakers choose to engage in these days, it became obvious that they could not be supported without a draft unless the reserves were deployed much more like "regulars." Indeed, a new Total Force Strategy ultimately forced recognition of the fact that reservists were carrying much of the load and were dying in the effort. The GI Bill, stingy even to "regulars," was slow to adjust to this new reality. Progress was painfully slow.

Second, it is important to recognize that we are in a new, better, world for veteran education. Things are better. We must remember the past lest it be repeated, but it does no good to address current issues overburdened by the baggage of the past. It is time to help a new generation of professors, administrators, fellow students and Veterans Administration staffers make college the best it can be for veterans.

We were lucky. Trends were positive and progress toward a Total Force GI Bill was being made, but there was no catalyst to enable a genuine revolution in veteran education. In spite of an active Partnership for Veterans Education that consisted of the leaders in the National Higher Education Associations and the leaders of the national Veterans Advocacy Organizations, only incremental improvements to the GI Bill were possible.

The 2008 election produced a weak House Veterans Affairs Committee leadership that focused on peripheral political issues. The Senate Veterans Affairs Committee had never been an effective advocate for education and the Senate Armed Forces Committee was wedded to DoD positions that were never favorable to the GI Bill. The Department of Veterans Affairs, slow to outgrow the subordinate authority of the old Veteran Administration, still followed DoD's lead.

Amazingly, an articulate veteran and former Secretary of the Navy, James Webb, was elected to the Senate from Virginia. He had not succeeded as Reagan's Navy Secretary. He was too independent, and behaved more like a dyspeptic artist than an effective political team player. He did not listen well and bucked political reality. It turns out that these traits were exactly what veterans needed. He rammed through a Bill that longtime veteran education advocates were convinced could not succeed. They would have advised something much less ambitious, but he did not ask them.

Webb struck at the right time: national guilt was at its peak over the treatment of "Wounded Warriors" and over the rising scandal of unequal treatment of reserve veterans with multiple tours in the combat zones. Years of agitation by advocates in higher education and the powerful veteran advocacy organizations in the Partnership for Veterans' Education had helped to wear down anti-veteran attitudes in the Congressional leadership. (OMB, Congressional Committee, and DoD staffers were unmoved, but helpless in the face of a new political reality.) The enormous cost of Webb's Bill, and the cost of about everything else in those days, did not seem to be an obstacle to policymakers. Go figure.

Let's not look this Gift Horse in the mouth. What we have here, finally, is a GI Bill that can fulfill the commitment that the nation makes to every recruit. The educational opportunity is real. Now is the time to focus on steps that can be taken to make the most of this opportunity.

There is need for action in the Department of Veterans Affairs and in Academe.


## Cultural Reform in Veterans' Affairs

The Department of Veterans Affairs (DVA) is well meaning and staffed with people who genuinely want to help veterans. Many are veterans themselves. The problem is that they work in a culture that is firmly stuck in the past. Always months late and many dollars short, this culture now clearly has more GI Bill than it can manage.

In the post-WWII era there were cases of abuse of the original G.I. Bill that left an ugly, and seemingly indelible, mark on VA and DVA administrators. An attitude emerged that seemed to say that veterans lie and steal and must be watched at all times. This permeated the old Veterans Administration and the Congressional Committees. It won't go away. This attitude led over the years to stifling rules and regulations that have been largely untouched by modern technology and concepts of management. The result has been unhappy veterans and a system of managing them that, put simply, does not work. Problems such as delays in processing claims, endemic at the old VA and persistent at the new DVA, could become absolutely crippling in managing the complex new GI Bill.

Congress stifles imagination and initiative at VA. No agency is more minutely managed. Committees with no apparent ideas on improving educational opportunity for veterans, tenaciously insisted on excessively tightfisted management of the few dollars the veteran was entitled to receive.

The DVA has become a timid rulemaking body, an abject subordinate to a veteran-unfriendly OMB, the Veterans Affairs Committees, and DoD, instead of a policymaking Cabinet Department created to fulfill the nation's responsibilities to veterans. DVA's Lawyers have disproportionate power to kill ideas in this environment. Absolutely no new idea escapes the scrubbing of hidebound DVA lawyers and senior staffers who make certain that anything new has to fit old ways and entrenched views and prejudices in OMB and DoD. Ideas cannot breathe on the top floor. DVA is a terrible place to have an imagination.

Reform is possible. The new DVA Secretary has already spoken of a need to address DVA "culture" on the handling of PTSD cases. Culture, of course, is a problem in managing veteran health care as well as in education. It will take vision and resolve to fix DVA culture. (Remember: this DVA Secretary, as Chief of Staff of the Army, had the vision and the guts to be right when the Secretary of Defense was dead wrong.)

The new GI Bill presents an opportunity to break old molds and outdated attitudes in veteran education. Hopefully, the Secretary will perceive this opportunity. The country is in the mood to see veterans treated logically and fairly, and increased participation in the G.I. Bill process by younger, savvy, players will inevitably increase pressure for reforms. The more active role of modern academe, which is heavily invested in new technology, can have a positive effect. Leadership in

Congress is crucial. Today, unlike the past, hope for reform lies more in the Senate Defense and Veteran Committees than just those in the House. This may help. Academe must stand up and be counted

It would be easy to be cynical about academe's recent conversion regarding veterans, given its past attitudes. It is true that colleges and universities, attracted by the smell of federal money and pressed by tightening of state funding, are getting the message that serving veterans is a very good idea. But there are also more positive forces at work that bode well for veterans.

A refreshing attitude among senior college and university administrators is emerging. The national higher education associations have supported positive actions to take into consideration the special needs of veterans on campuses. Academic support for the Partnership for Veterans Education was strong. There were constructive policies on ensuring that Soldiers in college called to active duty were fairly handled by colleges. The American Association of State Colleges and Universities has included a strong statement on veterans in its policy papers. Wal-Mart sponsored a competition for grants to colleges with new, positive, approaches by colleges to serving veterans, a competition that included dozens of institutions that was managed by the American Council on Education. Some college presidents have already stood up to be counted.

As the new GI Bill becomes institutionalized, there will be increasing opportunities for colleges and universities to participate. They can relegate veteran outreach to an obscure, underfunded and underappreciated corner of the university as in the past, or they can recognize the educational and social value of these opportunities at the policymaking level of their institutions. There needs to be "Command Attention" to veterans at every college and university. Leaders in academe were shamefully slow to support the Post-WWII GI Bill. This is a mistake that must not be repeated.

There has long been an active institution in academe dedicated to the education of active duty military members. Servicemembers Opportunity Colleges (SOC) has managed a Consortium aimed at facilitating attempts by men and women on active duty to attend civilian colleges and universities and earn regionally accredited civilian degrees. Hundreds of colleges and universities agree to military friendly SOC policies on credit transfer, acceptance of military vocational learning that is creditworthy, and support of highly integrated and articulated degree programs. SOC has tried for years to extend this effort to veterans as much as possible, but the outreach to veterans has lacked resources and strong backing by policymakers. Now the landscape is changing, and there is real potential here. More on this below.

Join the Revolution in Academe!

A conceptual revolution has taken place in higher education. Adult and Continuing Education, not the care and feeding of 18-year-olds, is already becoming the guiding concept. This, of course, applies readily to veterans who are adult students and not recent escapees from Mom's apron strings. Perhaps because the country got by with confusing veterans with adolescents after World War II, the confusion still exists. It is time to fix this.

The philosophy of Adult Learning is a work in progress, but fundamental change is in the air and some important facts are becoming clear. Adult students come to higher education with experience and education under their belt. Some of this is creditworthy. They need different doses of some subject matter than a green 18-year-old must have. This confounds academics that are absolutely positive that every link in every curriculum chain is critical for every student. Adult learners have an idea why they are in college. Their focus on their future place in the world of work imposes reality and relevance on academics that they are unaccustomed to.

This is healthy, and it portends great change in academe. Adult learners, including veterans, cannot simply be tacked on to the outmoded academic structure for 18 to 22-year olds.

Veterans are adult learners who come from a unique and demanding workplace. Many have growing families and must hold outside jobs. Most are prepared to work on varying schedules and in varying learning modes not compatible with the laid back working days of American college students and professors. Academe is beginning to adjust to these realities for civilian adult students who are becoming the majority on some campuses. It is time for the administration and management of veteran education, in academe, in Congress, and in the Veterans Department, to adjust policies to the Adult and Continuing Revolution in higher education.


Join the Management Revolution!

It is high time that the Department of Veteran Affairs becomes at least as efficient as Home Depot. Large transactions are common in the retail world on the signatures of people who have not volunteered to be shot at for their country. If fraud happens, it gets discovered and it is dealt with.

Why haven't the management concepts of the big retailers and credit card companies penetrated the Veterans Department, even though such concepts have gained some acceptance at such progressive bastions as the IRS? See the discussion above about entrenched attitudes about veterans and the stifling policies of the Committees in Congress, and the ever-lurking lawyers who have the DVA Secretary's ear.

The concept of Management by Exception is decades old, but it has never seen the light of day at DVA. Companies learned that letting people operate under the assumption of competence, integrity, and loyalty, and punishing transgressions quickly and fairly was far more efficient and productive than assuming the worst and spending resources to enforce normal, honest behavior. Why hasn't the notion of "Management by Exception" ever occurred to the VA? Instead of assuming that every veteran and every educational provider is a potential crook, why not set up effective processes to spot and punish lawbreakers?

Reflect a moment on the government's "exposure" to fraud. The maximum a veteran could "steal" is an entitlement earned by serving his country! Does it make sense to have a backlog of claims for something that has been earned, especially when the total possible claim is for relatively small amounts? It would be interesting to see a comparison of the cost of processing, and delaying, a claim for an education entitlement and the cost of the entitlement itself.

The GI Bill could be managed like a debit card and withdrawals from a veteran's entitlement be appropriately authorized and recorded. Let Master Card do it if the government cannot figure it out. (Let GEICO to do it: "its so easy a Caveman could do it.")

The Rules and Regulations for the GI Bill make the federal tax code look transparent. A sweeping change is needed. The Byzantine accumulation of micromanaging generations of public servants should be swept away and replaced by a new, brief, simpler set of rules. Again, the opportunity to do so has been ushered in by the new GI Bill. Management reform to match the boldness and imagination of the new GI Bill is needed. The Department of Veterans Affairs has never risen to act like a real Cabinet Department, and this is an opportunity to do so and propose serious policy alternatives to the past. History does not inspire confidence on this score. Perhaps, like the Webb Bill itself, reform to get the most out of the potential of the new GI Bill may have to come from outside.

Join the technological revolution!

This should go without saying in the 21st Century. A visit to DVA regional management centers will make it clear that it must be said. Handling of information is far behind the times. This writer can testify that many in DVA have tried to modernize the technical facets of administration without much success. Veteran educational staffers' efforts at technological upgrade fall victim to the low priority of Educational Services. At DVA, Health Care rules, and it sucks up most of the resources. It did precisely that on computer system upgrade at DVA.

There needs to be prompt and significant attention to upgrading technology in educational management if DVA is ever to discharge its duties under the new GI Bill.

But more needs to be said. It does little good to computerize bad practices. The reasons that the DVA is always behind in handling educational claims of veterans are only partly technological. Too much information is demanded too often. There are far too many complex rules for fairly straightforward management problems. It is no wonder that time consuming decisions must be made one at a time by an analyst. The bottom line here is that technological upgrade must be done in conjunction with an overhaul of the regulations and procedures, and the "culture."

Recognize what veterans bring to the table

Colleges long insulted veterans, and their military service, by offering college credit only for physical education after years in the military, often in high-tech jobs that the professoriate could only imagine. It was an accurate assessment of what academics thought about military service—a kind of extended gym class.

As noted above, Servicemembers Opportunity Colleges (SOC) has made much progress at changing this attitude in academe. Hundreds of academic institutions give credit for creditworthy learning while in the military. The American Council on Education evaluates such learning, lending credibility and integrity to the process.

The problem for veterans is that many of them choose to matriculate at colleges and universities that either do not usually serve active duty servicemembers or will not apply SOC's practices to veterans. It is time to form a seamless web between recognition of military learning of active duty servicemembers and that of veterans. This will require a serious, programmatic effort. For many years, efforts to accomplish this by jawboning, common sense, and appeals to fairness have made very modest progress. The responsibility of DVA to monitor credit recognition for veterans has been half heartily and ineffectively managed.

A fact of life must be confronted here. DoD has a strong interest in the education of active duty military members and discharges its responsibilities for active duty military education well. DoD's interests fade when the servicemember becomes a veteran for good reason: DoD's mission is warfighting. DoD has never been the primary advocate for veterans, and it should not be. This is why we have a Department of Veterans Affairs, and why it is at the Cabinet level. The Partnership that DoD has developed over the decades with higher education needs to be emulated by DVA.

A credit recognition regime for veterans, very much like that for active duty servicemembers needs to be created. This regime would recognize the realities that both veterans and the academic institutions face. Some of these realities are different for veterans and the colleges they attend than for active duty members. What is needed is a separate Program that is sponsored jointly by DVA and the national higher education associations. It should be managed in higher education in the manner that SOC is managed. The cost would be low, because strong new policy, tailored to veterans, is needed more than programmatic structure.

Improve care for veterans in college

Veterans bring notable strengths to the classroom that should be recognized. They also have vulnerabilities and weaknesses that must be addressed. Many of them will spend their immediate post-service years on campuses, so the nation's responsibility to care for veterans falls at least partly to colleges and universities. It is their duty.

Veterans are very special adult learners. Many have served in Hell, and they carry the burden with them.

College counseling and health care service must proactively address the need here. It is the nature of these vulnerabilities that they may or may not readily manifest themselves. (The need for proactive policies on psychological problems is not limited to veterans, as colleges have recently learned.)

It should not be necessary to point out that veterans with physical handicaps must be accommodated. Accommodating the physically handicapped is firmly entrenched in both the Politically Correct and the law. It only needs to be added that injured veterans have been handicapped in especially traumatic ways, and their care is complex and urgent. Handicapped veterans did their duty. Colleges must do their duty, too.

Finally, advocates of educating veterans need to aggressively take advantage of the fact that we are at a key juncture. There is a new, very promising GI Bill. Veterans can actually attend college on it! Colleges and universities are changing their attitudes and they have powerful incentives to do better. Congress has awakened to the nation's responsibilities. The public is on board.

It remains to get the administrative, managerial and academic policy houses in order. These are daunting tasks, given a lamentable history. Leadership at the U. S. Department of Veteran Affairs, role models in academe, and continued attention in Congress are sorely needed.

# Bibliography
For readers interested in veterans education

Ackerman, R. & DiRamio, D. (Eds.) (2009) In Creating a Veteran-Friendly Campus: Strategies for Transition and Success New Directions for Student Services, No. 126, Wiley Periodicals.

Ackerman, R., DiRamio, D., & Garza Mitchell, R. L. (2009) Transitions: Combat veterans as college students. In Ackerman, R. & DiRamio, D. (Eds.) Creating a Veteran-Friendly Campus: Strategies for Transition and Success. New Directions for Student Services, No. 126, Jossey Bass: San Francisco..

Allen, B. S. Jr., Herrmann, D., & Giles, S. L. (1995). Vietnam as a class war: Myth or reality.
Sociological Spectrum, 14, 299-311

American Council on Education. (2008a). Serving those who serve: Higher education and America's veterans. Retrieved March 5, 2009, from
http://www.acenet.edu/Content/NavigationMenu/ProgramsServices/MilitaryPrograms/serving/Veterans_Issue_Brief_1108.pdf

American Council on Education (2008b). Student Veterans Speak Out About Their College Experience: Senator Hagel Frames Discussion on Veterans and Higher Education. Conference on "Serving Those Who Serve: Higher Education and America's Veterans" Georgetown University. June 5.

American Council on Education (ACE) (2008c) Severely Injured Military Veterans ACE supported a Fulfilling Their Dreams project in which veterans with severe injuries are assisted in their return to civilian life. Retrieved on March 20, 2009 from
http://www.acenet.edu/Content/NavigationMenu/Programs Services/MilitaryPrograms/veterans/in   dex.htm-69k-Cached-Similar pages

American Council on Education (2008d). A Transfer Guide: Understanding Your Military Transcript and ACE Credit Recommendations. Military Programs: Washington D.C.

American Council on Education (ACE), American Association of Small of Student Affairs Administrators in Higher Education Administrators (2009) From Soldier to Student. American Council on Published by the American Council on Education for Military Programs: Washington D.C.

Armstrong, K., Best, S., & Domenici, P. (2006). Courage after fire. Berkeley, CA: Ulysses Press.

348

Association of Veterans Education (2006). Association of Veterans
    Education Certifying Officials. A NonChartered Organization .
    National Headquarters Address, 9813 104th Avenue Ottumwa, IA
    52501. Retrieved from
    http://www1.va.gov/vso/inde.cfm?template=viewreport&Org_ID
    =338-13k-Cached
Asch, B. J., Kilburn, M. R., & Klerman, J. A. (1999). Attracting
    college-bound youth into the military:    toward the development
    of new recruiting policy options. Rand Mongraph (Number:
    MR-984-OSD): RAND Distribution Services. Retrieved on
    March 22, 2005 from
    http://www.rand.org/about/
Baechtold, M. & De Sawal, D. M. (2009). Meeting the needs of women
    veterans. In Ackerman, R. & DiRamio, D. (Eds.), Creating a
    Veteran-Friendly Campus: Strategies for Transition and Success. New
    Directions for Student Services, No. 126, Jossey Bass: San
    Francisco..
Bauerlein, M. (2004). Liberal groupthink is anti-intellectual. Chronicle of
    Higher Education, November 12, 2004
Bauman, M. (2009) The mobilization and return of undergraduate
    students serving in the National Guard and Reserves. In
    Ackerman, R. & DiRamio, D. (Eds.), Creating a Veteran- Friendly
    Campus: Strategies for Transition and Success New Directions for
    Student Services, No. 126, Jossey Bass: San Francisco.
Black, T., Westwood, N. J., Sorsdal, M. N., & Michael. M. N. (2007).
    From the Front Line to the Front of
    the Class: Counseling Students Who Are Military Veterans. In J.
    Lippincott and R. A. Lippincott, Ruth A. (Eds.) Special
    populations in college counseling: A handbook for mental
    health professionals. (pp. 3-20). Aleandria, VA: American
    Counseling Association.
Boscarino, J. A., (2006). Eternal-cause mortality after
    psychological trauma: The effects of stress exposure and
    predisposition. Comprehensive Psychiatry, 47, 503-514.
Bound, J. & Turner, S. (2002). Going to War and Going to
    College: Did World War II and the GI Bill  Increase
    Educational Attainment for Returning Veterans? Journal of
    Labor Economics. 20, 4, 784-816.
Burkett, B. G. (1998). Stolen valor: How the Vietnam generations
    were robbed of its heroes and its history. Sunnyvale, CA:
    Verity Press.

Clausewitz, C. v. (2006). On War (C. J. J. Graham, Trans.). London: Project Gutenberg EBook.

Cook, B. J. & Kim, Y. (2008) From Soldier to Student: Easing the Transition of Service Members on Campus. Lumina Foundation.

Dean, C. (2000). Nam Vet: Making Peace with your past. Wordsmith Publishing.

Defense activity for non-traditional education support agency. (2004). Voluntary education fact sheet fy03. Retrieved on June 9, 2005 from http://www.dantes.doded.mil/dantes_web/library/docs/voledfacts/FY03.pdf.

Department of Veterans Affairs (2008) The Post-9/11 Veterans Educational Assistance Act of 2008 . VA Pamphlet 22-09-1 Retrieved on October 2008. from http://www.GIBILL.VA.GOV/GI Bill Info/programs.htm

Department of Veterans Affairs (2007). 38 CFR Book C Schedule for Rating Disabilities on October 6, 2007 from Department of Veteran Affairs. (2004). National survey of veterans. Washington, D.C.: National Center for Information Analysis and Statistics.

Digest of Education Statistics (2008) Table 231. Number and percentage of attendance: 2003–04    for veterans and non-veterans. National Center for Education Statistics.

DiRamio, D. & Spires, M. (2009) Partnering to assist disabled veterans in transition. In Ackerman, R. & DiRamio, D. (Eds.), Creating a Veteran-Friendly Campus: Strategies for Transition and Success. New Directions for Student Services, No. 126, Jossey Bass: San Francisco. Published online in Wiley InterScience (www.interscience.wiley.com) • DOI: 10.1002/ss.319

DiRamio, D., Ackerman, R., & Mitchell R. L. (2008). From combat to campus: Voices of student-veterans. NASPA Journal, 45(1), 73-94.

Editors (2009) How Old Are Most Veterans? Diversity Inc - Dec 8. http://diversityinc.com/content/1757/article/6973/?

Emmons, M. (2006). Traumatic brain injury: The 'Signature wound' of wars in Iraq and Afghanistan. Oakland Tribune. Retrieved Nov. 12, 2008. http://nl.newsbank.com/nlsearch/we/Archives=113840p]. Dec. 26, 2006.

Ephron, D.(2007). Forgotten heroes. Newsweek, Mar. 5, 2007, pp. 29–37.

Ford, D., Northrup, P., & Wiley, L. (2009) Connections, partnerships, opportunities, and programs to enhance success for military students. In Ackerman, R. & DiRamio, D. (Eds.), Creating a Veteran-Friendly Campus: Strategies for Transition and Success. New Directions for Student Services, No. 126, Jossey Bass: San Francisco.

Geraerts, E., Kozaric-Kovacic, D., Merckelbach, H., Peraica, T., Jelicic, M., & Candel, I. (2007) Traumatic memories of war veterans. Consciousness and Cognition: An International Journal, 16, 170-177.

Government Officials (2008). Educating Veterans on Entitled Benefits, Protecting Veterans' Rights, and Initiating Needed Reform (Inside the Minds). The Changing Landscape of Veterans Affairs, Aspatore Books Staff.

Grinnel Leadership (2006). Battlefield to Boardroom: America's Top Companies Actively Seek to Hire Service Members. Chapel Hill, N.C., March, Vol. 17, No. 06.

Hall, W. C. & Schweizer, P. (2005). Campus radicals vs. our vets. National Review Online.Retrieved Aug 29, 2005, from http://www.nationalreview.com/comment/hall_schweizer200508 290810.asp

Hart, A. R. III (2000). An operations manual for combat PTSD. Lincoln, N. E.: iUniverse.

Herrmann, D. J. (2007) Investigations into the Treatment of Servicemembers by Indiana Higher Educational Institutions. Terre Haute, IN: Veterans Higher Educational Group.

Herrmann, D. J. Hopkins, C., Wilson, R. B. & Allen, B. (2009) Educating veterans in the 21st Century. North Charleston, South Carolina :BookSurge.

Herrmann, D. J., Raybeck, D., & Wilson, R. (2008). College Is for Veterans, Too. The Chronicle of Higher Education, November 21.

Hillen, J. (1999). Must U.S. Military Culture Reform? Orbis-Philadelphia, 43(1), 43-58.

Hunter, R. & Tankovich, M. B. (2007) The Army National Guard The You Can Guide to Paying for your College Education, 2nd Printing. Washington, D.C.: Uniformed Services Almanac, Inc. http://virtualarmory.com

Indiana Employer Support of the Guard and Reserve (INESGR) (2007) Investigations into Services of Indiana Higher Education to Members of the of Guard and Reservists.

Johnson, T. (2009). Ensuring the success of deploying students: A campus view. In Ackerman, R. & DiRamio, D. (Eds.), Creating a Veteran-Friendly Campus: Strategies for Transition   and   Success. New Directions for Student Services, No. 126, Jossey Bass: San

Francisco.

Kingsbury, A. (2007). American Council on Education's new pilot program for wounded veterans. U.S. News & World Report. 143, 71-71.

Kotok, A., (2008). Student-Veterans Come Marching Home: Their Return to Studies, http://sciencecareers.sciencemag.org/career_development/previo us_issues/articles/2008

Lokken, J. M. Pfeffer, D. S., McAuley, J. M. & Strong, C. (2009). A statewide approach to creating veteran-friendly campuses. In Ackerman, R. & DiRamio, D. (Eds.), Creating a Veteran-Friendly Campus: Strategies for Transition and Success. New Directions for Student Services, No. 126, Jossey Bass: San Francisco.

Malkin, M. (2008). It's time we quit coddling anti-military militants. Home News Tribune Online 03/13/08

LoPresti, E. F., Mihailidis, A. & Kirsch, N. (2004). Assistive technology for cognitive rehabilitation: State of the art. Neuropsychological Rehabilitation, 14, 5-39.

Manguno-Mire, G., Sautter, F., Lyons, J., Myers, L., Perry, D., Sherman, M., Glynn, S., & Sullivan, M. (2007). Psychological Distress and Burden Among Female Partners of Combat Veterans With PTSD. Journal of Nervous and Mental Disease, 195, 144-151.

Mason, P.H.D. (1990). Recovering from the war: A woman's guide to helping your Vietnam vet, your family, and yourself. New York: Penguin.

McBain, L. (2009). "When Johnny [or Janelle] Comes Marching Home;" National, State and Institutional Efforts in Support of Veterans' Education. Perspectives. American Association of State Colleges and Universities, Summer, 2008.

McGrevey, M. & Keher, D. (2009) Stewards of the public trust: Federal laws that serve service members and student veterans. In Ackerman, R. & DiRamio, D. (Eds.), Creating a Veteran-Friendly Campus: Strategies for Transition and Success. New Directions for Student Services, No. 126, Jossey Bass: San Francisco.

Mettler, S. (2005). Soldiers to citizens: The GI Bill and the Making of the Greatest Generation. Cambridge: Oxford Univ. Press.

Milliken, C.S., Auchterlonie, J.L., & Hoge, C.W.(November 14, 2007). Longitudinal Assessment of Mental Health Problems among Active and Reserve Component Solders Returning from the Iraq War. JAMA, 298 (18), 2141 2148.

Minnesota State Colleges and Universities (2008) Health and health related behaviors: Minnesota Postsecondary Student Veterans. Boyton Health Service.

Murray, W. (1999). Does Military Culture Matter? Orbis Philadelphia, 43(1), 27-42.

National Center for Education Statistics (2008) . Number and percentage of attendence: 2003–04; veterans and non-veterans. Table 231. Digest of Education Statistics.

National Veterans Legal Services Program (2007). Veterans Benefit Manual. Retrieved on October 24, 2007 from http://www.nvlsp.org/Information/inde.htm

NAVPA (2006). National association of veterans ' program administrators. Retrieved on March 21 2007 from http://www.navpa.org/web_membership.htm   26k   Cached   –Similar pages.

NAVREF. (2006). National association of veterans ' research and education foundation. Retrieved on March 21, 2007 from http://www.navref.org/   14k   Cached   –Similar pages

North Carolina University (2007). Seminars on how veterans are a protected class. Retrieved on December 11, 2008 from http://www.ncsu.edu/equal_op/education/oeo_programs.html.

Powers, J. T. (2008a) Campus Kit for Colleges and Universities.. Student Veterans of America. Retrieved from www.studentveterans.org.

Powers, J. T. (2008b) Campus Kit for Student Veterans. Student Veterans of America. Retrieved from http//www.studentveterans.org.

Pryor, J. H. Hurtado, S.  DeAngelo, L., Palucki Blake, L., & Tran, S. (2009), The American Freshman: National Norms Fall 2009.  The Cooperative Institutional Research Program (CIRP) Higher Education Research Institute, UCLA. http://www.heri.ucla.edu.

Quillen-Armstrong, S. (2007). Course to help transition veterans into civilian life. July 5., Community College Times Web site: Retrieved on July 16, 2007 from http://www.communitycollegetimes.com/article.cfm?ArticleId=417.

Radford, A. W. and Wun, J. (2009). Issues tables: A Profile of military servicemembers and veterans enrolled in post secondary education from 2008 9. Retrieved December 15, 2009, from http://nces.ed.gov/pubs2009/2009182.pdf

Rumann, C. B. & Hamrick, F. A. (2009) Supporting student veterans in transition. In Ackerman, R. &      DiRamio, D. (Eds.) Creating a Veteran-Friendly Campus: Strategies for Transition and Success. New Directions for Student Services, No. 126, Jossey Bass: San Francisco.

Roth-Douquet, K. & Schaeffer, F. (2006a). AWOL: The Unexcused Absence of America's Upper Classes from Military Service—and How It Hurts Our Country, New York: Collins.

Rentz, E. D., Martin, S. L., Gibbs, D. A., Clinton-Sherrod, M., Hardison, J. & Marshall, S. W.. (2006). Family Violence in the Military: A Review of the Literature. Trauma, Violence, & Abuse, 7, 93-108.

Schram, M. (2008) Veterans under siege: How America Deceives and dishonors those who fight our battles. New York: St. Martins. Retrieved on September 14 from http://www.veteransforamerica.org/home/vfa/

Seal, K.H., Bertenthal, D., Miner, C.R., Saunak, S., & Marmar, C. (2007). Bringing the War Back Home, Archives of Internal Medicine, 167, 476 482.

Servicemembers Opportunity Colleges. (2004). What is SOC? Retrieved on February 5, 2005, from http://www.soc.aascu.org/socgen/WhatIs.html.

Servicemembers Opportunity Colleges (SOC). (2007a). Retrieved on Aug 25, 2007 from http://www.soc.aascu.org/

SOC (2007 to 2009) SOC Pamphlet. Dantes, Pages 1 to 32.

Smilkstein, R. (2002). We're Born to Learn: Using the Brain's Natural Learning Process to Create Today's Curriculum. Corwin Press.

Sternberg, M., MacDermid Wadsworth, S., Vaughan, J., & Carlson, R. (2009). The higher education landscape for student service members and veterans in Indiana. West Lafayette: Military Family Research Institute at Purdue.

Stiglitz, J. E. & Bilmes, L. J. (2008) The Three Trillion Dollar War: The True Cost of the Iraq Conflict. New York: Norton, W. W. & Company.

Summerlot, J., Green, S M (2009). Student veterans organizations. In Ackerman, R. & DiRamio, D. (Eds.) Creating a Veteran-Friendly Campus: Strategies for Transition and Success. New Directions for Student Services, No. 126, Jossey Bass: San Francisco.

Tanielian, T. & Jaycox, L. H. (2008). Invisible wounds pf war: Psychological and cognitive injuries. Their consequences, and services to assist recovery (Monograph MG 720 CCF)/ Santa Monica, CA: Rand Corporation.

Tanielian, T. & Jaycox, L. H., Schell, T. L., Marshall, G. N., Burnam, M. A., Eibner, C., et al. (2008). Invisible wounds of war: Summary and Recommendations for Addressing Psychological and cognitive injuries. Monograph MG 721 CCF) / Santa Monica, CA: Rand Corporation.

Trewyn, R. A. & Stever, J. A. (1995). Academia: Not so hallowed halls for veterans. Journal of the Vietnam Veterans Institute, 4, 63-75.

U.S. Department of Education. (2009). U.S. Department of Education Database of Accredited Postsecondary Institutions and Programs. Retrieved November 10, 2009, from http://ope.ed.gov/accreditation/

Veterans Administration (2006a). A Brief History of the VA. Office of Construction & Facilities. Retrieved on January 15, 2007 from http:www.va.gov/facmgt/historic/Brief_VA_History.asp - 19k

354

Veterans Administration (2006b). History of the Department of Veterans Affairs. Retrieved on January 15, 2007 from http:www.va.gov/facmgt/historic/Brief_VA_History.asp - 19k

Vietnam Era Veterans Readjustment Assistance Act of 1974; Title 38 United States Code Section 4212.

Wenger, D., Rufflo, M., & Bertalan, F. J. (2006). ACME project, internet-based systems that advocate credit for military experience and analyze options for veterans in career transition. Proceedings of the IEEE International Conference on Advanced Learning Techniques, IEEE The Computer Society.

Whealin, J.M. (2004). Warzone related stress reactions: What veterans need to know. A National Center for PTSD Fact Sheet. Iraq War Clinician Guide. Department of Veteran's Affairs, National Center for PTSD.

Williamson, V. (2008) A New GI Bill: Rewarding our Troops, Rebuilding our Military. Iraq and Afghanistan Veterans of America, issue report.

Zoroya, G. (2007). Military prodded on brain injuries. USA Today, http://www.usatoday.com/news/washi